WHEN HENS CROW

WHEN HENS CROW

The Woman's Rights Movement
in Antebellum America

SYLVIA D. HOFFERT

INDIANA UNIVERSITY PRESS

Bloomington and Indianapolis

The paper used in this publication meets the minimum
requirements of American National Standard for Information
Sciences—Permanence of Paper for Printed Library Materials,
ANSI Z39.48–1984.

Manufactured in the United States of America

Library of Congress Cataloging–in–Publication Data

Hoffert, Sylvia D.
When hens crow: the woman's rights movement in
antebellum America / Sylvia D. Hoffert.
p.   cm.
Includes bibliographical references (p.   ) and index.
ISBN 0–253–32880–2 (cloth: acid–free paper)
1. Women's rights —United States—History—19th century.
2. Women in politics—United States—History—19th century.
3. Feminism—United States—History—19th century. 4.
Language and languages—Sex differences. I. Title.
HQ1236.5.U6H64   1995
305.42'0973'09034—dc20   94–44083

1 2 3 4 5 00 99 98 97 96 95

In Memory Of
Anna Barbara Pressler Miller
1890–1973

When legislators bold invade
The laws which they themselves have made;
When the parson 'gainst the Bible preaches,
And modest virgins wear the breeches;
When women scorn domestic cares,
And bold intrude on men's affairs,
Aspiring with mistaken pride
The war-horse of the world to ride,
Then will wild chaos come again,
And Eve with the old serpent reign;
A second time will pay the price
Of wit, by loss of Paradise.
The world tail foremost will advance,
Like Freedom in regenerate France;
By going backwards all come right,
And men grow blind by too much light.

[Prophecy from an Old Book]
Published in the *New York Daily Times*
December 28, 1852, page 2

CONTENTS

ACKNOWLEDGMENTS

I began work on this book in the summer of 1987 while attending a seminar for teachers sponsored by the National Endowment for the Humanities entitled "The Scottish Enlightenment and the American Constitution." During that summer I had the opportunity to spend three weeks at Princeton and two at St. Andrews University in Scotland studying the connection between the ideas of the Scottish Enlightenment and the founding of the American republic.

The directors of that program were John Murrin of the History Department at Princeton and Eleanor Kingsbury, an energetic Scotswoman who at the time was headmistress of Springside School in Philadelphia. Their efforts provided me with a summer filled with massive amounts of reading, access to two impressive research libraries, the pleasure of living temporarily among a community of scholars dedicated to teaching and intellectual discourse, and a new research project. To them I will always be grateful. Although the subject of women's history was rarely mentioned during those five weeks, this book evolved from discussions with my fellow seminar participants about the uses of language and the impact of Scottish Enlightenment philosophy on American life.

I wish to thank Mary Kelley, Ruth Bloch, Dennis Pilant, Mary Baumlin, Jane Hoogestraat, Meagan Dorsett, Matthew Mancini, Steve Vaughn, John Murrin, M. Jeanne Peterson, and Richard Kohn for their encouragement and for reading and commenting upon parts of this book. I also wish to thank the National Endowment for the Humanities, the Council for Basic Education, and Southwest Missouri State University for the financial support necessary to finish it. The help of Pat Holland of the Stanton-Anthony Papers at the University of Massachusetts–Amherst, the archivists of the Sophia Smith Collection at Smith College, and the staffs of the interlibrary loan departments at Southwest Missouri State University and the University of Missouri–St. Louis as well as the editors at Indiana University Press was invaluable. Gary L. Bunker provided me assistance in locating illustrations. *Journalism Quarterly* allowed me to republish parts of chapters four and five. The Boston Public Library, the Sophia Smith Collection, the Syracuse University Library, the Vassar College Library, the Mable Smith Douglass Library at Rutgers, the Huntington Library, the Houghton Library, the Schlesinger Library, the Massachusetts Historical

Society, and the Rare Book and Manuscript Library at Columbia University gave me permission to quote from manuscripts in their collections. Finally, I would like to thank the members of my family, especially my daughter Mindy, whose response when I announced that I had begun research on a new book was, "You mean you're going to write *another* book?" In the name of scholarship, they each again sacrificed the time and attention I might otherwise have given them.

WHEN HENS CROW

INTRODUCTION

Let me begin with a fable. "There once lived in a Farm Yard a great many Roosters and Hens, and it chanced one morning that a young Hen with a very fine voice began to crow. Thereupon all the Roosters hurried together and solemnly declared that there was nothing so dreadful as a Crowing Hen! Now there was in the Yard a Rooster who had always been feeble and could only cackle, but when the Hen mentioned this, the Roosters shook their heads and said, 'Females do not understand Logic.'" The moral to the story: "There is a great deal of difference between a Cackling Rooster and a Crowing Hen."[1]

This fable is instructive on a number of levels. It testifies to the control that men traditionally have had over public discourse and by extension public life (the right to "crow"). It suggests that "crowing" (male language) is not only different from but better than "cackling" (female language). It attests to the ability of some women to appropriate male language and express themselves with a clarity and eloquence that is unexpected and to the ease and predictability with which that appropriation evokes a strong response. It stands as witness to the cohesiveness of the male community and its determination to protect the prerogatives of men against the incursions of presumptuous women. It testifies to man's need to know that, whatever his inadequacies, he is different from woman. And it stands as witness to the wish on the part of some to silence women's public voices, as well as to their unwillingness to participate in public debate with women. It was from within this sort of cultural context that a group of articulate male and female reformers in the mid-nineteenth century collectively began to challenge the ideas that men and women were inherently different and that American public life and the discourse that characterized and accompanied it should be a male preserve.

The American woman's rights movement represents one of the most notable and dramatic examples of an attempt, in this case by a small cadre of both male and female activists, to organize efforts to improve the legal, economic, political, and social status of women. Thus, it is not surprising that as widespread interest in the history of women emerged in the 1970s, scholars turned their attention to the movement. The result was that the story of the Seneca Falls convention became well known, the significance of reform influences in general and abolitionism in particular to the development of the woman's rights movement were generally acknowledged, the movement's goals were identified, and the names of its most prominent leaders, while they may not have become household words, became at least familiar to the well-informed.

Despite their predictable interest in woman's rights activism, however, pioneers in the field of women's history tended to concentrate on something other than the woman's rights movement during the antebellum period. In her survey of the movement, Eleanor Flexner, for example, devoted only a few pages in two short chapters to its organization between 1848 and 1860. Keith Melder, looking back to the early nineteenth century, concerned himself with those factors that contributed to the development of the movement rather than with the movement itself. And Ellen Carol DuBois used the antebellum movement as the starting point from which to trace the subsequent development of organized feminist activism.[2] Others who followed focused on the philosophy and activities of the movement from the point of view of individuals like Elizabeth Cady Stanton, Susan B. Anthony, and Lucy Stone.[3]

This book looks at the leaders of the antebellum woman's rights movement as a group and is concerned with broadening our understanding of the ideology of the early woman's rights movement, the way that the woman's rights vanguard expressed that ideology, the strategies that they devised to attract attention to their message, and the response that their message elicited from some of those who were exposed to it. It argues that they accomplished a good deal during the first twelve years of the movement's existence. First, those who led the movement developed an ideology and a public language or idiom that helped women move beyond the limits placed on them by the domestic ideal and Republican Motherhood. They also developed strategies guaranteed to elicit responses to their demands which created a political culture that could no longer ignore the participation of women.

Throughout the ages, communication for women, most of whom were excluded from public life and thus from public discourse because of their gender, was largely confined to the private sphere. Certainly, there were exceptions. Queens and noblewomen, by virtue of their rank, both spoke and wrote for a public audience. Women with an intellectual bent published books of poetry and prose, sometimes under their own names and sometimes under the names of others. Women testified in court, participated in public demonstrations, led armies, lobbied legislators, and circulated petitions. They did so as individuals and sometimes in groups.

But women never had the opportunity to contribute to public language, to debate public issues, or to participate in public affairs to the same degree that was possible for most men. The degree of their exclusion and their consciousness of it varied depending on time, circumstance, and place. That is what makes the meeting that took place on Sunday, July 16, 1848, so significant. On that day Elizabeth Cady Stanton, Jane Hunt, Martha Coffin Wright, and her sister Lucretia Mott sat around a mahogany table in Mary Ann McClintock's parlor in Waterloo, New York, quite conscious of their exclusion and quite determined to create a collective public language for all American women, thus building on the efforts of those individuals who had spoken out before on behalf of the female sex. They were equally determined to force American men not only to listen to their message but to acknowledge their political competency and the legitimacy of their message by responding to it.

They spent that day writing a series of documents that they intended to present to the first woman's rights convention scheduled to be held three days later in the Wesleyan Chapel in Seneca Falls, three miles away. By Wednesday they had completed their task, and they presented to the audience of the convention a Declaration of Sentiments, modeled after Jefferson's Declaration of Independence, which specified the disabilities that women suffered in American society. In that document they asserted that "men and women are created equal," that women had the same "inalienable rights" as men, and that women had the right to withdraw their "allegiance" from any government that denied them their rights and to demand the institution of a new government which would protect their rights. They blamed men for denying women such things as the vote, the right to control their own property, guardianship of their children, and equal opportunities in education and employment. Those who participated in the convention responded by passing a series of twelve resolutions asserting women's right to redress of their grievances. Those resolutions set forth five quite specific goals. They demanded that any statute or legal precedent that placed women in a position of inequality with men be invalidated, they insisted that men be held to the same standards of moral behavior as women, they claimed for women equal access to education and economic opportunity, they demanded that women be granted the right to vote, and they asserted women's right to speak in public from both podium and pulpit in order to pursue their goals.[4] The Declaration of Sentiments called for changes in law and social custom as well as in the attitudes upon which both were based.

The speeches and documents presented at the Seneca Falls convention in 1848 set forth the goals of what was eventually to become the organized feminist movement in the United States.[5] The Declaration of Sentiments was a document born of frustration and indignation as well as of optimism and hope. Most of the ideas it expressed had been articulated before, sometimes privately (as in Abigail Adams's 1776 plea to her husband to "remember the ladies") and sometimes in public (as in Mary Wollstonecraft's *A Vindication of the Rights of Woman* [1792]).

Public protest about the inferior status of women in the English-speaking world can be traced back to the seventeenth century. Early British feminists established a construct that defined women as a sociological group and argued that the condition of woman was a product of social convention rather than nature. But those early protesters apparently had little if any direct influence on the generations that followed them.[6]

The same cannot be said for those in the eighteenth century who critiqued the condition of women. Eighteenth-century British feminists, responding to the continued subordination of women, not only demanded that educational opportunities for women be improved but also exploited the increasing respectability of sentiment to undergird their demands that women be granted more rights.[7] Their protests were continued in nineteenth-century America by such notables as Frances Wright, Sarah and Angelina Grimké, and Ernestine Rose, who spoke out eloquently in public against the subjugation of women. Their appropriation of the right to lecture from podium and platform caused a great uproar among the clergy and among others who understood, whether consciously or not, that women's right to speak established the foundation of their right to extend their participation in public affairs. It was this controversy combined with the legislative debate over the right of New York women to control their own property and the experience of women who had confronted gender discrimination from within the abolitionist and other reform movements that provided the impetus for the Seneca Falls convention in particular and feminist protest in general during the antebellum period.[8]

The Declaration of Sentiments and the speeches given in support of its resolutions struck a responsive chord in those who attended the convention and brought derision from some but not all of the representatives of the popular press.[9] In an age when for all practical purposes American women's claim on public rhetoric was tentative at best, the presentation of the Declaration of Sentiments can best be described as the first organized attempt to build on previous individual efforts by women like the Grimké sisters to create an idiom through which women could express themselves politically as a group and articulate an ideology which would help to extend their right to participate in public life.

The ideas of the early feminists and the way in which they chose to express those ideas were of primary importance in directing the early public debate on the subject of woman's rights. But some aspects of the ideology that they developed and the language that they used to express their discontent have only begun to receive the attention that they deserve. That is unfortunate because, as I will argue, both verbal and nonverbal language and the ideas that they expressed were the single most important weapons of the early woman's rights movement. They represented the desire and determination on the part of woman's rights advocates to identify themselves, to describe the female experience, and to trace their history as well as to renegotiate gender relations in all aspects of American life. In the absence of a national organization, they served as the organizing principles which held the movement together before the Civil War. Moreover, the transformation of society that woman's rights activists envisioned was expressed in words long before it began to take place in fact. Their ideology and the way they chose to express it was

Woman's Rights.

By suggesting that female woman's rights advocates were crowing
hens, journalists attempted to humiliate them and belittle their
efforts to improve the status of women in American society. From
Nick Nax, January 1858, p. 285. Courtesy American Antiquarian
Society, Worcester, Massachusetts.

dissonant, provocative, and compelling enough to elicit a response from
those who were exposed to it. It was the resulting discourse that established the basis for the pursuit of gender equality in the United States and
full participation for women in economic and political life. For these
reasons, the ideology and language of the early woman's rights movement
and the response that it evoked merit closer attention by historians.

This study of the early debate over woman's rights has been informed by
a number of intellectual perspectives. The first is that of intellectual

historians who, since the 1950s, have moved from the study of the history of ideas to the study of the history of discourse. Influenced by research in the fields of anthropology and linguistics, they directed the attention of historians not only toward identifying the language or languages that were used to discuss political questions but also toward analyzing the cultural significance of the use of distinctive political vocabularies. Labeled contextualists, their study of discourse lent itself to a discussion of cultural symbolism as expressed in language and demanded an investigation of both verbal and behavioral response. It also encouraged historians to try to explain why certain vocabularies were used at particular times and in specific cultural contexts.[10] The work that they have done, however, has been largely confined to the study of male political rhetoric. I hope to apply some of their insights to the study of those who led the woman's rights movement.

More recently, poststructural critics such as Jacques Derrida, Michel Foucault, and others have directed the attention of scholars to a theory of language that suggests that, once uttered or written and presented to an audience, words lose their context, their authors lose control over their meaning, and words take on a life of their own as they are absorbed and recontextualized by various audiences. The end result is that the intention of the author can be lost.[11] Not surprisingly, these ideas have prompted considerable debate in the academic community. For purposes of this study, they serve as a constant reminder of the need to be sensitive not only to what speakers said and writers wrote but also to the way their message was received and interpreted.[12]

The third scholarly tradition to which I owe a debt is that of the sociolinguists who have concerned themselves with the study of gender and language. Much of their work is based on Edward Sapir's premise that language is a product of culture.[13] They argue that because language is a product of culture it gives meaning to the structure of culture. They see words as tools that allow us to organize and interpret what we experience in a specific society.[14] In general, however, because they see language as a culturally specific symbol system, they consider it unlikely to be used as an instrument of cultural change,[15] a view with which I disagree. Nevertheless, their work provides a means of conceptualizing the way language is used in a society where men and women are socialized differently.[16] It also offers a starting point for analyzing what the early woman's rights advocates were attempting to do as well as why and how others responded to those attempts.

Their research has important implications for studying the leaders of the woman's rights movement who were attempting to broaden the political role of women in the antebellum period. The degree to which boys and girls were socialized to occupy separate spheres before the Civil War influenced the way they were taught to express themselves. Because the public political roles for women were limited before the Civil War, there was no reason to teach female children to express themselves in that milieu.[17] Therefore, the language of most women did not have the same political dimension as did the language of most men. That being the case, women could not effectively articulate their grievances and demand redress until they had legitimized their right either to use the same political language that men used or to create a political idiom of their own.

Because it was exclusive, political language was both a resource and a symbol of identity for men. It represented a source of power that was gender-specific.[18] The fact that men discussed politics in public—and the *way* that they discussed the subject—linguistically connected them to political power in the same way that fraternal, athletic, and military language connected them with their clubs, teams, and regiments. It provided them with what sociolinguists would call "competency," an asset derived by one member of a group from being able to communicate with other members of a group using an idiom specific to that group.[19] Political language, therefore, carried with it political competency and served as an instrument which helped men to establish and maintain their masculinity.

When a small cadre of women, supported by sympathetic male support-ers, laid claim to the right to use political language, they both challenged male political and social hegemony and exposed the tenuousness of the mid-nineteenth-century definitions of maleness. By rejecting domestic metaphors as a way of expressing their demands, woman's rights advocates laid claim to an enhanced place for women in the public world rather than confirming their traditional place in the home. In essence, they asserted the right to express themselves in a language to which, because of their previous exclusion, they had no claim and in so doing forced their audi-ences to reassess the meaning of gender in America. The debate that followed was, therefore, as much a debate over what it meant to be a man and a woman as it was over whether or not women should be granted more rights.

Feminist historians have added yet another dimension to the study of discourse. Scholars such as Carroll Smith-Rosenberg have argued that women avoid the oppression of language by modifying and changing its meaning in order to fulfill their own needs, express themselves in their own way, and achieve their own ends. By directing attention toward images and metaphors, this model encourages us to try to understand the ways in which "words both reflect and alter the world in which they are spoken."[20]

Smith-Rosenberg and others have also enhanced our understanding of the cultural context from which the movement for woman's rights arose. They describe a context characterized by a complex interaction of a number of factors which together set the stage for public political protest on the part of women and the men who supported their demand for equal rights. Among the most important of those factors were the rise of commercial capitalism, the beginnings of industrialization, and the growth of towns and cities. These developments affected the lives of women in a number of ways. First they began the process of removing economic production from the home and thus changing women's domestic roles. This process relieved middle- and upper-class women of some kinds of productive labor. They paid at least two prices for that relief. One was that, as Jeanne Boydston has pointed out, the work they continued to do in the home was marginalized—if not in reality, at least in terms of public perception. The second was that they became increasingly dependent upon those male breadwinners willing to support them and their children. Popular authors also subjected them to a set of prescriptions, described by Barbara Welter as the "cult of true womanhood," that designated the domestic sphere as woman's proper place and demanded that middle-class women, black as well as white, also exhibit such characteristics as piety, purity, and submission to male authority.[21] Nancy Cott and others have suggested, however, that the female culture that developed from gender segregation may have contributed to a refined sense of gender identity among women from which the demand for equal rights could evolve.[22] For less privileged women, the rise of commercial capitalism and industrialization meant that they often found it necessary to seek employment outside the home. While they too established a distinctive female culture, that culture was significantly different from that of women in the middle and upper classes.[23] Economic development also brought about changes in the law which affected women. States like New York led the way in attempts to make regulations involving debt, bankruptcy, and liability more responsive to changing economic conditions. One of the results was the passage of laws granting married women the right to more control over their property.[24]

The growth of towns and cities began the process of concentrating and making more visible social problems such as poverty and drunkenness, thus making them hard to ignore. At the same time it brought together large numbers of women with the sense of moral superiority and disinterested social responsibility, time, and energy to organize benevolent societies in order to deal with those problems.[25] That propensity was encouraged by the social activism of religious groups like the Quakers as well as by the religious revivals of the Second Great Awakening and the spread of evangelical Protestantism, whose millennial vision demanded that true Christians, men and women alike, work to improve the world.[26] The reform movements which resulted welcomed women's participation even while they typically segregated them. In many cases, it was their experiences within those reform movements that forced activists to confront and respond to discrimination based on gender. Indeed, among the most important precipitating events leading to the Seneca Falls convention were the 1840 split in the American Anti-Slavery Society over the participation of women in the organization and the exclusion of female delegates from the World Anti-Slavery Convention in London that same year.[27] Despite this problem, however, benevolent societies and reform movements responding to the effects of social and economic change provided women with an unprecedented opportunity to develop their leadership, fundraising, and public speaking skills and made them aware of the limitations of relying on moral suasion to achieve their goals.[28]

The existing political culture also set the stage for the rise of the woman's rights movement. As Linda Kerber has pointed out, the political culture created after the American Revolution encouraged women to carry out their political roles within the home as Republican Mothers by training future republican citizens. But while Republican Motherhood limited women's political role, it also encouraged an improvement in women's educational opportunities, opportunities that would eventually lead women to take an interest in issues not directly related to either housekeeping or child rearing.[29]

The early nineteenth century was also characterized by an increase in the numbers of white men who could vote.[30] As long as there were restrictions on the numbers of men allowed to participate in political activities, the exclusion of women did not seem quite so egregious. But with the advent of universal, white, adult, manhood suffrage, the exclusion of women from voting and holding office was magnified since it placed them on a par with children, slaves, Native-Americans, convicts, and the mentally incompetent as the only groups left who were denied the vote.

All of these factors combined to produce the kind of climate necessary to encourage some women to develop a consciousness of the inequities to which they were being subjected. Personal circumstances determined which aspects of gender discrimination triggered feminist consciousness and brought individual women into the woman's rights movement. For Elizabeth Cady Stanton it was the restrictiveness of life as a housewife in Seneca Falls combined with her earlier resentment of laws which oppressed women, social custom that denied them access to higher education, and the lack of opportunity for women like Lucretia Mott to participate as equals with men in the World Anti-Slavery Convention.[31] For Susan B. Anthony it was experiences like the public humiliation of being refused the right to speak from the floor of a Sons of Temperance meeting.[32] For Lucretia Mott it was things like the realization that in her Quaker school male teachers earned twice as much as female teachers.[33] And for Lucy Stone it was her anger at being denied the right to vote as a member in the affairs of her church and the attitude of Congregational ministers toward women who wished to speak in public.[34]

The experience of the men who participated in the woman's rights movement was somewhat different. For men like Gerrit Smith, Samuel May, and Wendell Phillips, sensitivity toward gender discrimination came from their association with female friends and family members, their reform activities in abolition and temperance, and their outraged sense of justice when faced with the consequences of the belief that women were not the equals of men.[35] But for men and women alike, it was the anger that resulted from their personal sensitivity to discrimination based on gender that encouraged them collectively to seek social, economic, and political change by participating in the early woman's rights movement.

Early woman's rights activists, working within this context, depended upon ideas expressed both verbally and nonverbally rather than on institutions and organizations to try to change their world. These so-called strong-minded women and their male supporters appropriated an inherently sexist political philosophy and a political language created by men to serve their own ends. After identifying the leaders of this reform movement and discussing their relationships to one another and how they attempted to maintain those relationships, we will turn to an examination of aspects of the ideological origins of their demand for equal rights, the metaphors they used to express their ideas, the composition of their audience and how it was cultivated, and how some of those in that audience interpreted the message and responded to it.

Using woman's rights speeches, convention proceedings, tracts, pamphlets, newspaper reports and editorials, and articles from reform periodicals as well as the personal papers of such leaders as Lucretia Mott, Elizabeth Cady Stanton, and Susan B. Anthony, we will address a number of issues. The first concerns the role of both verbal and nonverbal forms of communication in cementing the casual network of friendship and reform sympathies that served as the basis for group identity and solidarity among the early leaders of the woman's rights movement. The second is an attempt to explain how early woman's rights advocates were able to move beyond the ideology and rhetoric of Republican Motherhood to demand an enhanced public political role. That ideology erected two barriers to expanding woman's political life. First, it defined her political role as private and therefore thwarted the efforts of women to expand their political activities into the public sphere. It also defined her political role in terms of her relationship with others. I will argue that in order for women to move beyond the ideology of Republican Motherhood, they had to embrace a different philosophy, one filtered through the natural rights doctrine of John Locke, early utilitarianism, and common sense philosophy of the Scottish Enlightenment. The resulting hybrid ideology provided those who became woman's rights advocates with a way of conceptualizing a political role for women that was not dependent upon domestic relationships or woman's work in benevolence, and allowed women to separate themselves from men, children, home, and church, and to claim the rights of citizenship based on the principles of individualism and self-interest rather than on the principles of self-sacrifice.

Many studies of the woman's rights movement are more concerned with its goals and tactics than they are with an in-depth analysis of its ideology.[36] Those scholars who do address the issue of its ideology argue convincingly that a number of influences such as evangelical Protestantism, Romanticism, Transcendentalism, and abolitionism combined with Enlightenment ideas and the principles of natural rights to bring about the early woman's rights movement.[37] But those who acknowledge feminist indebtedness to Enlightenment philosophers do not elaborate enough either to identify explicitly which of their ideas were the most significant or to explain in detail how those ideas were used by those who spoke out for the cause of woman's rights before the Civil War. Some even conclude that the Enlightenment provided women with little guidance in their attempts to establish for themselves a political persona in the new republic or argue that its legacy was "an extraordinarily confusing one."[38] More recently, Rosemarie Zagarri has challenged these assessments by illustrating how Scottish Enlightenment philosophers like Adam Smith and David Hume contributed to the concept of Republican Motherhood, but she does not carry her analysis beyond the early national period.[39] It is my intention, therefore, to try to enhance our understanding of how Enlightenment philosophy, particularly ideas derived from early utilitarianism and the Scottish Common Sense School, read both in the original and in diluted popularized versions, helped woman's rights activists justify their claim to equal social and political rights and economic opportunity.

Those who were most active in speaking out for the cause of woman's rights before the Civil War rejected metaphors most closely associated with woman's traditional sphere of home and benevolence in favor of the metaphors of nature, combined with those referring to the oppression of slavery, architectural renovation, machines, the millennium, and war, to express their discontent and articulate their reform ideology. This combination of metaphors provided them with a language which bound them together as a group and provided them with an especially effective way to promote their cause by rhetorically placing women in contexts that had traditionally been controlled and dominated by men. It also helped them to establish their political competency and provoked those in their audience to reassess their ideas about gender roles and relations.

Finally, I will focus on the way early woman's rights advocates cultivated their audience and the response they elicited when they made their demands public. The audience that was most publicly articulate in its response to the demands of these reformers and, therefore, the one that can be most systematically studied was composed of journalists representing two different kinds of periodicals: the newspapers of the penny press and reform journals. Newspapers had traditionally been an important weapon in the political arsenal of men. They became even more important in the mid-nineteenth century when, because of the development of paper and printing technology, new marketing techniques, and the rise of literacy, newspapers could be published and sold quickly and cheaply. Political in focus but not necessarily partisan, they increasingly contained human-interest stories as well as political and commercial information.[40]

Historians of the woman's rights movement have observed in passing that before the Civil War the popular press was generally contemptuous of woman's rights advocates and did little or nothing to help their cause.[41] But a systematic study of the matter using primary sources indicates that this assessment is not entirely accurate. The attention of newspaper editors was critical for the promotion of woman's rights demands. Silence on the part of the press would have condemned the movement, which had no official press of its own, to obscurity if not virtual invisibility as far as the general public was concerned. The leaders of the woman's rights movement intuitively understood that fact and quite consciously developed strategies designed to assure that newspaper editors reported their activities and responded to their demands. By manipulating the penny press and its male editors, woman's rights activists succeeded in directing toward themselves and their message the kind of attention that was crucial to the advancement of their interests and made male newspaper editors, both sympathetic and unsympathetic, unwitting and sometimes unwilling accomplices in the effort to gain more rights for women.

Careful analysis of the amount and kind of newspaper coverage directed towards the woman's movement in the Northeast and middle sections of the country before, during, and shortly after the convocation of woman's rights conventions in the antebellum period indicates that descriptions of and editorial comments upon woman's rights activities were extensive and that the editorial policies of daily newspapers in cities like New York, Philadelphia, Boston, St. Louis, Chicago, and Cleveland represented a broad range of opinion concerning the issue of more rights for women.[42] Some papers like the *New York Daily Herald* were indeed contemptuous. But others like the *New York Daily Times* reported the activities of woman's rights advocates straightforwardly. And still others like the *Philadelphia Public Ledger and Daily Transcript*, the *New York Tribune*, and the *Chicago Daily Tribune* were generally supportive. The important point is that papers all over the northern half of the country reported and commented upon those activities. The result was that the penny press in those sections played a significant role in diffusing information about the status of women and the demand for more rights. By doing so, it served the movement as its most important conduit to the general public and helped to legitimize the claims of women for enhanced social, economic, and political opportunities by promoting discussion of them.

Woman's rights advocates had to exert less effort to attract the attention of the editors of reform journals like *The Lily, The Sibyl, The Una, Frederick Douglass's Paper*, and *The Liberator*. And, not surprisingly, historians have emphasized the importance of these journals to the early woman's rights movement.[43] Periodicals like these could be counted on to support any number of reforms. *The Lily* edited by Amelia Bloomer, for example, promoted dress reform and temperance as well as woman's rights. The purpose of *The Liberator* was to advance the cause of abolition, but its editor William Lloyd Garrison also supported equal rights for women. Reform editors gave space to the cause of woman's rights when they could. But I will argue that their willingness to promote the cause was not as significant as the attention that the issue of woman's rights received in the penny press. The editors of journals like *The Lily* and *The Una* were faced with low budgets and limited circulation and were to some degree dependent upon stories printed in the penny press for information about the movement. Penny press newspapers had daily, biweekly or triweekly, and weekly editions. They were hawked on the street as well as sent through the mail to subscribers. Reform journals, unlike large circulation dailies, were normally published weekly, bimonthly, or monthly and were sold primarily through subscription. They also differed from the large circulation newspapers in that they tended to speak primarily to those already predisposed to support the demands of woman's rights advocates. Their major contribution to the cause, therefore, was limited primarily to cultivating those already interested in reform and to preserving the loyalty of the committed.

This study is confined to the period before the Civil War because in the very beginning there was among those who led the woman's rights movement comparatively little public disagreement about their goals and strategy. At no other time in their history did the most active woman's rights advocates speak so much with one voice. This does not mean that they always agreed with one another. Disagreements were to be expected given the fact that the point of reference from which they approached the cause of woman's rights sometimes differed. Some, like Elizabeth Cady Stanton, approached feminist issues from a singularly secular point of view. Others, as we shall see, placed the movement in the context of the coming millennium. Some were determined to try to establish the fact that men and women were the same as a basis for claiming equality of rights. Others found it difficult to give up the idea that men and women were different and insisted that women should be given more rights because they were morally superior to men. Some were willing to combine the struggle for political rights with dress reform and temperance. Others objected to that kind of inclusiveness. The early woman's rights movement was also characterized by the kind of squabbling and pettiness that sometimes erupts in groups whose members work closely together and feel passionately about what they are doing. But despite their differences, the leaders of the movement only occasionally criticized each other in public. And when they did, those criticisms tended to reflect their commitment to the spirit of debate or their need to clarify the issues rather than any really deeply felt antagonism. In the beginning, their desire to gain as much support as possible required a degree of tolerance that would not characterize the movement after the war. The differences that would eventually divide them lay just below the surface.

Indications that their ability to maintain tolerance for difference was limited became clear at the 1860 national convention when Elizabeth Cady Stanton, despite warnings from some of her friends, raised the issue of divorce. But in 1861 woman's rights advocates were as distracted by disunion and the possibility of war as the rest of the nation, and they agreed among themselves to cancel their annual convention. During the war, voices raised for the cause of equality for women were largely silent or focused on the more immediate problem of supporting the war effort and working for the abolition of slavery. And after the war, the movement split between the National Woman's Suffrage Association and the American Woman's Suffrage Association, organizations that would spend most of the rest of the century competing rather than cooperating with each other.[44]

Before the war and the split in the movement that followed, women gained more control over their property, took advantage of increased educational and economic opportunities, and claimed their right to speak out on their own behalf. They did not achieve equality before the law. They also failed to gain the right to vote. But they were able to engage influential men in widely disseminated public political discourse on the subject of woman's right to full participation in all aspects of American life. It was their success in maintaining that discourse that established a political competency for women that went beyond the one which had been granted to them by the ideology of Republican Motherhood. That discourse was a prerequisite for any significant improvement in woman's political, economic, and social status. Because of it, woman's interests could not be disregarded. Along with the kind of petitioning and lobbying long associated with women's work in the area of benevolence and reform, it served as a bridge that linked the private political role assigned to women after the American Revolution to the increasingly public one they would eventually assume in the twentieth century.

I

THE ADVOCATES

In an 1852 editorial commenting on the participants of the woman's rights convention held in Syracuse, New York, James Gordon Bennett of the New York *Herald* asked rhetorically, "Who are these women?" and then proceeded to identify them as generally unattractive and disagreeable "hens that crow."[1] Those "hens" and the men who worked with them to advance the cause of woman's rights before the Civil War formed a fairly homogeneous group and established a strong network of social relationships.[2] At the same time, however, their personal commitment to individualism encouraged them to set limits on the degree to which the group that they identified themselves with could control their voices and behavior. That individualism led them to reject the opportunity to establish any sort of formal organization. It also led them into and then out of a commitment to wear reform dress. In the end, it was their social network, their ideology, the verbal symbols that they devised to express that ideology, and the cooperation required to attract attention to their cause which held them together so that they could pursue their reform work effectively.

Many individuals participated at one time or another in the various local, state, and national woman's rights conventions held before the war. But the vanguard of that group was composed of about twenty-three men and women who had the time, energy, money, and commitment to participate in at least three national conventions including those early ones held in 1848 in Seneca Falls and Rochester.[3] Of that group fourteen were women. Susan B. Anthony, Antoinette Brown Blackwell, Paulina Wright Davis, Abby Kelley Foster, Frances Dana Gage, Harriot Kezia Hunt, Lydia Ann Jenkins, Jane Elizabeth Hitchcock Jones, Lucretia Coffin Mott, Clarina I. Howard Nichols, Abby Price, Ernestine Potowski Rose, Elizabeth Cady Stanton, and Lucy Stone all appeared in person and spoke out in support of woman's rights or sent letters to be read at three or more of the eleven national conventions that followed the Seneca Falls convention. Less active on the national level but no less committed were women like Martha C. Wright, Angelina Grimké Weld, and Elizabeth Oakes Smith.

The other nine were men, a fact that testifies to the degree to which the antebellum woman's rights movement, like abolition and temperance, was characterized by cross-gender cooperation and collaboration.[4] Charles Burleigh, William H. Channing, Frederick Douglass, William Lloyd Garrison, Horace Greeley, Thomas Wentworth Higginson, Samuel J. May, Wendell Phillips, and Gerrit Smith all either joined their female colleagues on the podium or sent letters expressing their support for the cause to be read by others. Parker Pillsbury, Theodore Parker, Henry Ward Beecher, George William Curtis, and others also spoke compellingly in support of woman's cause but participated less frequently in what might be considered the national debate over woman's proper role in society and politics.

These men and women had a great deal in common. Most of them were middle-aged: Lucretia Mott, born in 1783, was the oldest of the group. Almost all of them were married and had children. All but Frederick Douglass were white, and all but Ernestine Rose were native-born. All of them had either formally or informally educated themselves. Their religious affiliations varied. A great many of them were Quakers or Unitarians. Most were liberal Protestants of one sort or other. They were middle-class reformers, mostly from New York and New England, whose interest in improving society led them into a variety of reform movements ranging from dress and prison reform to abolitionism and temperance work as well as feminism.[5]

It would be hard to overestimate the importance that this participation in social reform activities played in the development of the early woman's rights movement. Reform work provided women the opportunity to develop public speaking, fundraising, and administrative skills as well as a network of individuals who could be counted on to support them both emotionally and materially. As Ellen Carol DuBois has pointed out, the abolitionist movement was particularly important to the development of early feminism. It provided them with an egalitarian philosophy, an organizational structure, financial support, a ready-made constituency, an opportunity to enlarge the definition of woman's "proper sphere" despite the censoriousness of the clergy, and the belief that agitation and provocation was their primary responsibility.[6]

The activist networks that woman's rights supporters formed as a result of their participation in reform movements were based on family relationships augmented by physical proximity, mutual interests, and the kind of personal sacrifices that reform work demanded of each of them. Susan B. Anthony, for example, was introduced to William Lloyd Garrison, Frederick Douglass, and Wendell Phillips in her father's household. She met Elizabeth Cady Stanton through Amelia Bloomer, the editor of the reform paper *The Lily*, with whom she worked in the cause of temperance. Elizabeth Cady was the cousin of Gerrit Smith and through him met various prominent abolitionists including the man she married, Henry Stanton. It was when she accompanied her new husband to the World

Anti-Slavery Convention in London that she met Lucretia Mott. Ernestine Rose worked with Paulina Wright Davis as well as Stanton in the New York campaign to provide married women with property rights. Before she became involved in the woman's rights movement, Jane Elizabeth Jones had accompanied Abby Kelley Foster on an abolitionist speaking tour. Antoinette Brown met Lucy Stone at Oberlin, and, before she began to support woman's rights, joined Bloomer and Anthony on a tour intended to promote the cause of temperance. Both Stone and Brown married into the Blackwell family.[7]

This network of like-minded reformers, formed over the years, was fluid and could be welcoming and inclusive. This is not to say that it was immune from squabbles, bickering, and petty jealousies, but that woman's rights advocates were eager to recruit others to their cause. Some like Frances Gage initiated their own membership into the group by appearing at the Syracuse national convention in 1852 prepared to give an unsolicited speech. The only person she knew when she arrived was Samuel J. May.[8] Others found a sponsor from among those whose commitment to the cause was well established. Paulina Wright Davis, for example, acted as Elizabeth Oakes Smith's patron when she wrote in a letter to Elizabeth Cady Stanton, "She [Smith] is not as ultra as some among us. But we must accept her for all that she is. We need every possible shade and variety of lecturers and workers in this great movement. . . . She will bring a great many to think and reason on the subject and will throw none back. She will never indulge in any personalities and hence, unlike Abby Foster, never offends a hundred where she converts one." Such an endorsement, she no doubt hoped, would promote the influence of Smith within the inner circle of feminist activists.[9] Susan B. Anthony was introduced to Elizabeth Cady Stanton in 1851 while on her way to a temperance meeting. Stanton immediately welcomed her as a recruit into the woman's rights movement, and they became fast friends.[10]

During the ten years or so before the Civil War these reformers contributed to the cause of woman's rights by performing such public political rituals as writing letters to editors, giving speeches, conducting petition drives, raising money, editing and publishing essays and articles on woman's rights, and calling conventions on the local, state, and national levels. Planning a national convention began immediately after the previous convention adjourned. Beginning in 1850 ad hoc committees rented public halls, arranged for speakers, and prepared a slate of officers for the consideration of convention participants. A few weeks before the convention began, members of the committee sent out a "call" to reform periodicals as well as newspapers in order to inform those who might be interested where and when the convention would take place. Early conventions were intended to be open forums where questions regarding the status of women could be discussed by those in the audience as well as those on the speakers' platform. Later conventions had a somewhat more formal agenda. Typically a presiding officer called the meeting to order and presented a slate of new officers to the audience. After installing the new officers, the audience listened to reports on the condition of women, speeches, letters from those who found it impossible to attend the meeting, and debates over resolutions presented for consideration.

Response to calls for national conventions was encouraging. Attendance at the Seneca Falls convention numbered a little over one hundred. By 1853, woman's rights advocates could fill several thousand seats in major metropolitan areas.[11] As the ideas advocated by woman's rights activists began to spread, new converts began to take action. Emily Collins, for example, was so inspired by the Seneca Falls convention held in July of 1848 that within three months she and fifteen or twenty of her neighbors had formed a Woman's Equal Rights Union in their county in a remote area of the state of New York. They met in each other's homes every two weeks to discuss issues relevant to the movement such as the need for a newspaper, lecturers, and fundraising. Together they organized petition drives and encouraged men to discuss the issue of woman's rights in their debating clubs.[12]

Woman's rights leaders also considered the possibility of formally organizing themselves. In 1851, for example, Elizabeth Oakes Smith suggested to Paulina Wright Davis that they and some of their more "judicious" female colleagues form some sort of "sisterhood" modeled after a masonic organization. Davis wasn't particularly enthusiastic about the idea. "I hate organizations," she wrote. "They cramp me. I never like to work for their machinery. But this may be useful if it is made subservient to the object," she concluded.[13] There is no evidence that Smith's plan was ever implemented despite the fact that, as Tocqueville observed, Americans had a great propensity for forming associations.

What is particularly telling about Davis's comments regarding Smith's suggestion is the degree to which others in the movement agreed with her about the disadvantages of formally organizing themselves. In the spring of 1852, Antoinette Brown wrote to Lucy Stone about the possibility of forming a national society to promote the cause of women. She was ambivalent about the idea, determined to preserve the right of all of the cause's supporters "to act independently." At the same time, however, she was afraid that if they did not organize themselves around the inclusive and broad general principle of gender equality, someone with narrow views would organize a group that would "shame the cause and retard its progress." Then, she predicted, the movement would fragment when rival organizations were formed.[14]

The issue arose again that fall at the Syracuse convention where convention participants debated it on the third day. After presiding officer Lucretia Mott announced that the convention would discuss the possibility of forming a permanent national organization, Rev. Samuel J. May, pastor of the Unitarian Church in Syracuse, read a letter from Angelina Grimké Weld opposing the idea. Weld's objections were based upon the idea that there was a difference between what she called natural or divine organization, which allowed the world to progress automatically from one state to another, and artificial or human organization, which did not. She had a number of objections to associations established by humans. In her view, once formed, organizations took on a life of their own. They killed the reform spirit and stifled independence of thought. They prevented change from occurring through a *"crystallization"* process whereby old ideas were allowed to become fixed and immutable. They had no "safety valve" to encourage creativity. Like poison, she wrote, human institutions such as the church and the state destroyed life and debilitated their members. Such artificial organizations with their "tests of membership" and rigidity of doctrine demanded that individual interests be sacrificed for the benefit of the group. In doing so they "paralyzed" the wills as well as the minds of their members. "It [the organization] builds walls around itself for its own protection" and becomes more conservative by "shutting out that natural and healthful collision with outside influences" which tended to energize and stimulate its members, she wrote.[15]

After May finished reading Weld's letter, a convention participant, Mary Springstead, offered a motion from the floor to organize a permanent woman's rights society. A long debate ensued among various leaders of the movement, most of whom agreed with Weld that organizations did nothing but restrain the individual and discourage creative thinking.[16] Dr. Harriot K. Hunt, for example, opposed a national organization on the grounds that institutional authority arbitrarily restrained individuality. "Spontaneity" was more natural, she said. It "will organize, vitalize, and render efficient." Woman's rights advocates needed no artificial connection. "We are organized and linked together like nature, and electrical sympathy is the only safe organization," she argued.[17]

Ernestine Rose agreed. Organizations were as constraining as "Chinese bandages," she said. Her experience was that "political, moral, and religious bodies" were "the incubus of our nature." They put "shackles" on the intellectual freedom of their members. "The moment a man has intellectual life enough to strike out a new idea, he is branded as a heretic," she said. Like Hunt, she argued that the "magnetism of the cause" was all that was needed to unite them.[18] Lucy Stone was as suspicious of organizations as the others. She reminded the audience that "like a burnt child that dreads the fire, they had all been in permanent organizations, and thus dreaded them. She had [had] enough," she said, "of thumb-screws and soul screws ever to wish to be placed under them again."[19]

Only a few supported the idea of a permanent organization. Their arguments were based on the belief that a national association would make their efforts more systematic and efficient.[20] But they failed to convince convention participants. So when the debate ended, the convention voted to adopt a motion by Davis not to form a national organization but to encourage woman's rights supporters to hold local and state conventions at least once a year.[21] And until after the Civil War, the woman's rights movement was directed by a largely self-appointed central committee whose membership was passed around to those with the time, energy, and expertise to manage the various activities of the movement.

The result of the debate over forming a permanent national organization is not really surprising. Many woman's rights advocates came to the movement with anti-institutional biases. Those with abolitionist backgrounds were aware that both church and state tolerated and sometimes even defended the existence of slavery. And both were held responsible for the subjugation of women. Woman's rights activists petitioned state legislatures for equity under the law and struggled against the prejudice of clergymen who opposed the right of women to speak out in their own behalf or on behalf of others. Moreover, their experience in reform organizations only confirmed their belief that formal associations did little to encourage the participation of women on an equal basis with men. The opposition of some male delegates to admitting women to equal participation in the American Anti-Slavery Society in 1840, a conflict which resulted in a permanent split in organization, was only one of the more dramatic humiliations to which female reformers were constantly subjected.

Female temperance advocates faced similar discrimination. In January of 1852 when Susan B. Anthony, representing the Daughters of Temperance, attempted to address an assembly of temperance advocates in Albany, New York, she was advised that while women were welcome to serve as delegates to the convention, they were expected to listen rather than participate in the proceedings. Five months later, Anthony along with Amelia Bloomer, this time serving as a representative of the Woman's New York State Temperance Society, were denounced from the floor as representatives of "'a hybrid species, half man and half woman, belonging to neither sex,'" when they attempted to take their seats at the Men's New York State Temperance Convention held in Syracuse.[22]

Those kinds of humiliating incidents would continue. The year after the debate at Syracuse, Antoinette Brown was refused the right to sit on the platform at the World's Temperance Convention held in New York. Brown had been appointed a delegate to the convention by both the South Butler [New York] Temperance Association and the Rochester [New York] Toronto Division of the Sons of Temperance. When she reached New York City, she heard some discussion about whether the convention would indeed admit women as delegates. Determined to "test the matter" she went to Metropolitan Hall and presented her credentials to the secretary on the platform and took her place in the audience. Gratified when the convention voted to receive all authorized delegates without regard for color or sex, she attempted to return to the platform to thank the convention; but presiding president Neal Dow refused to allow her to speak. The next day she returned to the convention, and Dow recognized her; but delegates on the floor prevented her from speaking by disrupting the meeting for three hours. The president finally cleared the hall and informed the delegates that they would be allowed to retake their seats and vote in the convention only after their credentials had been checked. When the convention reconvened, the delegates voted against allowing women to speak.[23]

During the debate in Syracuse, Elizabeth Oakes Smith had pointed out that a permanent organization would provide woman's rights advocates with a structure within which to establish contacts with one another, contacts that were of crucial importance in promoting their cause.[24] But this advantage did not impress the leaders of the early woman's rights movement because most of them had begun their reform careers as members of abolitionist or temperance organizations and had therefore already established the kind of personal networks that a formal and permanent woman's rights society could provide. Moreover, the commitment of woman's rights advocates to the ideology of individualism precluded the kind of collectivism that formal organization seemed to require. As we shall see in the next chapter, until women moved from an ideology based on belief in the selflessness of womankind to an ideology based on the assumption that the pursuit of self-interest for women was legitimate, they would not be able to argue effectively for an expansion of a public role for themselves. This ideology of individualism combined with their already well-established personal acquaintance with one another and their sometimes humiliating experiences in the organizations of various other reform movements led them to reject the idea of establishing a permanent national woman's rights society. They were willing to work within a reform community composed of like-minded kin and friends, but they had no intention of placing themselves in the position of being responsive to the collective demands of an organization. Community allowed them the choice of fighting for equality both in their own way and in informal cooperation with others. Organizational collectivity demanded discipline, encouraged group decision making, and was likely to require submission to the will of the majority. Community allowed them to make individual choices. They feared that collectivity would not. Their unwillingness to sacrifice themselves for the benefit of the group, even a group whose goals they generally endorsed, stood as testimony to their commitment to the principles of individualism and the preservation of their own personal self-interest even as they pursued advances that they felt would serve the interests of all women and society in general.

This rejection of formal collectivism did, however, pose a potential threat to the ability of woman's rights advocates to communicate with the general public as well as to maintain stability and preserve unity within their movement. They attempted to maintain their sense of community in part through letter writing, personal visits to each other's homes, committee work, and public advocacy. Added to these activities were other symbols that could be used to publicly testify to their feminism and commitment to the cause. Among the most important, as we shall see in chapter 3, were the literary metaphors that woman's rights advocates used as verbal symbols in their speeches, tracts, essays, and letters. But they also tried using the visual metaphor of clothes to draw attention to the woman's rights movement, enhance their sense of community, affirm their commitment to the cause, and force those who saw them to reconsider their attitude toward gender roles in American society.

Because they were pioneers and because appearing in public to support the cause of feminism was unconventional, those who participated in the early woman's rights movement were from the beginning very sensitive and self-conscious about their personal appearance.[25] They understood implicitly that clothes have meaning, that they can be used to communicate complex messages that testify to such things as the wearer's social class, gender, personal relationships, political opinions, and attitudes toward the body.[26] Some of them were determined to try to use the metaphorical power of clothing to promote the struggle for equal rights.

Shortly after the Seneca Falls and Rochester conventions Elizabeth Cady Stanton learned that Richard Hunt, a mutual friend and supporter, had criticized the hat that she had worn to deliver her maiden speech in support of woman's rights. According to Lucretia Mott, Hunt had found Stanton's hat to be too "theatrical." Hunt was concerned that what Stanton wore might interfere with her audience's ability to focus on her ideology and rhetoric. Mott must have agreed since she suggested that a bonnet that reflected "Quaker simplicity" might be more appropriate.[27] Part of their concern, no doubt, arose from the fact that both of them were Quakers, a religious denomination that traditionally insisted on plain dress as a form of self-discipline. This insistence had served them and their religious forbears well as, among other things, a potentially effective strategy for disarming those hostile to them. Their criticism was meant to suggest to Stanton that presenting herself in plain and conventional clothing might soothe the visual sensibilities of her listeners while she stimulated their intellectual and cultural ones. They asked that she use her appearance to confirm her femininity, respectability, modesty, and ingenuousness. Her clothes, their suggestion implied, could serve as a kind of masquerade that might temper and render more palatable the effect of her unconventional demand for gender equality.

STRONG-MINDED "BLOOMER."—"Now, do, Alfred, put down that foolish Novel, and do something rational. G(
and play something You never practice, now you're married."

The Bloomer costume captured the imagination of illustrators who used it to provoke speculation about how giving women more rights might influence gender roles. *Harper's New Monthly Magazine*, January 1852, p. 286. Courtesy of the Library of Congress.

A little over two years later, however, some in the vanguard of the woman's rights movement rejected the approach suggested by their Quaker colleagues. By wearing reform dress in public, they adopted an alternative strategy, one that visually announced their membership in a group committed to the principle that women's social, economic, and political roles as well as their minds and bodies should be freed from artificial restraints of conventions which helped to deprive them of power and influence outside the home.

Elizabeth Smith Miller, the daughter of Gerrit Smith, was among the first to wear what became known as the Bloomer dress. She appeared in Seneca Falls wearing the outfit in the winter of 1850–51. Her version of the outfit combined pantaloons similar to those worn by the Turks with a dress with a short skirt that fell loosely from the shoulders. The costume was much more comfortable to wear than more conventional dress which constricted the body and draped it with yard upon yard of fabric. It allowed a woman to move freely about and to carry things in both hands while going up and down stairs. And since it did not sweep the ground, it stayed relatively clean.

Elizabeth Cady Stanton and her friends and neighbors adopted the dress, and soon it was being promoted by Amelia Bloomer in her temperance paper called *The Lily* published in Seneca Falls, New York. The July 1851 issue of the paper contained an illustration of the so-called "new costume" which had appeared previously in a Boston periodical called the *Carpet Bag*. Two months later, Bloomer printed a woodcut of a daguerreotype of her own costume. And in the January 1852 issue she published two fashion plates to illustrate a Bloomer costume suitable for wear in the wintertime which she informed her readers was "warmer, with a smaller amount of clothing, than the old style." Moreover, she pointed out, "there are no long skirts to gather up mud and snow, and whip it upon the ankles."[28] The campaign to promote popular acceptance of this new fashion was as much an attempt to promote the health, comfort, and freedom of movement of women as it was to make a political statement. And its supporters were determined that it be presented to the public as an expression of "good taste."[29]

The costume attracted considerable attention and almost immediately became associated with the struggle for woman's rights. Because of its distinctiveness, it provided woman's rights advocates with a visual symbol which testified to their personal, social, and political opinions. As Jane Swisshelm, editor of the *Pittsburgh Saturday Visiter* put it, "the whole question of woman's political and social position was mixed up with . . . the length of her petticoats."[30]

Newspaper reporters collaborated with woman's rights advocates in popularizing the symbol by describing with some regularity the clothes that woman's rights speakers wore at their conventions. In 1853 the *New York Daily Times* told its readers that "Mrs. [Amelia] Bloomer was attired in a suit of brown satin, cut, of course, in the most approved style of her own costume. Miss Anthony was dressed in a similar costume—material, black silk. Rev. Antoinette Brown (not considering the Bloomer costume to harmonize with the dignity of her office) wore ordinary long skirts."[31] A similar story appeared in the Philadelphia *Evening Bulletin* the next year. "Miss Lucy Stone," the reporter wrote, "was dressed in a rich Bloomer costume made of black silk velvet and fine black cloth. Her pantaloons were made of the last material and her feet were enclosed in a pair of patent leather shoes."[32]

Bloomers, however, were not the only new style of dress adopted by advocates of woman's rights. In 1853, Stanton carried dress reform one step further by designing for herself a short dress worn with high boots rather than Turkish pants. The dress fell one inch below the top of the boots. She reported that she had received compliments on her new costume but was unable to convince others to adopt it.[33]

While they lasted, Bloomers and short dresses were more than just provocative visual metaphors representing the demand that women be granted equal rights. Wearing reform dress publicly demonstrated a woman's commitment to independence of thought and action. In the absence of a formal organization, it helped to establish and maintain a sense of community among those who supported the cause. It also provided woman's rights advocates with a way of testifying to and measuring the extent of their commitment to the cause. In that sense, willingness to wear Bloomers served as the very kind of test of membership that those who opposed formal organization so feared. It testified in a visual public way to the degree to which a woman was willing to sacrifice herself to make a political statement. Stanton, for example, wrote that she was afraid that her insistence on wearing reform dress in public might even result in the loss of her kin.[34]

Failure to wear Bloomers or short dresses in public could cast doubt on one's level of commitment or effectiveness as an advocate of woman's rights. Elizabeth Oakes Smith, who remained unenthusiastic about wearing reform dress, failed in her bid to become president of the woman's rights convention held in Syracuse in 1852 partly because of the way she dressed. Susan B. Anthony, a strong supporter of the Bloomer costume, played a significant role in preventing her nomination. Smith attended the meeting in a fashionable "short-sleeved" and "low-necked" embroidered dress. Anthony objected to her appearance on the ground that dressed as she was she "could [not] represent the earnest, solid, hardworking women of the country." Anthony's argument won the day. Lucretia Mott was nominated as president. Smith was relegated to a vice-presidency.[35] Anthony's friend Elizabeth Cady Stanton likewise expressed some concern about the ability of those who refused to adopt reform dress to convincingly promote the cause of woman's rights when she commented that she would have found Lydia Fowler's lectures more convincing if she had not appeared before her audience with her "waist lined with whale-bones."[36]

Paulina Wright Davis, like other woman's rights advocates who resisted wearing reform dress, felt compelled to try to defend her decision to wear conventional clothing in public in order to preserve her status as a woman's rights leader. She was perfectly willing to martyr herself for the cause, she assured Stanton, but she was determined to decide for herself how she would go about doing it and argued that adoption of reform dress was more likely to hinder than to help her to promote the interests of women.[37]

The adoption of reform dress also served as a way to acknowledge at least implicitly the degree to which conventional dress made genteel and respectable women invisible and unnoticed in public. Women's clothes obscured their bodies, subtly testifying to their restricted access to public life and equality with men. When woman's rights leaders donned the Bloomer costume and its variations, they publicly testified to their refusal to any longer tolerate that status.

Reform dress helped them to communicate that message by obscuring the line between a woman's private life and her public one. It drew attention to women's bodies and the clothing that covered them, thus making them a topic of public discussion. Wearing short dresses and

Bloomers in public allowed female woman's rights advocates to embody, quite literally, their demands and their right to express them freely and seek redress of their grievances. Unlike conventional dress, reform dress did not restrict, control, and discipline the body. Bloomers allowed the female body to reveal its natural expanse and contours. In a visual way, reform dress unleashed female physicality and placed it before the public eye.

Because wearing Bloomers in public directed attention toward women and made them visible, the costume helped to promote discussion of the demand that women's public roles be expanded. But in doing so, it also made public figures of those who donned the outfit and encouraged outsiders and strangers to intrude into the private space of their lives. The experiences of Stanton and Lucy Stone illustrate the point. In June of 1851, Stanton reported to her friend Elizabeth Miller that her husband Henry's political opponents had made her choice of clothing an issue in his recent political campaign. "My name was hawked about the streets and in all the public meetings," she wrote. She reported that two men had been brought to blows over a hat that she had worn and others had severely criticized her choice of dress. "Street urchins," she complained, verbally abused her. The question of her dress continued to haunt her in the form of a popular ditty sung in the streets at the end of the campaign:

> "Heigh! ho! the carrion crow
> Mrs. Stanton's all the go;
> Twenty tailors take the stitches,
> Mrs. Stanton wears the breeches."[38]

Conspicuous she was. Embattled she felt. Suffer for the cause she did. But at the same time, her clothes made her as much a part of the political process as her husband and his political cronies. Her choice of costume had inadvertently provided her with a public opportunity to testify to a political philosophy that was as disconcerting and even offensive to the unsympathetic and uninformed as the clothes that she wore. Despite the personal discomfort that resulted from all this attention, she remained at least temporarily committed to this visual testimony to her campaign to free women from the bonds of convention that enslaved them.

Stanton was not the only one to suffer for the cause. Lucy Stone reported that she was "annoyed to death by people who recognize me by my clothes." She wrote to Susan B. Anthony that when she traveled in the costume, perfect strangers felt compelled to sit next to her and "*bore*" her with their prattle. Moreover, she found that when she went out to see the sights in a new city dressed in the reform dress, "a horde of boys pursue me and destroy all comfort." She was convinced that if she dressed more conventionally, she would again become invisible and would not be subjected to such unwelcome intrusions.[39] But like Stanton she was willing to pay the price that accompanied her determination to testify in a visual way to her commitment to woman's rights, at least for the time being.

What both Stanton and Stone discovered was that choosing to wear unconventional dress in public was a powerful weapon but a double-edged sword. Wearing Bloomers on the street freed their bodies, made them visible, allowed them to testify to their commitment to the cause, brought public attention to the issue of woman's rights, and enhanced their place in public life. At the same time, however, they found that these same clothes deprived them of the privacy and invisibility that wearing conventional dress would have assured them. Their costume gave strangers and "street urchins," who harassed them on trains and sidewalks and bandied about references to their most private relationships, license to intrude into their personal space and private lives. The result was that while both women remained committed to their right to dress as they wished, they began to reassess the degree to which this form of exhibitionism was worth the sacrifice of their privacy. They learned in a very personal and dramatic way what any politician or popular entertainer could have told them, that public life sometimes carries with it a heavy price.

Eventually, one feminist leader after another began to abandon the practice of wearing the Bloomer costume in public. As they did so, the usefulness of dress as a visual sign of one's political and social philosophy as well as of community and commitment declined. Some were more persistent than others. Anthony, for whom the importance of dress as a symbol of freedom and community was of paramount concern, resisted the return to wearing conventional clothes in public. She pursued a vigorous campaign to prevent her friends and co-workers from discarding the controversial costume but to no avail. By the spring of 1854, Stanton had given up wearing short skirts in public. Anthony noted her disappointment when she reported to Stone that Stanton's "petticoats have assumed their former length, and her wardrobe cleared of every short skirt." Anthony regretted Stanton's decision. "Everyone who *drops* the dress," she complained, "makes the task a harder one for the few left,"[40] and she continued to hold out despite pressure from both Stanton and Stone.[41] But by 1855 even she had returned to wearing long skirts.[42]

Distressed by this turn of events, Gerrit Smith tried to extend the life of reform dress as a visual metaphor and political symbol by attempting to renew in print the debate over its role in the struggle for female equality. In December of 1855, he wrote a letter to his cousin Elizabeth Cady Stanton criticizing the female vanguard of the woman's rights movement for rejecting the Bloomer costume. Conventional female dress, he wrote, was a symbol of woman's "helplessness and degradation." It imprisoned and crippled the female body by depriving women of the power to take care of themselves and to achieve economic independence. It rendered them "unfit . . . for the vast majority of human pursuits" and reduced them to "plaything[s] and doll[s]."[43] For Smith, the willingness of woman's rights advocates to continue their efforts to free women's bodies from the bondage of conventional clothing was a test of their moral courage and persistence. Failure to do so, he feared, would not bode well for attempts to achieve such goals as political and economic equality.

Smith's letter, which was published in reform periodicals like *Frederick Douglass's Paper* and *The Sibyl* and as a broadside, brought a flurry of responses from the female leaders of the movement.[44] Stanton, of course, felt compelled to answer his challenge immediately. In collaboration with Martha Coffin Wright, she wrote a reply which was also published in a number of periodicals including the Rochester [New York] *Tribune*, *The Lily*, and Frederick Douglass's abolitionist paper and printed as a broadside. Stanton pointed out that while a woman's dress might be an important symbol, it was only a symbol. A change in dress, she argued, would not change the condition of women any more than the right to wear pants changed the condition of slaves in the South. Moreover, she pointed out that decisions about matters of dress tended to be both personal and capricious. The ultimate goal of the movement, she asserted, was to so change American society and the institutions and laws upon which it was based that any woman, whether married or not, would be guaranteed the right to her own person.[45]

Smith replied privately in a letter to Stanton assuring her that the basis of their disagreement over the issue of woman's dress was a matter of perspective and strategy rather than substance. He agreed with Stanton that the ultimate goal of the movement should be gender equality. But he maintained that achieving that goal had to be done in stages. And he was convinced that the first stage was to enable women to become economically independent of men, a condition that was impossible to achieve as long as women's clothes imprisoned their bodies and hindered their freedom of movement.[46]

The public debate that Smith initiated among woman's rights advocates lasted for about ten months. Frances Gage's response, published in *Frederick Douglass's Paper*, argued that what women wore was of considerably less import than the issue of who controlled their bodies, wages, and thoughts.[47] Months later in October of 1856 Sarah Grimké responded to Smith in *The Lily*. A Quaker, and therefore more conservative in matters of dress than either Stanton or Smith, she argued in her letter that while the Bloomer costume was very practical "for walking in the country, through bushes and brakes, jumping fences, working in the garden, and all sorts of domestic labor," it was as inappropriate for a woman to wear the outfit "when quietly seated at home, or passing about a city" as it was for "a farmer who is visiting his friends or spending a few days in New York" to wear his working clothes "or appear in the parlor in his shirt sleeves."

THE DRESS CIRCLE AT A CONCERT—FRONT ROW.

In the late 1850s, editors of popular periodicals like *Harper's Weekly* caricatured the extravagance of the dresses worn by middle- and upper-class women just as they had poked fun at the Bloomer costume earlier in the decade. *Harper's Weekly*, August 1, 1857, p. 496. Courtesy of the Library of Congress.

While she acknowledged that freedom of movement was necessary for any woman who aspired to enter such heavy trades as shipbuilding, most women, she felt, were more likely to find economic opportunity in the kinds of newly emerging handicraft trades, clerking, and sales jobs that were increasingly open to them. Such jobs, she pointed out, required manual skill and quickness of mind, qualities that were not necessarily inhibited by the kind of clothes a woman wore. Her main criteria for selecting appropriate dress therefore included any garment that was "simple, uncostly, convenient, and healthy."[48]

By the time Grimké responded to Smith, the debate over reform dress among the vanguard of woman's rights advocates had been reduced to a discussion over the practical significance of clothing. For them, its usefulness as a visual metaphor and political statement was ending. During the next few years, the job of directing public attention to the matter of woman's dress was left to illustrators and cartoonists who caricatured fashion in such popular periodicals as *Harper's Weekly Magazine* and *Frank Leslie's Illustrated Newspaper* and those who carried on the cause by organizing the National Dress Reform Association.[49] By 1859 few if any of the female vanguard of the woman's rights movement wore Bloomers in public. That fact was duly noted in the press when the *New York Daily Herald* announced that Bloomers were no longer being worn on the platform of national woman's rights conventions.[50]

That woman's rights advocates should have resorted to the use of clothes as a symbol of their oppressed status and as a metaphor for their demands for freedom testifies to the degree that they had internalized the idea that clothes were a visual representation of gender. In American society the clothes that men and women wore were distinctive. The clothes that most people chose to wear testified to the kind of body that the clothes covered. As Joan Wollach Scott has pointed out, the source of social, economic, and political inequality between men and women in Western culture has been located in their bodies. Access to the full rights of citizenship and public life was in both theory and practice dependent on the possession of certain physical characteristics.[51] The Bloomer costume and its variations, deemed unfeminine by the general public, provided those who were willing to adopt it a way of publicly announcing that they were no longer willing to allow their bodies and the clothes that represented those bodies to serve as the source and symbol of their inequality and invisibility. Gerrit Smith said as much when he predicted that if women were to discard conventional dress, men would have to acknowledge woman's "transmutation into his equal."[52] The freedom that Bloomers and short dresses gave to women represented the freedom that men had to pursue the economic, social, and political opportunities that were available to them. By wearing unconventional clothing, female woman's rights reformers challenged the American public to reconsider their attitudes toward gender roles and the meaning of the human body as well as to acknowledge the right of women to equality with men.

In the end, however, conformity in dress, like membership in a permanent organization, was sacrificed on the altar of individualism and self-interest. The men and women who supported the cause of woman's rights were willing to spend their time, money, and energy promoting the feminist cause. They were willing to sacrifice their personal reputations and private resources in order to gain for future generations greater access to economic, political, and educational opportunity. But they were determined to decide for themselves what price they would pay for their participation in the movement and how they would conduct their struggle to achieve gender equality. Before the Civil War, the ties that bound them together were ultimately limited to those of friendship and mutual respect, combined with an ideology and an accompanying language that could be used by each of them in their own way to provoke and sustain public discourse on the subject of the status of women in America.

II

THE IDEOLOGY

The ideology of the early woman's rights movement was designed to justify the demand that women be given the opportunity to expand their participation in American social, economic, and political life, to challenge prevailing attitudes toward gender roles, to fundamentally transform American society and the male dominated infrastructure that supported it, and to make such changes palatable to those outside the movement. When Elizabeth Cady Stanton, Susan B. Anthony, and Matilda Joslyn Gage looked back on their role in the early woman's rights movement from the perspective of the early 1880s, they wrote that they had been eclectic in their appropriation of ideas in their attempt to formulate a coherent woman's rights ideology. Their intent had been to weave together a set of principles designed to promote the cause of "individualism" as a way of improving the condition of womankind.[1]

As others have pointed out, the early leaders of the woman's rights movement brought with them to the cause intellectual baggage derived from their work in other reforms. Thus, the ideology which helped to bind together the network of woman's rights advocates in the years before the Civil War was, not surprisingly, a hybrid one which combined ideas from a number of sources including abolitionism, Romanticism, utopian socialism, evangelical Protestantism, transcendentalism, republicanism, John Locke's theory of natural rights, and the Enlightenment to justify their demands for equal rights.[2] None of these intellectual traditions had originally focused on the status of women. They had been designed to accommodate male needs, to address their concerns, to promote their interests, and to stabilize the political, economic, and social systems that they had created. Because there were no other ideological and discursive structures available to them, woman's rights advocates had to express themselves within male-defined intellectual frameworks and discourse. The need to appropriate political and social philosophies designed by men testified to women's traditional intellectual and political marginality. But while men may have created and up to this point remained largely in control of Western intellectual life, they did not control the way the intellectual traditions that they had created were applied. When woman's rights advocates appropriated male political and social philosophies and applied them to the female experience, they did so in ways that expanded their meaning in order to produce an ideological framework that could be used as the basis for legitimizing the political, social, and economic empowerment of women and to create a political culture that could no longer restrict woman's participation.

One of the most difficult problems faced by early woman's rights advocates was how to bridge the gap between prevailing attitudes that demanded from women the sacrifice of self for the benefit of others and the kind of pursuit of individual self-interest that was at the core of the demand for equal rights. In order to do this, they explicitly rejected the limits that the prevailing ideologies of Republican Motherhood, domesticity, and benevolence placed on women and modified and reinterpreted the theories of republicanism and natural rights along with early utilitarian ideas as well as those of the Common Sense School of the Scottish Enlightenment in order to make women a more integral part of American social and political culture.

Among the most powerful and influential political ideologies in the early nineteenth century was that of republicanism, whose language expressed the ideals of civic humanism with its emphasis on the need to subordinate private interests to the public good. Republicanism offered women two political roles. The first was the role of the republican wife. The second was that of the republican mother. Both roles were infused with political meaning since their underlying assumption was that virtuous women were required to perpetuate republican values and institutions. But the significance of that meaning was limited in the sense that the political role it offered to women was dependent upon their relationships to men and susceptibility of men to their influence. Thus, it was female influence within relationships with others rather than direct female participation in public affairs that served as the basis for women's political life. Nevertheless, as Linda Kerber has pointed out, while republicanism and the language that accompanied it limited political opportunities for women, it also encouraged them to develop such characteristics as independence and self-sufficiency, characteristics which Kerber argues were critical in helping them eventually to carve out for themselves a larger political role.[3]

The expectations accompanying what Barbara Welter has called the "cult of true womanhood" demanded piety and moral rectitude from women. According to its tenets, women were expected to assume complete responsibility for running a household and child care and to subordinate themselves and their personal interests to the authority and interests of their husbands. While this set of prescriptions tended to confine the activities of middle- and upper-class women to the domestic sphere,

Nancy Cott and others have suggested that it also produced a shared sense of female identity among them which, among other things, eventually found public expression as women began to participate in various reform and benevolent activities.[4]

The ideology of benevolence was built on the idea of a "female sphere" produced by the cult of domesticity and was encouraged by the rise of evangelical Protestantism. Charity work and participation in reform activities provided women with a socially acceptable way to expand their activities beyond the household in order to bring about the moral regeneration of society. It was through their work in benevolence that many women came to understand the ways in which their opportunities to play significant roles outside the home were limited.[5]

The ideologies of republicanism, domesticity, and benevolence had at least one thing in common. Each of them demanded that women sacrifice their own interests in order to promote the interests of the state, members of their own families, and society at large. The ideology of republicanism asked that women not only inculcate the selfless principles of civic virtue in their children but dedicate their own lives to those principles as models for their children to follow. The ideology of domesticity asked women to restrain their selfish impulses and subordinate their own personal desires and needs to the needs of their households, husbands, and children. And the ideology of benevolence encouraged women to sacrifice the few moments not consumed with performing the duties of wife, mother, and housekeeper to help those in their communities who were less fortunate than themselves.

One of the main things that differentiated women's participation in the woman's rights movement from their participation in other reforms and benevolent activities like abolition, temperance, and poor relief was the degree to which the struggle for woman's rights represented a rejection of the prescription that women should be selfless. While its goals were altruistic in the sense that they were designed to achieve equality for women in all social classes and ultimately to improve society as a whole, women's demand for improved educational and economic opportunities and political equality was based unabashedly on the principles of individual self-interest.

Well-educated and well-read, the middle-class reformers who became active in the woman's rights movement before the Civil War were exposed to a wide variety of intellectual traditions. Elizabeth Cady Stanton's intellectual training illustrates the point. In her youth she studied mathematics, Greek, and philosophy with the Rev. Simon Hosack (1755–1833), a conservative Presbyterian minister who had attended the University of Glasgow.[6] Later her brother-in-law, Edward Bayard, a graduate of Union College in Schenectady, New York, tutored her in political economy, law, and history as well as philosophy.[7] Her contact with her father's law office and his clerks meant that she grew up with a familiarity with the law and the legal position of women, a position that was only confirmed when she read Sir William Blackstone, James Kent, and Joseph Story on the subject.[8] At Emma Willard's Troy Female Seminary she studied the moral philosophy of William Paley and Dugald Stewart.[9] It was during this time that she attended the revival meetings conducted by Charles Grandison Finney. As an antidote to the religious enthusiasm that she experienced under the influence of Finney, her family removed her from school temporarily and Bayard tried to divert her with the novels of Sir Walter Scott, James Fenimore Cooper, and Charles Dickens as well as the works of the Scots phrenologist George Combe. Her journal entries after she left Willard's school include Romantic references from the works of Lord Byron, Samuel Taylor Coleridge, John Dryden.[10]

After 1838 Stanton spent an increasing amount of time with her cousin Gerrit Smith and his family at their home in Peterboro, New York, absorbing the reform ideas that he and his friends espoused. It was there that she met the abolitionist activist Henry Stanton in 1839. After their marriage in 1840, they left for England to attend the World Anti-Slavery Convention, where she met Lucretia Mott with whom she read and discussed Mary Wollstonecraft's *Vindication of the Rights of Women* as well as the ideas of Frances Wright and Thomas Paine.[11] By the time her honeymoon was over, she had become a Garrisonian abolitionist.[12]

Early woman's rights advocates like Stanton were also exposed to political language as it came to them filtered through contemporary plays, newspapers, orations, poems, essays, and short stories. Fourth of July programs commonly included a reading of the Declaration of Independence, for example, which served to remind those who listened that those who had led them in revolt against British political authority had been committed to the concepts of social contract and natural rights.[13]

But as we have seen, the political legacy of the American Revolution for women was the insistence that their most important contribution to the political life of the new republic was to take place within the home, where, as republican wives and mothers, they were expected to train their sons and daughters to become ideal citizens. In order to legitimize claims for a political role beyond that granted to women by that political legacy with its emphasis on self-sacrifice, woman's rights advocates had to begin to develop a philosophy that allowed them to move beyond the prescriptions of civic humanism. They needed to redefine their place in society as well as their political role and relationship to the state.

To help them do this, the leaders of the early woman's rights movement grafted onto the rhetoric of republicanism the language of natural rights filtered through early utilitarianism and the debates among Scottish Common Sense philosophers. In doing so, they placed their movement squarely within the republican tradition and its sensitivity to the dangers that the concentration of power posed to the liberty of the individual. At the same time, they appropriated social contract theory to establish their own sense of history, and the language of utilitarianism as well as that of the Scottish Common Sense School and its British popularizers to assert their right as individual women to pursue their own self-interest. This combination enabled them to assert their right to move beyond the limits that Republican Motherhood and the ideologies of domesticity and benevolence placed on their social, economic, and political lives and legitimize their desire to seek advances designed to benefit themselves.

Throughout the period between 1848 and 1860, woman's rights advocates used the rhetoric of republicanism both to expose male hypocrisy and to connect themselves to the principles upon which the government was based. In 1850 Horace Greeley charged that no "sincere Republican" could possibly refuse "the demand of Women to equal participation with Men in Political Rights."[14] And two years later Antoinette Brown accused "men who claim to be Christian Republicans" of being "guilty of absurd inconsistency and presumption" when they denied women the right to participate in government.[15] At the last convention held by woman's rights supporters before the Civil War, woman's rights advocates were still justifying their claims to equal political status with men on the principles of republicanism. "The essence of republican liberty," they reminded their audience, "is the principle that no one class shall depend for its rights on the mercy or justice of any other class."[16] Such rhetoric served as an ideological and linguistic bridge that connected women to the political tradition of the founding fathers.

But they also used republican rhetoric to direct attention toward the dangers inherent in the concentration of power. By suggesting that the concentration of political and economic power in the hands of men constituted a tyranny against women, they attempted to enlarge the way that the ideals of republicanism could and should be applied to the category of gender.

Leaders of the woman's rights movement worked on the assumption that the prevailing male ideology of power distribution viewed power as a limited resource. Their assumption was confirmed when Henry Raymond of the *New York Times* published an essay in his paper describing the effects of accepting the demands of woman's rights supporters. Their demands, he announced to his readers, "conflict with, and if secured, will tend to diminish, the rights of masculine mankind." If they had their way, he continued, men would be deprived of their "grand prerogatives."[17]

Woman's rights advocates understood perfectly that they were engaging in what others would perceive to be a win/lose conflict and that men would be unlikely to grant willingly political, social, and economic rights to women because they believed that to do so would be to diminish their own power in direct proportion to the degree that the power of women was enhanced. Wendell Phillips pointed out to the audience of the Tenth National Woman's Rights Convention in May 1860 that those in power had never been known to grant privilege to the powerless "out of love" but only out of "fear." His conclusion that "you must force the upper classes to do justice by physical or some other power"[18] echoed the voice of Lucy Stone, who at a similar convention in 1853 had warned that it was inexpedient for women merely to ask for their rights. "Women," she argued, "must not wait for men to give. . . . We may ask indeed; but shall we receive? Better for us to adopt the shorter method and take."[19]

The problem was that while woman's rights supporters could and did expose the evils of the concentration of political, economic, and social power in the hands of men, they were unlikely to find comfort in Phillips's observation and were in no position to follow Stone's advice. Their solution to the problem was to try to separate the idea of rights from the idea of power. They argued that their claim to equal rights could not threaten the source of male power because those rights and the power inherent in possession of them could not legitimately be appropriated by another individual. As Paulina Wright Davis put it at the first National Woman's Rights Convention in Worcester, Massachusetts, in 1850, "The rights and liberties of one human being cannot be made the property of another." The rights they demanded, she argued, could neither be salvaged nor purchased because they were "inalienable."[20] Antoinette Brown echoed her sentiments when, three years later at another woman's rights convention, she reminded her audience that it was "a very common idea that this movement is antagonistic to the rights of men." That idea was "mistaken and unfortunate," she continued. Where the rights of citizens were concerned, "That which is mine is not my neighbor's; that which belongs to woman cannot belong to her brother."[21]

What woman's rights supporters attempted to do, then, was to remind their listeners that while the concentration of power led to the tyranny of men over women, the diffusion of power could guarantee that the principles of republicanism would be preserved and the unity of society enhanced. The most articulate expression of that view was delivered by Elizabeth Cady Stanton in her "Address to the New York State Legislature" in February 1860. The thrust of her argument was that the power that accompanied the possession of rights was a limitless resource: "Though the atmosphere is forty miles deep all round the globe," she observed, "no man can do more than fill his own lungs. . . . Though rights have been abundantly supplied by the good Father, no man can appropriate to himself those that belong to another." She declared that giving women equal rights would in no way diminish the power of men. "Those in power," she continued, always suffer "a kind of nervous unrest . . . whenever new claims are started by those out of their own immediate class." She was convinced that the powerful tended to believe "that rights are very much like lands, stocks, bonds, and mortgages, and that if every new claimant be satisfied, the supply of human rights must in time run low." Their view was wrong, from her point of view. "You might as well carp at the birth of every child," she concluded, "lest there should not be enough air left to inflate your lungs; at the success of every scholar, for fear that your draughts at the fountain of knowledge could not be so long and deep; at the glory of every hero, lest there be no glory left for you."[22]

Given the fact that women were in no position to take the power that they wanted, Stanton found it inexpedient to threaten, bully, or embarrass the members of the state legislature. Instead she shifted the terms of the debate by changing the assumptions upon which the discourse concerning woman's rights was based. By suggesting that power was a limitless, asexual resource, she could argue that it was an integrative or incorporating rather than a separating or disruptive force, a force that could be used to unify society and to enable each of its members to more effectively discharge his or her duties. Expecting women to fulfill their social and civic obligations without equal rights was, as Clarina Nichols put it, like trying "to make brick without straw."[23]

Attempting to apply John Locke's language of natural rights to the condition of women posed some problems for woman's rights advocates. Locke's language described the original state of nature for all adult humans as a "state of perfect freedom" and "equality," where power in the family was "parental" rather than "paternal" and where marriage was a "voluntary contract" between two equals.[24] For Locke, individuals in the state of nature sacrificed some of their rights in order to establish a government that could protect their life, liberty, and property. Citizenship was derived from a social compact creating that government. And while there was nothing in Locke which explicitly excluded women from that compact and from citizenship, the rights of citizenship which were preserved as a result were reserved for men for all practical purposes. Presumably, when women sacrificed their rights for the benefit of social order, they gave up their inalienable ones as well as their alienable ones. Therefore, as Carole Pateman has pointed out, trying to apply contract theory to women in the conventional way was (and still is) problematical at best.[25]

The problems of whether or how to apply the idea of a social contract to American women were evident even before the Revolution began. Thomas Jefferson and the members of the Second Continental Congress appropriated Locke's political philosophy and language when in the Declaration of Independence they wrote that "men" were "created equal" and had "certain unalienable (sic) rights" including those of "life, liberty and the pursuit of happiness" and that governments derived "their just powers from the consent of the governed."[26] While their starting point was the citizenship that derived from the original compact, the citizenship that they envisioned was confined to the male gender.

Publicly, those who established the new republic and wrote its constitution and laws all but ignored the implications that natural rights
philosophy and social contract theory had for American women. James
Otis was exceptional when he asked in a pamphlet published before the
American Revolution, "Are not women born as free as men?" and "If . . .
all were reduced to a state of nature, had not apple women and orange girls
as good a right to give their respectable suffrages for a new King as the
philosopher, courtier, *petit-maître* and politician?"[27] If anyone responded
publicly to his question, that response has been lost to the historical
record.

That does not mean, however, that early American politicians were
unaware of those implications or had given them no thought in private. In
the spring of 1776, John Adams and his wife debated the need to "remember the ladies" when he and his colleagues wrote a new set of laws for the
government that they were creating.[28] During the same period, he wrote a
letter to James Sullivan in which he considered the implications of the
theory "that the only moral foundation of government is, the consent of
the people." In that letter, he asked rhetorically, "Whence arises the right
of the men to govern the women, without their consent?" He resisted the
temptation to argue simply that women as a group were by virtue of their
sex either incompetent or unqualified to participate in public life (he was
not Abigail's husband and Mercy Otis Warren's friend for nothing). He
concluded that as many reasons could be given for excluding some men as
for excluding some women from participation in affairs of state. Some
women might be too delicate or too busy with "domestic cares" to play a
significant political role, but, he pointed out, there were also many
propertyless men "in every society" who were "too little acquainted with
public affairs to form a right judgment, and too dependent upon other men
to have a will of their own."[29]

Another revolutionary, Richard Henry Lee, was forced by his sister to
consider the practical effects of denying the vote and direct representation
to property-owning women when she complained to him in 1778 that
"widows were not represented" by those who taxed them. He acknowledged that granting women the right to vote had "never been the practice
either here or in England" because it was considered either "out of
character" or unnecessary. Nevertheless, he claimed that he had no
objection either in practice or in theory to their voting and pledged that he
was willing readily to give his "consent to establish" their right to
represent their own interests.[30]

Clearly the exclusion of women was troublesome to some. But while an
occasional American statesman may have been willing to apply his understanding of Lockean political philosophy to women in private, none did
anything of a permanent nature to share with women the power that
derived from the possession of natural rights. Those who ratified the 1790

constitution in the state of New Jersey, for example, did give women the right to vote, but that right was withdrawn in 1807.[31]

Early woman's rights advocates, nevertheless, found Locke's political philosophy and language useful.[32] First, it allowed them to place their demands within the respected and familiar American political tradition that had been established through the Declaration of Independence and provided the opportunity to demand increased rights for women based on their humanity, which was not in question, rather than on the nature of their citizenship, which was.[33] The founding fathers had used the language of natural rights to argue for the protection and preservation of their prerogatives as citizens. Women could not start from the same place. While no one was likely to deny that they were citizens, it was clear that female citizenship was not the same as male citizenship and that men and women in practice had different civic duties and prerogatives. Woman's rights advocates, therefore, had to use Locke not to argue for the preservation of their rights but to gain their rights in the first place.

In their Declaration of Sentiments, woman's rights advocates appropriated the language of the Declaration of Independence and changed very little of it. They proclaimed that women had been created equal to men and that both sexes had been "endowed by their Creator" with the same rights. It was on this basis that they demanded "the equal station to which they" were "entitled."[34] Twelve years later, Elizabeth Cady Stanton repeated their commitment to Lockean principles when she began her speech to the New York legislature with a reminder that "every individual comes into this world with rights that are not transferable."[35] Their main points were to claim that their citizenship could not be viewed as an extension of that of their husbands and to deny that families headed by those husbands were legitimate representative democracies.

But the most important contribution of the ideology of natural rights to the woman's rights movement was to provide them a distinctive framework for conceiving the past which not only reflected but contributed to their sense of gender identity. Lester Cohen has convincingly argued that men like Thomas Jefferson and James Wilson, who both signed the Declaration of Independence, and the "revolutionary historians" like Mercy Otis Warren and Jedidiah Morse, who followed them, understood the theory of natural rights as a historical or processive theory. According to Cohen, they transformed natural law into a historical process by viewing natural rights as original rights guaranteed by experience through history. For them, natural law was a part of the historical process rather than merely "a static body of immutable principles." They viewed British policies as having threatened both abstract rights and historical practice.[36] It was a practice that consisted of the process of negotiating and renegotiating the original contract between the governors and the governed in order to defend and preserve liberty. In British history that negotiation process had resulted in the signing of the Magna Carta and the Bill of Rights, both of which guaranteed natural rights in practice. For the signers of the Declaration of Independence, the usurpations and tyranny of George III in Parliament were merely one more example, albeit the most recent example, of actions that threatened the "rights of Englishmen."[37] They were determined to protect what they labeled their natural rights and were willing to break political ties with Britain in order to do so. They were able to place their experience within a history of repeatedly successful attempts to preserve natural rights against repeated attempts on the part of the government to usurp them.

Years later when Stanton and her friends wrote the Declaration of Sentiments, they did not bring with them any way of distinguishing between recent or past injustice. Men had from the beginning denied women their natural rights. According to the Declaration of Sentiments, "The history of mankind is a history of repeated injuries and usurpations on the part of man toward women having in direct object the establishment of an absolute tyranny over her."[38] The charges against American men listed so explicitly there were not new. They were perpetual. They were the same tyrannies that women had always been subjected to: deprivation of political rights, legal rights, and economic and educational opportunity. When it was applied to women, natural law had no tradition except in the most abstract sense. The natural rights of women had been usurped from the beginning of historical time and little had been done since then to change the situation. Women had participated in no process of negotiation and renegotiation in an effort to preserve their rights. They could not view themselves as protecting or defending their natural rights because they had no sense that those rights had been established by or for them in historical practice. Their rights had not been established, protected, and preserved through time. As Gerrit Smith put it, "The object of the 'Woman's Rights movement' is nothing less than to recover the rights of woman."[39]

Thus, when women claimed their natural rights the concept took on a new meaning. The only way natural rights for women could be understood was if those rights were viewed as a set of static, fundamental principles which had never changed and were universally applicable. In this new context, natural rights was historical in a sense that was different from that of men. For women and their sympathizers, the language of natural rights did not describe the same kind of change, dialectic, innovation, cycle, growth, and development that were features of men's historical sense. Their concern was to identify the indignities to which women had always been subjected. The time frame was not the issue for women that it was for men. By claiming the ideology of natural rights and by appropriating its language while at the same time implying that women's past experience vis-à-vis natural rights was different from that of men, early

woman's rights advocates declared their independence from male experience and history and established a basis for developing their own historical
consciousness as women. In this way they were able to adapt male
political philosophy and language to a female frame of reference and use it
to meet female needs.

Sensitive to the distinctiveness of their historical experience, they
began to expose the exclusive nature of what had been defined by men as
historically significant. Early woman's rights advocates such as Susan B.
Anthony were incensed by the inattention men paid to female experience
and accomplishments. "Why is it," she asked, "that the pages of all history
glow with the names of illustrious men, while only here and there a *lone
woman* appears, who, like the eccentric camel, marks the centuries?"
Male historians, she complained, make "a goodly show" of the achievements of other men, but "no writer will a little time bestow" on the
"worthy acts" of women.[40]

Their response was to adapt the male definition of what was historically
significant to the female experience and create a historical model that was
more inclusive. Early woman's rights advocates were perfectly willing to
capitalize on the achievements of women who could serve as examples of
those whose birth or exceptional abilities had allowed them to overcome
the disabilities that gender placed on them. These women were historically significant not because they had rights but because they had achieved
historical significance without them. They were powerful politicians like
Victoria, Isabella, Elizabeth, and Maria Theresa or intellectuals like Margaret Fuller or Mary Wollstonecraft. Their names belied the claim that
women could not compete with men. Therefore woman's rights advocates
did not hesitate to use their names in their speeches to demonstrate that,
if given the opportunity, women could exhibit great eloquence, intellect,
patriotism, and, in the words of Ernestine Rose, the same "self-sacrificing
devotion to the cause of humanity" that was characteristic of male
worthies. Rarely did a woman's rights convention pass without the litany
of their names being recited.[41]

Of equal importance to their argument, however, were women whose
historical significance was their lack of achievement. These women were
important because, deprived of their right to liberty and property and the
right to pursue happiness, they found it impossible to participate in those
activities that had traditionally been defined as historically significant by
men. Referred to as "a worthy woman of my acquaintance," "a young
woman," "a mother of three children," "a widow," or "a case," they may
have been anonymous, but they were much more representative than
women worthies; and their experiences were discussed in detail. It was
their condition as women, not their identity, that was historically significant. Their historical experiences were gender-specific in the sense that
what they endured testified to the general vulnerability and helplessness

of women who, denied their natural rights, found it impossible to protect their own interests.

It was because of their shared experience of helplessness as women that they deserved a historical role. Their stories deserved to be told not because they were exceptional but because they were unexceptional. They were like the "worthy woman" described by Clarina I. H. Nichols to the audience at the 1851 National Woman's Rights Convention in Worcester whose property, controlled by her husband while he lived, was given by the state to his brothers and sisters when he died. They were the mothers Antoinette Brown placed in the historical record when she described "a mother of three children" whose alcoholic husband, about to die and leave his family "penniless," appointed his relatives instead of his wife the guardians of their children. And they were the widows whose story Frances Gage recorded for posterity when she described the inability of a bereaved wife to find employment to support herself.[42] Their histories were significant because without equal rights before the law and equal opportunities to compete with men, all women faced the possibility of being deprived of their property, losing custody of their children, and dying in poverty because of the lack of economic opportunity. Thus woman's rights advocates enlarged the definition of what was historical in order to include the experience of most women as well as the experience of women worthies. In doing so, they expanded a practice they had begun as abolitionists and temperance workers, whose publication of slave narratives and exposés on the consequences of drunkenness made a place in the historical record for African-Americans and the victims of alcohol abuse. By continuing to create an inclusive historical model, they added an important weapon to their arsenal of arguments which was designed to recover the natural rights that women had been denied.

Thus, woman's rights activists were able to use the ideology and language of John Locke to connect themselves to a respected and familiar political tradition, to allow them to demand rights for women based on their humanity rather than on their citizenship, and to provide them with a distinctive framework for conceiving and reporting the past. Scottish Enlightenment philosophy combined with a strong dose of early utilitarianism was appealing to them for other reasons.

Debates among Scottish moral and common sense philosophers in the eighteenth century arose partly as a response to the effects of the Act of Union of 1707 under which Scotland gave up its sovereignty and became a part of Britain. While union with England deprived Scotland of any future independent political identity and distinct national history, it brought with it economic advantages by allowing Scotland to become an integral part of the expanding commercial economy of her southern neighbor. The intellectual community in Scotland, which included such notables as Adam Smith, David Hume, Francis Hutcheson, and Dugald Stewart, was not hostile to this change. Its members did not attempt to challenge the political arrangements established in 1707. They accepted Scotland's loss of independence and welcomed the economic opportunities that union brought with it. The focus of their intellectual activities was to promote economic change by providing it with a secure and clearly articulated ideological foundation. They sought to work out a way to relieve the tensions inherent in the move from an agrarian economy to a commercial one by providing an intellectual framework for understanding and rationalizing economic change and controlling the social dislocations that could be expected to accompany it.[43]

The political and economic context in which they found themselves led them to approach these problems in ways which were useful to the woman's rights advocates in the United States, a country which was by the late 1840s, like Scotland a century earlier, experiencing an expansion of commerce. First, union with England discouraged Scottish philosophers from placing their intellectual discussion in a national context. The framework of their discourse on the relationship between politics and economics tended to be universal rather than culturally specific. As John Robertson has pointed out, philosophers like David Hume were concerned with "the progress of society in general . . . the common problems of developing, commercial societies" rather than with "the condition of Scotland or even Britain in particular."[44] They also made a real attempt to distinguish between those human characteristics that derived from nature or biology as opposed to those that were a product of socialization.[45] Because their perspective was so wide and they were so sensitive to the importance of culture in determining the way humans behaved, the language of the Scottish Enlightenment philosophers and the scope of their discourse not only allowed for but in some ways encouraged the applicability of their ideas to women as well as men.[46]

Secondly, they tended to focus their attention on the question of how to preserve virtue in a commercial society, or to put it another way, how to resolve the conflict between self-interest and public responsibility. Their resolution of the question led them to change the definition of virtue. Virtue was no longer defined, as it had been in the republican tradition, as dependent upon the sacrifice of the self for the benefit of society and the use of reason. The key to success in a commercial economy characterized by free competition, minimal state interference, and emphasis on individual rights, was not selflessness but the pursuit of self-interest. Virtue, they claimed, could be expressed through the pursuit of self-interest for the betterment of society. Adam Smith was, of course, one of the strongest proponents of this view.

But while Scottish intellectuals like Smith argued that individuals had a right to be autonomous and independent and acknowledged the right of individuals to work out their own destiny, they also recognized that self-interest needed to be balanced by some force to prevent it from becoming oppressive to the general good. They found that balance in the interaction inherent in the conduct of social relationships and the applicability of what they called "sensibility" to the conduct of public affairs.[47]

These ideas had great potential for serving as one of the ideological bases for developing a rationale to promote the political, economic, and social advancement of women. One of the reasons that women had been denied their rights in the past had been because their behavior was believed to be a response to emotion rather than reason. As Genevieve Lloyd has argued, the whole concept of reason in Western culture has been male in focus. It has been, she says, "a cultural ideal which has defined itself in opposition to the feminine."[48] French Enlightenment philosophers, like Diderot and Rousseau, were only carrying on the legacy of Western philosophy when they pictured women as fundamentally flawed for this reason.[49] Scottish Enlightenment philosophers like David Hume and Adam Smith, however, redeemed sentiment, declaring it neither trivial nor capricious but essential as a way of balancing the tendencies of self-interest that could be expected to motivate behavior in a commercial society.[50] Thus, the Scottish Enlightenment provided a more nurturing intellectual environment for the development of American feminist ideology than did the French Enlightenment by emphasizing the importance of those very characteristics that had traditionally been associated with the female character.

Moreover, Scottish intellectuals argued that virtue based on sensibility had to be nurtured through the very kinds of social relationships that dominated the lives of American women, those to be found among friends, in voluntary associations, and in the family. All of these were the very milieu in which women, denied equal access to the public worlds of politics and commerce, had the greatest influence. It is not surprising, then, as Ruth Bloch has pointed out, that after the Revolution Americans were willing to accept the idea that public virtue could be defined in terms of sensibility and that such virtue was recognized as feminine. Nor is it surprising, given the consistency with which men throughout the ages had dominated the right to participate in public affairs, that at the time this feminization of public virtue "hinged on the exclusion of women from institutional public life."[51] What early woman's rights advocates had to do was to argue that it was as legitimate and appropriate for women to pursue self-interest as it was for them to mediate its effects through sentiment and sociability. In this way they could move beyond the ideology of Republican Motherhood and its demand that they sacrifice themselves for the good of the state.

The two authors whose works were most likely to have served as a starting point for the development of both this ideology and language were William Paley and Dugald Stewart. William Paley (1743–1805), the archdeacon of Carlisle in England, published his *Principles of Moral and*

Political Philosophy in 1785. It immediately became a standard text for Cambridge University students and went through fifteen editions before Paley's death in 1805.[52] Paley's treatise was assigned reading in most American colleges during the post-revolutionary period as well as in the leading schools for girls.[53] As we have already seen Elizabeth Cady Stanton read Paley at Emma Willard's school. Julia Ward Howe, more interested at the time in chemistry than in moral philosophy, remembered the tedium of having to memorize long passages from his book at Miss Catherine Roberts's Day School for Young Ladies in New York City. Others like Antoinette Brown read him on their own with somewhat more enthusiasm.[54]

Paley was not judged an original thinker. He was committed to the principles of natural rights as defined by John Locke, and he espoused a variety of moral philosophy based on a principle of utilitarianism that anticipated Jeremy Bentham. According to Paley, virtue consisted of "doing good to mankind, in obedience to the will of God and for the sake of [one's own] everlasting happiness." He believed that "whatever is expedient is right" and that it was "the utility of any moral rule alone, which constitutes the obligation of it." "We can be obliged to nothing, but what we ourselves are to gain or lose something by," he wrote.[55] While he rejected Locke's idea of a social compact, he agreed that "men" were born with natural rights which consisted of "life, limbs, and liberty, his right to the produce of his personal labour; to the use, in common with others, of air, light, water."[56] His attitude toward marriage illustrates his utilitarian orientation. Marriage, he felt, served society in that it promoted private comfort, allowed for the production of children, divided up women among men thereby eliminating a "source of contention" and by implication discouraged fornication. Marriage organized society into families, made people settle down and establish a secure state, and encouraged industry.[57] He also argued that while nature had "made and left the sexes of the human species nearly equal in their faculties, and perfectly so in their rights," the Scriptures had ordered the subordination of wife to husband in order "to guard against those competitions which equality, or a contested superiority, is almost sure to produce." Expediency rather than nature, he argued, had dictated that civil government be founded on paternal authority.[58]

His views posed a direct challenge to the likes of moral sense philosopher Francis Hutcheson, who maintained that moral judgments were spontaneous and derived from the sentiments rather than reason and that virtue was characterized by "disinterested benevolence." Paley argued that moral sense was culturally determined rather than innate. "Upon the whole," he wrote, "it seems to me, either there exist no such [moral] instincts as compose what is called the moral sense, or that they are not now to be distinguished from prejudices and habits; on which account they cannot be depended upon in moral reasoning."[59] Like Adam Smith, Paley believed that self-interest could be used to benefit society as a whole.

Unlike Smith, however, Paley tended to focus more on individual self-realization than on social good.

Dugald Stewart (1753–1828), who held the chair of moral philosophy at the University of Edinburgh after the retirement of Adam Ferguson, was a student of both Ferguson in Edinburgh and Thomas Reid in Glasgow.[60] Stewart's works represented a synthesis of the ideas of the Scottish Common Sense School begun by Reid and popularized by James Beattie, a school that began as a response to the skepticism of David Hume. Hume rejected the use of reason in favor of sensibility as a way of discovering truth because reason could not describe a reality that had no basis in experience. Thomas Reid rejected both Locke's idea of *tabula rasa* and Hume's conclusions and suggested that great truths could be discovered through the use of a combination of reason and innate common sense. That combination allowed sensations to be sorted out and placed into a context informed by human experience.[61]

The Common Sense School created by Reid and Stewart had wide appeal in the United States. Stanton studied Stewart's work at Emma Willard's, and it, like Paley, was taught in all American colleges in the first half of the nineteenth century.[62] Also like Paley, Stewart appeared on the reading lists of Americans whose tastes in literature reflected the time they were willing to spend contemplating serious religious and philosophical questions. Susan Mansfield Huntington, the daughter of a Connecticut minister and the wife of another, after having read Stewart was impressed enough with what he had to say to recommend him to a friend: "Have you read Dugald Stewart's Philosophical Essays?" she asked in a letter. "He is generally esteemed, I believe, one of the greatest men of the present age."[63] Stewart had appeal to Americans because the principles of Scottish Common Sense philosophy were, in the words of scholar Terence Martin, "safe, stabilizing, and conservative."[64]

Stewart was familiar with Paley, referred to him directly in his *General View of the Progress of Metaphysical, Ethical, and Political Philosophy Since the Revival of Letters in Europe*, and was in complete agreement with him that self-interest served a positive function and could be used to benefit society.[65] Individuals, Stewart believed, were morally obliged to attend to their own interests. In *Outlines of Moral Philosophy*, he argued that "a steady regard, in the conduct of life, to the happiness and perfection of our own nature, and a diligent study of the means by which these ends may be attained, is another duty" of the virtuous person. He distinguished self-interest from selfishness, maintaining that selfishness was not the motive for human action but the effect. An act was selfish only if it placed individuals in opposition to others and thereby disconnected them from society.[66]

The liberal tradition espoused by these British intellectuals was also popularized by such authors as Mary Wollstonecraft, Jane Haldimand

Marcet, and Harriet Martineau. In 1792 Wollstonecraft published her *A Vindication of the Rights of Women*. In her treatise, Wollstonecraft insisted that women's "first duty is to themselves." Pursuing their own self-interest, she insisted, would not prevent them from fulfilling their obligations to society as mothers and their duty to the state as citizens.[67] Regard for her work declined after the publication of William Godwin's biography of her life, and her ideas were attacked in print by individuals such as Yale professor Benjamin Silliman.[68] Nevertheless, those interested in improving the status of women continued to find inspiration in her words.

Twenty-four years after the publication of Wollstonecraft's *Vindication*, Jane Marcet, an English gentlewoman, published a book containing a series of conversations between "Mrs. B." and her young friend Caroline. These conversations provided a palatable medium through which Marcet attempted to explain to "young persons of either sex" the principles of political economy as developed by such notables as William Blackstone, Adam Smith, and William Paley.[69] Sixteen years after that, Harriet Martineau began publishing a nine-volume series of stories called *Illustrations of Political Economy* designed to illustrate the ideas of James Mill, Adam Smith, Jeremy Bentham, David Ricardo, and Thomas Malthus.[70] Both Marcet and Martineau intended their books to appeal to a mass audience, and both books went through numerous editions in Britain and the United States.[71] They were widely read and helped to legitimize the belief that a strong sense of individualism combined with the pursuit of self-interest could be of benefit to society.[72]

Popularized by such authors as Wollstonecraft, Marcet, and Martineau and filtered through the American educational system, utilitarianism and the philosophy of the Common Sense School was vital to the formation of the early woman's rights movement. Middle-class reformers like Stanton and her friends found themselves in a world in which, among men, the conflict between civic virtue (duty to the community) and liberal individualism (pursuit of personal interests) was being resolved in favor of liberal individualism.[73] It remained to women to pass on the legacy of the republican civic virtue tradition through their obligations as mothers. As long as they deferred to a tradition which measured virtue in terms of the sacrifice of self-interest, there was little chance that they would actively or effectively seek a political role other than that which had been extended to them in their domestic sphere.

Paley and the Scottish Enlightenment philosophers were a part of an intellectual tradition that focused on the relationship between private interests and public responsibilities. This problem was central to women because up to this point the traditions of republicanism, domesticity, and benevolence had made the public display of selflessness the only legitimate basis for women's participation in affairs beyond the home. Woman's rights reformers appropriated those aspects of utilitarianism and Scottish philosophy which emphasized the acceptability of the pursuit of self-interest for the benefit of society as a whole—and the need to balance self-interest with sensibility—in order to claim a more significant role in public life.[74] Selectively using these ideas, early woman's rights advocates could claim legitimacy for the belief not only that women had the same natural rights as men but also that they had a right to take an interest in and promote those things that would enhance their own well-being. When women pursued their own interests, they would argue, society as a whole would benefit. So between 1848 and 1861, they focused on the ideas provided to them by the utilitarian individualism of Paley and Stewart, as well as by Locke's language of natural rights, and incorporated them into both the Declaration of Sentiments and their early speeches.

They began by calling the document that they presented to the Seneca Falls convention a "Declaration of Sentiments." In doing so they publicly rejected the idea that public life was confined only to men who could claim a natural propensity to be reasonable. They claimed instead the right to discuss politics and power using a language with which their gender had long been associated. They used the language of sensibility, given intellectual respectability by the Scottish Enlightenment philosophers, to lay claim to qualities of public virtue long viewed as distinctively female and demanded the right of women to practice of those virtues in the public as well as the private sphere.

In their resolutions, they noted that while claiming for himself strength of intellect, "man" had willingly accorded "to woman moral superiority" and argued that such virtue should qualify them for expanded political roles as well as religious, economic, and social ones.[75] They ignored tradition which had assumed that the prerogatives of citizenship should be based solely on one's ability to reason. The power of centuries of Western philosophy which denied or ignored the intellectual abilities of women was too strong. Lucretia Mott acknowledged that power when she wrote to Stanton, "Thou wilt have hard work to prove the intellectual equality of woman with man—facts are so against such an assumption in the present stage of woman's development." The best strategy, she counseled, was never to "*admit* inferiority" even if they could not "*prove* equality."[76] So instead woman's rights advocates argued that reason without sensibility was inadequate for the conduct of public affairs. As Elizabeth Cady Stanton succinctly put it at the National Woman's Rights Convention in Worcester, Massachusetts, in 1850, "There must be a great national heart, as well as head."[77]

Secondly, in their declaration and speeches they argued that the pursuit of personal interests was both an integral part of the law of nature and "superior in obligation to any other" and that any law which conflicted with that principle was "of no validity."[78] In her speech supporting the

Declaration of Sentiments at the Seneca Falls convention, Stanton declared that there could be "no happiness without freedom."[79] Following the lead established at Seneca Falls, Abby Price, speaking at the 1850 National Woman's Rights Convention in Worcester, declared, "We shall assume that happiness is the chief end of all human beings; that existence is valuable in proportion as happiness is promoted and secured; and that, on the whole, each of the sexes is equally necessary to the common happiness, and in one way or other is equally capable, with fair opportunity, of contributing to it. Therefore each has an equal right to pursue and *enjoy* it."[80] A few years later Antoinette Brown Blackwell, speaking before the Tenth National Woman's Rights Convention, eloquently restated these principles: "I believe . . . that the highest laws of our being are those which we find written within our being; that the first moral laws which we are to obey are the laws which God's own finger has traced upon our own souls. Therefore, our first duty is to ourselves, and we may never, under any circumstances, yield this to any other."[81]

Early woman's rights advocates demanded rights to which they felt entitled as individuals. By refusing to make the claim that acquiring those rights would necessarily make women better wives, mothers, or daughters, those who supported woman's rights explicitly rejected the political role formulated after the American Revolution which had established familial relationships and the sacrifice of self as the basis for and boundary of women's political identity and power. In the process they also began to go beyond the role given to women by Paley and Scottish Enlightenment philosophers who, while they may have been willing to honor women for their sensibility, had no intention of challenging gender roles or providing the basis for expanded political rights for women.

Determined to devise a strategy both to appeal to those who were inclined to support them as well as to disarm those who would oppose them, woman's rights advocates were anxious to assure their listeners that a woman's right to pursue her self-interest was not intended to fragment society by making women independent of men and that their claim to more rights would in the end benefit society as a whole. "Every person, man or woman, is an integer . . . a whole person," argued Theodore Parker. But, he assured his audience, "the rights of individualism are not to be possessed, developed, used, and enjoyed by a life in solitude, but by joint action."[82] Paulina Wright Davis agreed. While she was willing to admit that the reforms that they were proposing were "radical," she argued that the movement had no intent of arming "the oppressed against the oppressor, or of separating the parties, or of setting up independence, or of severing the relation of either." They sought changes, she claimed, that would bring to women "liberty without its usually associated independence."[83]

Woman's rights advocates claimed the right of women to establish their own autonomy, seek personal happiness, and pursue their own interests. They also rejected relationships as the basis for their citizenship. But at the same time, they argued that female autonomy and the pursuit of self-interest would promote the public good. Their first job was to redefine society to include women. "Society," argued Ernestine Rose in 1852, was typically viewed as being composed of "the male sex only." "Statesmen," she observed, "never include women in their solicitude for the happiness of society."[84] Once women were included as those who constituted society it followed that laws which oppressed them could never "promote the highest good of society," argued Elizabeth Cady Stanton. "The best interests of the community never can require the sacrifice of one innocent being—of one sacred right."[85] Granting women their natural rights was "for the good of all," stated Lucy Stone at the 1853 woman's rights convention in New York City. "The race will be benefited, for the development which is the result of the use of *all* the powers, is gain to the race, as much as to the individual."[86] Their claims were not selfish (as defined by Stewart) since, while they represented what women perceived to be their self-interest, they were not designed to separate them from the rest of society but rather to integrate them more fully into it.

In a general sense the pursuit of self-interest meant the same thing to woman's rights advocates as it did to the members of the male political community. It meant that individuals had the right to identify their own needs and use whatever resources were available to fulfill them. There were some differences, however, in the way that many men and woman's rights advocates conceptualized the pursuit of self-interest. Woman's rights advocates like Theodore Parker and Lucy Stone emphasized the importance of self-interest as an incorporating concept which would not only allow independence but also encourage co-operation and help to unify society. They hoped that its pursuit would enhance community life, not fragment it. This was in direct contrast to those whose practical pursuit of self-interest in the world of business and politics tended to focus on individualistic and sometimes anti-social competition. Secondly, for supporters of woman's rights the context for the pursuit of self-interest was gender. They emphasized the fact that women were denied political and legal rights as well as equal economic opportunity because they were female. They demanded that women as individuals and as a group be granted such things as property rights, access to divorce, and custody rights over children. In contrast, the context for the expression of self-interest among men before the Civil War was much more likely to be consciously based on class, party, economic interests, or sectional loyalties than on gender. Even when gender became an issue in the course of political life and debate, it was not likely to be the primary concern. When the legislators of the state of New York passed the Married Women's Property Act in 1848, for example, they were not as much concerned with what it would do to protect women as they were with how it would protect the economic interests of the propertied.[87]

Early woman's rights advocates looked to a wide variety of intellectual traditions in order to develop an ideology that would serve their purposes. By focusing the ideology of republicanism away from its emphasis on self-sacrifice and toward its emphasis on the dangers of concentration of power, and then combining it with the ideologies of natural rights, sentiment, and self-interest, they were able to move beyond the restrictions that Republican Motherhood and its corollaries placed on female citizens and justify women's claim to equal rights with men. At the same time they also created their own political idiom, one that legitimized a place for women in the world of politics as well as history. Their demands and the rhetoric they used to express them added a feminine dimension to public discourse that up to this point had been but a whisper and in doing so helped to further integrate women into American public life.

III

THE LANGUAGE

Drawing upon their experience in reform and having adopted an ideology designed to justify their claim that social, economic, and political power should be more equitably distributed, early woman's rights advocates began the process of creating a language of public protest that could serve their particular interests and help them achieve their goals by linguistically redefining and expanding the parameters of women's roles in society. Their language, like their ideology, represented a rejection of the restrictions that Republican Motherhood, domesticity, and the ideology of benevolence placed on women and allowed them to place women side by side with men as equal participants in public as well as private life. Their language, like their ideology, was designed to provoke those in their audience to reconsider their attitudes toward gender roles and to encourage them ultimately to support the idea of gender equality.

The language that the leaders of the woman's rights movement used to express their discontent and demand redress of their grievances was first and foremost a public language, a language clearly intended to place the woman's rights movement and its advocates in the world outside the home. Their rhetoric was filled with metaphors that placed the issue of more rights for women within the context of the important public questions and events of the day.[1] Sensitive to the condition of the oppressed because of their close association with abolition, they compared the position of women to that of slaves and referred to conventional roles for women as confining enclosures. A part of a world attempting to deal with the legacy of religious enthusiasm as well as the social and political problems associated with rapid economic development and geographic expansion, they pictured themselves as the architects and builders of a new world order which would welcome the equal participation of women in public and private affairs. Products of a culture in which technological development was causing rapid change in economic life and social relations, they compared society as it was then constructed to a poorly designed machine. Residents of a nation recently victorious in a war against Mexico and a country in which political relationships tended to be adversarial, they used military metaphors to describe their goals and formulate their strategy for achieving their objectives. Exposed to the language of the Romantics, they used references to nature in general and the sea, the weather, and horticulture in particular to place women in a context that drew attention to their power to both create and destroy.

This particular combination of metaphors, designed to enhance women's public roles, represented the determination of woman's rights advocates, male and female alike, to claim an equal place for women in the artificial world as well as the natural one. While their importance as child bearers, nurturers, and dispensers of charity was unchallenged, women's place in religious activities, business, and politics was restricted. Their roles in establishing institutions such as governments and religions that were intended to control and impose order upon human relationships remained unacknowledged. They could not point to great works of architecture designed and built by women to hold the forces of nature at bay. Such activities, if not always initiated by men, came to be controlled by them. The metaphors used by woman's rights advocates, therefore, represented a rhetorical effort to place women in contexts previously dominated by men and to harness the creative energy, skills, and intellect of women in the attempt to resolve the tension between the power of nature and the efforts of human beings to control and manipulate its creative and destructive tendencies for their own benefit. In doing so, they added a feminine dimension to public discourse which was an important first step in expanding woman's place in public life.

On a more practical level, the language of woman's rights advocates had a strategic component and, therefore, served their interests in various ways. Some of the metaphors that they used were resonant and reassuring. Some were dissonant and deeply disturbing. Combining metaphors allowed woman's rights supporters to speak to different constituencies while at the same time forcing their listeners to reassess popular attitudes toward the meaning of masculinity and femininity. Used by male and female woman's rights advocates alike, the combination of metaphors that they chose provided mid-nineteenth-century feminists with a way to begin to impose the modification of gender roles and relations on public consciousness. Like the visual metaphor of clothes, these linguistic metaphors served as a source of group identity and group cohesiveness. They also allowed woman's rights advocates to discount the significance of gender as a divisive factor within their own group.

Because their ultimate goal was to enhance woman's role in public life, it is not surprising that they rejected the language of domesticity and modified the languages of republicanism and benevolence in their attempts to do so. What is striking about the public documents and speeches of the early woman's rights movement is the degree to which metaphors describing domestic activities and references to female self-sacrifice are largely absent. Except to complain that woman's domestic work was underappreciated, woman's rights supporters rarely referred to the actual work itself. Missing from their speeches and essays were references to spinning or weaving, stirring or kneading, sweeping or dusting. They did not use metaphors alluding to conceiving, giving birth, nursing the sick, nurturing children, or assisting the poor and downtrodden. In 1853 Lucretia Mott, calling on women to speak out strongly on their own behalf, referred to the notion that a woman's "voice should be drawn as fine as a cambric needle."[2] And a year later, Helen Hazelwood wrote in an article entitled "Woman" that women should be allowed to use "the pen as freely as the needle."[3] But such brief references were the exception rather than the rule. When they were demanding an opportunity to participate more fully in public affairs, woman's rights advocates rarely used words describing those tasks and duties with which American women were most closely associated.

By rhetorically removing women from the home and placing them in the midst of the public issues of the day, early woman's rights supporters were not necessarily rejecting women's domestic role or discounting the importance of women's participation in benevolent activities. They were first of all simply using language to suggest that women's roles outside the home should not be limited. In linguistically distancing themselves from restrictions that traditional roles placed on women, they were also insisting that gender distinctions be discarded or redefined. By simply neglecting rhetorically to place women in a context where most in their audiences expected to find them, they rejected the convention that equated femininity with domesticity and selflessness and asked their listeners to do the same. Such a rhetorical strategy clearly had the advantage of providing the kind of dissonance and shock value required to attract attention to the cause of woman's rights.

One of the metaphors that woman's rights advocates frequently used to describe the general condition of all women and to force the American public to address the issue of gender equality in the public sphere was one that suggested that women were no better than slaves. "Woman is a slave, from cradle to grave," Ernestine Rose told her audience at the Syracuse convention in 1852.[4] Early woman's rights supporters were, of course, not the first to use the slavery metaphor in this context. In the eighteenth century, for example, Mary Astell wrote in her essay on marriage, "If all Men are born Free, how is it that all women are born slaves?" Similarly Daniel Defoe's Roxanna compared the state of married women to that of a slave because the marriage contract forced women to give up their "Liberty, Estate, and Authority."[5] And Mary Wollstonecraft's *Vindication of the Rights of Woman* was peppered with references to the enslavement of women.[6] That rhetorical tradition, combined with the fact that, as Jean Fagan Yellin and others have pointed out, many early woman's rights advocates were directly and deeply influenced by the abolitionist movement, provided them with a frame of reference from which to protest the status of women as well as a powerful metaphor to express their discontent.[7]

Women, in their view, were subject to social and economic as well as political and psychological enslavement. Lucretia Mott, for example, speaking before the 1853 woman's rights convention in New York, observed that "woman has long been the mere slave of social custom, the unreasoning victim of conventional cruelty."[8] Such language was not unusual for Mott. She was a leading antislavery advocate and used the analogy often when called upon to comment publicly upon the condition of women.[9] Other abolitionist-feminists appropriated the language as well. It projected an extremely powerful image. At the same convention, for example, Paulina Wright Davis blamed woman's economic condition for her slavery. "Poverty is essentially slavery," she asserted. "The women of the time, the women worthy of the time must understand this and they must go *to work*! . . . They must purchase themselves out of bondage."[10] And in a memorial adopted by the Salem, Ohio, woman's rights convention in April 1850, Mariana Johnson wrote, "We believe the whole theory of the Common Law in relation to woman is unjust and degrading, tending to reduce her to a level with the slave, depriving her of political existence, and forming a positive exception to the great doctrine of equality as set forth in the Declaration of Independence."[11]

Early woman's rights advocates understood the impact of the centuries of ideological indoctrination that compelled women to collaborate in their own victimization and to construct defenses to protect female self-esteem from the damage it would suffer if they were compelled to acknowledge their true condition. For this reason they argued that the slavery of women was as much a psychological bondage as it was a physical one. In 1848 Emma Willard pointed out that to give up a portion of the right to oneself is acceptable, "but to resign it wholly is to be a self-made slave."[12] Women are obliged to acknowledge their condition even when it does not seem immediately oppressive, wrote Lydia Jane Pierson in her letter to the Akron, Ohio, woman's rights convention in 1851: "Woman's condition is almost that of a chattel slave. When her bonds are woven of silk or twisted of flowers . . . she may smile and dally with them, deeming them ornaments, defenses even; but when those bonds are heavy chains of cold, hard iron, or braided thorns, with here and there a flower, what sophistry can persuade her that they are pleasant and beautiful?"[13] It was not just their condition but their complacent acceptance of it, according to Abby Price, that made them "basely slaves."[14]

Antislavery advocates never ceased to point out that slavery not only artificially imposed restrictions on physical movement but also discouraged the expression of creativity. Thus, it is not surprising that woman's rights advocates, many of whom also supported abolition, tended to refer to society, its institutions, and the prejudices which limited opportunities for women, as a confining physical enclosure—a house, a fortress, or a prison—and to their program for reform as a plan for the demolition, renovation, and reconstruction of the whole social, economic, and political structure. Speaking before the woman's rights convention at Worcester in 1851, for example, Paulina Wright Davis compared society to an "edifice" whose condition was in a state of disrepair. The "light and warmth of the rising day" were excluded from its "ancient turrets and battlements," she observed.[15] And Ernestine Rose, referring to the "thick and impenetrable fortress of prejudice," assured her audience that "if you once make an inroad in it, that space can never be filled up again; every stone you remove is removed for . . . good; and the very effort to replace it, tends only to loosen every other stone, until the whole foundation is undermined and the superstructure crumbles at our feet."[16] Woman's rights advocates intended, according to Elizabeth Oakes Smith, to "pull down our present out worn and imperfect structure of human institutions" and to "reconstruct it upon a new and broader" foundation in the form of a "perfect and harmonious temple."[17] Their goal was to supervise the construction of a world which would encourage both men and women to establish the proper balance between their physical and spiritual needs. The first step in that process was to expose the wrongs against woman, and thus lay the "corner stone" for reform.[18]

Their desire to create a world in which women would play a larger public role seemed to demand that they take immediate action. But there were some among them who understood the kind of planning required of master builders. While there was no doubt in her mind that they had the aptitude necessary to carry out their plans, Lucy Stone warned against beginning construction prematurely. Like any good builder, she argued, women and their supporters "could not put timbers together, and build a goodly structure, till they knew what materials they had."[19] Their vision, however slow to materialize, however, did not change. At the National Woman's Rights Convention in 1860, Elizabeth Cady Stanton suggested that they were in the process of building an "edifice" and Ernestine Rose used the same metaphor to explain that in laying out their "whole plan of rights" they should behave like an "architect who understands his business." Like great builders, they should mark "out not only every hall, and every room, but every niche and corner, every pantry and closet, and even where each specific piece of furniture is to be placed . . . before the first stone is laid for the edifice."[20]

For some, building that edifice was an important component in bringing about the moral regeneration of the world. While most of the leaders of the woman's rights movement cannot be considered religious evangelicals, they had Christian backgrounds and they lived in a world influenced by the revivalism of the Second Great Awakening and its demand that Christians work to build a new world in anticipation of Christ's second coming. Their fiercest opposition came from the clergy, who decried the kind of world they envisioned and attacked them from pulpit and podium, arguing that the basis for proscribing the activities of women was to be found in the Bible. It is not surprising, therefore, that when some woman's rights advocates described their vision of a world characterized by gender equality, they put it into a religious context. Woman's rights leaders like Lucretia Mott responded to clerical objections to expanding woman's roles by arguing that woman's inferior position was not God's work but the work of men who had misinterpreted the Bible and structured the hierarchies of religious institutions to devalue and exclude women. "It is not christianity but priestcraft that has subjected woman as we find her," she said at the National Woman's Rights Convention in Cleveland in 1853.[21] She and others like Antoinette Brown worked hard to convince those in their audiences that the kind of world in which women were denied equal rights was an unregenerate one.

Others argued that allowing women to develop their full potential was not just a way of improving society but was also a way to bring them all closer to the anticipated millennium. The legacy of the Second Great Awakening carried with it the conviction that each individual had to assume responsibility for his or her own salvation as well as the popular belief that one of woman's primary sources of power was her moral influence, an influence which, properly directed, could prepare the world for Christ's second coming. Some woman's rights advocates appealed to those anticipating Christ's return by suggesting that a precondition for the millennium was gender equity. So, according to Abby Price speaking at the woman's rights convention held in Worcester in 1850, when women were given equal rights, "a new era, glorious as the millennial morning, will dawn on earth, an advent only less radiant than that heralded by angels on the plains of Bethlehem."[22] The next year, a speaker at the woman's rights convention in Akron, Ohio, similarly described acceptance of the idea that men and women were equal as the "harbinger" of the "coming of the millennium."[23] It was, they argued, woman's efforts to work out their own salvation and then redeem and regenerate the world by demanding fair and equitable access to opportunity and protection of the law that would pave the way for Christ's second coming.[24]

Woman's rights advocates like Price took an inherently religious frame of reference and the language that accompanied it and secularized them both. For them, gender equality was a precondition for bringing about both a just society and eventually the millennium. At the same time, however, they were determined that the kind of regeneration they hoped to nurture through their work in the woman's rights movement would bring with it significant and immediate improvement in the everyday material well-being and legal status of women. They were willing to use the power of woman's moral influence and her work in altruistic activities to justify seeking changes that, while ostensibly intended to prepare society for the second coming, had an explicit this-worldly dimension and self-interested component.

The secular thrust of woman's rights rhetoric was also reflected in the tendency of its advocates to use mechanical metaphors to explain how restrictions on women affected social, economic, and political life. These metaphors projected an image of society as a machine made up of parts large and small, each essential to the efficient functioning of the machine. Products of a world increasingly influenced by engineering and technology, they pointed out that any machine whose parts were missing, improperly installed, or out of balance could not be expected to fulfill the use for which it was intended. H. H. Van Amringe in an essay read before the audience of the 1850 woman's rights convention held in Worcester, Massachusetts, claimed that the world was waiting for women to gain their rights. Like mechanical engineers, he explained, "we frame a governor for equalizing motion and accumulating power. The power thus accumulated is applied to the accomplishment of effects, for which the machine, without this *help*, would be incompetent." The world, he suggested, was like a machine which could not run at its greatest efficiency, or as he put it, "proceed to its highest destiny," without incorporating the power of women.[25] Emma Willard used a similar analogy. For those who designed a government not to avail themselves of the advice and counsel of women was comparable, she argued, to a "mechanician, who having a heavy weight to move by steam, should so miscalculate his force as to make no account of one half . . . as not even to take the pains to know whether it would be . . . a conspiring or an opposing force." Rhetorically, she asked, "What would you think" of such a "mechanician?" "The wise politician," she advised, should take account of the "power of female influence" and "in constructing the machinery of government he should not only guard against it becoming an opposing force, but he should provide a machinery by means of which it will aid to propel the political train in the right direction."[26] Likewise at the woman's rights convention at Worcester in 1851, Paulina Wright Davis observed that "a skillful mechanic never puts a wheel, or pulley, or spring too many in his machine; nor wastes material or power in making them too great or strong for their intended use." To fail to allow women to do whatever they were able to do, she argued, was to waste their potential to contribute to society.[27]

Mechanical metaphors linguistically provided for women a place in the midst of those who claimed the right to order and control the forces of nature for the benefit of society. Such metaphors gave women an active role in harnessing physical power and efficiently directing its use for the benefit of all. In that sense, it gave the self-interested demand for more rights for women a selfless and, therefore, benevolent dimension, one that was consistent with Scottish Enlightenment philosophers' insistence that self-interest be directed toward achieving goals that would benefit everyone. It also revised the rhetoric of republicanism in the sense that in emphasizing the dysfunctional effect that the improper concentration of power might have in technology, it subtly alluded to the importance of the kind of diffusion of power in government and society that was necessary to protect republican principles.

Perhaps the most dissonant metaphor used by woman's rights advocates before the Civil War was the metaphor of war. According to Paula Baker, military metaphors were commonly used by journalists in the nineteenth century to characterize male political behavior—elections were "battles," party workers were "soldiers," and parties themselves were "armies."[28] Her observation testifies to the degree to which the pursuit of politics, like the pursuit of war, was viewed as an exclusively male activity, one whose very language implicitly excluded women. In his study of American feminism in the post–Civil War era, William Leach characterized those with a feminist vision of a reformed society as having so much "disdain" for politics and political parties that they were unwilling to employ "the language of power, faction, or conflict" in their speeches or writings.[29]

Whatever may have been the case with respect to this metaphor after the war between the states, it was an important part of the language of woman's rights advocates before 1860. This is surprising given the fact many leading woman's rights advocates were Quakers and abolitionists who were, generally speaking, predisposed toward pacifism and who opposed military conflicts like the Mexican War because they believed it represented an attempt to expand the institution of slavery. Nevertheless, in the early years of the woman's rights movement, supporters of equal rights for women appropriated and exploited the metaphors of war to express their discontent, to devise their strategy for change, and to expand the opportunities for women to participate in the political life of the republic. They consciously and publicly defined their movement as a war or crusade filled with skirmishes and battles which would gain them eventual victory over those they perceived to be their enemies. Nancy Baird of Virginia summed it up when she wrote to the woman's rights convention in Worcester, "Your . . . work" is a "war with principalities and power, and *wickedness in high places*, a war with profound ignorance and long cherished prejudice. . . ."[30]

Woman's rights supporters appropriated the rules associated with the gentleman's code of honor by challenging their opposition with "glove" and "gauntlet."[31] They armed themselves with whatever weapons were available. In her speech before the Seneca Falls convention, for example, Stanton called upon American women to "buckle on the armor that can best resist the keenest weapons of the enemy."[32] That "armor," suggested

Lucretia Mott, was their dependence upon "Right, Truth, and Reason."[33]
At the second National Woman's Rights Convention in Worcester in 1851,
Ernestine Rose suggested that during their "crusade" they "must put on
the armor of charity, carry before us the banner of truth, and defend
ourselves with the shield of right against the invaders of our liberty . . .
until we have conquered."[34] And in 1853 Lucy Stone spoke of the "rod"
which they held in their hands and with which they would "smite" their
enemies.[35] Elizabeth Oakes Smith wrote to Stanton in 1852 that the
selection of weapons was an important one, implying that victory for
women would depend more upon intellect and strategy than on brute
strength. "You know," she reminded her friend, "it is not the battle axe
that does the greatest execution; the finely tempered blade may cut
through the flimsy straws of conventionalism, and specious error quite as
effectually."[36]

She like others in the movement believed that the vote would be
woman's most effective weapon and that their armory would be incomplete without it. The ballot, resolved the woman's rights convention in
Boston in 1855, would be "woman's sword and shield."[37] The vote, they
argued, would give women as a group both the power to attack their
adversaries and the ability to protect themselves against them. But the
vote, they acknowledged, would be the hardest weapon to acquire. "Depend on it," wrote Elizabeth Cady Stanton to president *pro tem* of the
Salem, Ohio, woman's rights convention in 1850, "this is the point to
attack, the stronghold of the fortress—*the one* woman will find most
difficult to take—*the one* man will most reluctantly give up." It might
take years, she warned, but they needed to "encamp right under its
shadow—spend all of our time, strength, and *moral* ammunition" on
obtaining it. She encouraged them to refuse to allow anything to "seduce
us from our position until that one stronghold totters to the ground." Once
that happened, she predicted, "the rest will they surrender *at discretion*."[38]

Like members of a military headquarters, they defined their goals. Like
generals in the field, they argued over and planned their strategy. Their
goal should be "conquest," declared A. D. Mayo.[39] They needed to "select
the points of attack," advised Paulina Wright Davis.[40] But selecting those
points of attack was not easy. While some like Stanton argued that they
should concentrate on getting the vote, others maintained that women
should first liberate themselves from their restrictive clothing. Jane
Swisshelm, for one, felt that dress reform would only distract them from
their main goal. In an editorial which appeared in her paper the *Pittsburgh
Saturday Visiter*, Swisshelm protested that she felt "equal to the task of
defending the cause of our sex single-handed against the united armies of
the world." But to complicate the campaign with the issue of dress reform
was to find herself "upon a sandbank, which has been all carefully
undermined." The woman's rights "army," which she assumed were her

"allies," seemed to be fighting "another kind of expedition altogether." They were "marching in full force" so that ladies could have "pantaloons." If they persisted, she continued contemptuously, "May heaven grant them beards—war to the knife and the knife to the hilt, bombardments, breast-works and cannonadings in defense of their right to the trousers!" But she had not "enlisted in any such war" and had no intention of assisting them in their efforts.[41]

While they argued over their strategy, they called their troops to battle. "Let her [woman's] firm and united ranks appear, with a white banner given to the breeze," advised Abby Price.[42] And having unfurled their banners, they were advised to "array" their "forces in order, and press on."[43] They would lead their troops to the field and attack, all the while sensitive to the fact that only the most dedicated would follow them. "This reform will be the sword of division," warned A. D. Mayo in a letter to the Syracuse convention. Those who expressed commitment to the cause but who had entered it "from any motive less exalted than consecra-tion to duty, [would] fall away in weariness and disgust."[44] They expected that their army like those of men would be plagued with the problem of desertion.

They had some sense of what it meant to participate in warfare. Their definition of the enemy was broad. They expected to suffer. Their partisan-ship was exclusive. "Both men and women will appear as antagonists, equipped with their warlike implements," warned Elizabeth Wilson in her letter to the 1850 Worcester convention. The enemy would "requisition" all the weapons at their command including "their faithful ally, the mob, with its heavy artillery, charged with brickbats and rotten eggs."[45] Accord-ing to the editor of *The Lily*, the first alert would be sounded by male newspaper editors "who feel it their especial duty to watch over the interests of their sex." They were, she observed, "already sounding notes of alarm, and calling upon their clan to prepare to resist the army of women that are coming against them in battle."[46] The "lords of creation" were "stationed on the watch towers" and could "sniff danger in the wind."[47] Those who did not stand with them, they would assume were against them. They warned their listeners that "those who do not enter the open arena to do battle for or against" them would not be allowed to remain neutral.[48]

They did not expect an immediate victory and recognized that their campaign would be long and tortuous. Matilda Gage warned them that "there will be a long moral warfare before the citadel yields." While they worked for the defeat of those who opposed them, they should, she advised, "take possession of the outposts."[49] Attacks on such outposts would take place at woman's rights conventions, dubbed the "Thermo-pylae" of "freedom" by Elizabeth Oakes Smith at Syracuse.[50] Like the Greeks in their famous attempt to resist the power of the invading

Persians, woman's rights advocates understood that they were outnumbered and appreciated the importance of choosing a defensible position. Unlike the Greeks, they expected opposition from both the front and the rear.

Once the outposts were taken, however, they would have to directly confront the enemy. "The enemy," warned Paulina Wright Davis, "disputes the possession of the 'good land' with us, and there are giants in the field against us, and the victory is not to be achieved by battles fought on this side of its borders. We must invade the disputed territory—we must go up individually and possess it."[51] They were David. Those who opposed them were Goliath. They were convinced that they had the skill and the intellect to overcome the social, political, and economic advantages of the enemy. With God on their side, they were sure of eventual victory. They acknowledged that they were carrying out "moral warfare" which demanded heroism in the face of a "solid phalanx" of opposition but which, they assured their audiences, would ultimately result in their capture first of the "outposts" and then of the "citadel" itself.[52]

The use of military metaphors no doubt reflected the fact that the U.S. had recently succeeded in expanding its borders by winning the Mexican War. The woman's rights movement emerged just as the war was ending. Because the war was fought in a land far removed from most Americans, its conduct had less immediacy for the civilian population than that of the American Revolution or the War of 1812. American cities were not threatened with invasion. Foreign troops did not occupy American soil. And yet because of the rise of the popular press and improvements in communication brought about by the development of the telegraph, American civilians were barraged with information about the war.

While the war had little immediate effect on the status of women, popular authors and their editors, not necessarily committed to feminist principles of gender equality, used the opportunity to remind their readers that women were as capable as men of heroic behavior and had been known to fight for their country when necessity demanded it. The Washington *National Intelligencer*, for example, reported that women were serving in the Mexican army. With tongue in cheek, it urged that the U.S. government recruit women to serve on the front. Characterizing women as "*instinctive* soldiers," it warned that encountering an angry woman, "when once fairly aroused," on the field of battle was as bad as encountering "so many tigresses."[53] Other periodicals issued reports of the determination of Dos Amades, the female commander of a company of Mexican lancers, to drive the Americans out of Mexican territory and the heroism of Ann Chase, the Irish-born wife of the American Consul in Tampico, who stayed behind in the city and supplied American troops with intelligence which led to its capture.[54] Sarah Josepha Hale, the editor of *Godey's Lady's Book*, one of the most popular women's magazines of the day, excerpted a paragraph for her "Editor's Table" from the New York *Home Journal* which reported not only that a battery had been named for Ann Chase for her heroism at Tampico but that "two companies of women" had "been armed and equipped as an ecclesiastical guard by the Catholic vicar of one of the valleys of Switzerland." If that were not bad enough, ran the New York editorial, "Mormon women" had recently been "formed into a regiment." Such things combined with the demand that women be given the right to vote and proposed revisions in law which would allow married women the right to control property seemed to portend "a sort of petticoat ascendancy."[55]

Hale's response to such news was predictable. In favor of efforts to provide women with more educational and economic opportunities, the editor of *Godey's* opposed other woman's rights demands. But she informed her readers that while she did not support attempts to gain the vote for women and certainly did not "advise ladies to enlist" in the army, she did regard the honors bestowed on Ann Chase as well deserved. Her interest in women's participation in war was not limited to one editorial, however. Hale also ran a series of twelve articles each concerned with women in the era of the American Revolution who in one way or another had exhibited the kind of "disinterestedness, courage, and constancy" which qualified them for heroic stature.[56] Whether she approved of women serving in the military or not, Hale through her editorial policy helped not only to remind her readers that women as well as men were capable of acts of heroism but also to legitimize women's participation in war.

Woman's rights activists, while perhaps more ambivalent than many about the Mexican War, nevertheless, like other citizens experienced it vicariously through reports in newspapers and periodicals. Their use of military language was, no doubt, in part a reflection of that vicarious experience. But military language came to them through another source as well—that of the evangelical Christian tradition.[57] It was a language used by ministers and hymn writers to call the religious to action as in the popular "Onward Christian Soldiers." Yet as Sandra Sizer has pointed out in her study of the rhetoric of revivalism in the nineteenth century, "Onward Christian Soldiers" was an exceptional hymn. Most battle hymns of the period were not hymns of conquest but rather hymns of defense that encouraged the faithful to hold steady against an enemy whose advance was persistent. More typical, according to Sizer, was a hymn entitled "Hold the Fort."

> Ho! my comrades, see the signal
> Waving in the sky!
> Reinforcements now appearing
> Victory is nigh!

See the mighty host advancing
Satan leading on:
Mighty men around us falling,
Courage almost gone.

CHORUS:
"Hold the fort, for I am coming,"
Jesus signals still,
Wave the answer back to heaven,
"By Thy grace we will."[58]

Considering the power of nationalism and religion in the mid-nineteenth century, it is not surprising that military metaphors would appear in the rhetoric of reformers. But in the case of the woman's rights movement, their use represented something more than merely bandying about words referring to current events or religious commitment. For them the use of military metaphors represented a linguistic attempt both to acknowledge the significance of the struggle they faced and to claim from men the right to participate in political debate and by extension politics itself including the politics of war. It was a demand that men acknowledge the political competency of women as a first step in incorporating them into the political structure.[59] By describing their activities as military campaigns, woman's rights advocates placed their political claims side by side with those advocated by men through their political parties, and modified the ideology and rhetoric of republicanism in such a way as to include women among those citizens who were perfectly willing and competent to fulfill their civic responsibilities by fighting to protect and preserve its democratic principles.

The use of military metaphors by women and those who supported their cause posed a deliberate and overt linguistic challenge to social, economic, and political patriarchy in America at a time when men were especially vulnerable. It represented a deliberate trespass onto turf dominated by men since time immemorial. Whether used to describe the evangelical efforts of "Christian soldiers" or the partisan struggles within local, state, and national government, language filled with military metaphors had been, up to this point, male language. Military language provided a way of characterizing what it meant to be manly in an age in which, according to E. Anthony Rotundo, the definitions of what constituted masculinity were changing.[60]

Manliness tended to be defined as much by how men differed from women as by what men were or thought they were.[61] From the middle ages through the eighteenth century, masculinity had been defined partly on the basis that men had the ability to reason while women did not. But by the Age of Jackson, Americans had rejected the importance of the power of reason in favor of what Scottish Enlightenment philosophers would have called sensibility, "the intuitive powers of the human heart,"[62] a characteristic long viewed as a feminine attribute.

During the same time period, the patriarchal power of fathers within the family was declining as mothers began to replace them as the moral authority and primary agents of early childhood socialization.[63] When woman's rights advocates appropriated military metaphors to express their political demands, they laid claim to an experience that had been with only rare exceptions reserved exclusively for men.

As literary critic Sandra Gilbert and others have pointed out, the significance of war as a male experience in Western culture has been and still is profound. War magnifies the power of men and the vulnerability of women and children by dividing society into the protectors and the protected. But while war offers men the opportunity to become military heroes and allows them to glorify their actions in the pages of history, it also makes them vulnerable. War temporarily removes men from control over women and thus brings into question their ability to compel female obedience to both themselves and the state. It encourages the mobilization of the female population and expands opportunities for them by removing men from civilian life and forcing women to accept roles and responsibilities normally defined as male. War kills sons, leaving daughters to survive and inherit property. War maims sons, husbands, and fathers who become dependent upon the care that women are expected to give. War destroys the edifices that men have built, the physical and public symbols of male power. In many ways war makes women central rather than peripheral figures.[64] But as long as women were excluded from combat, their centrality could be ignored or discounted. When they linguistically placed themselves in the midst of combat, woman's rights advocates magnified their centrality, asserted their competency, and forced their listeners to acknowledge them both.

From the male point of view, female participation in war was incongruous. Women were not and never had been central to either political or military life. So by using the metaphors of war, women were claiming the right to engage in combat at least on the discursive level and in that sense become like men. As in the case of adopting the Bloomer costume and its variations, they refused to continue to allow their female bodies to be the source of their social, economic, and political disempowerment. They adopted linguistically male characteristics complete with the symbols of their power and authority. Their banners, swords, and rods served as symbolic phalluses. The thrust of their rebellion was to act collectively to gain power. They made demands not only as individuals but also as an army. The language they used very specifically rejected the social conventions that divided male and female spheres and ignored traditional socialization patterns that reserved for men access to public power through force of arms if necessary. Crucially, this language not only disregarded but also directly challenged the social conventions that on one hand allowed men the right to express their anger and frustrations physically and on the other forbade women to do so and expected them to suppress such feelings. By using military language, women who spoke out in support of improving the condition of their sex forced their listeners to deal with their individual and collective rage as well as to direct their attention toward feminist social, economic, and political goals.

When woman's rights activists used military metaphors, they were angry and prepared for battle, but—in their own minds at least—the thrust of their militancy was not to destroy but to create. They did not want to replace existing economic, social, and political systems with entirely new ones. They only wanted to enlarge woman's opportunity to participate in the systems that already existed. Because their goals were limited in that sense, they were hopeful that they could be accomplished. They were prepared to nurture support for their cause rather than try to impose the changes they deemed necessary by force. They were willing to keep a rein on their militancy and hold it in reserve. But in the end, they were determined to use whatever weapon was available to them to challenge the gender conventions that reserved for men social, economic, and political power.

When they used the metaphors of nature to express their ideology they made their strategy clear. These metaphors allowed them to describe their grievances, goals, and strategies within a discursive structure that projected images that were on one hand benign, harmonious, evolutionary, and creative and on the other powerful, violent, and destructive. In an apparent effort to remind and reassure their audiences as well as themselves that woman's role in the evolution of the world typically had been creative and nurturing, woman's rights advocates such as Paulina Wright Davis promised their audience that they sought change "without violence or any form of antagonism." They claimed that they wanted merely "to replace the worn out with the living and the beautiful, so as to reconstruct without overturning, and to regenerate without destroying."[65]

They continued this line of argument when they pictured themselves as society's gardeners who spend their lives, attuned to the rhythms of nature, plowing, planting, weeding, and harvesting. Using organic metaphors, they argued that their only goal was to nurture the growth of their society and its institutions and laws so that women could have equal opportunity to pursue their self-interest for the benefit of all. "Governments are not made; they grow," Wendell Phillips assured his audience at the 1856 woman's rights convention. "They are not buildings like this, with dome and pillars; they are oaks, with roots and branches, and they grow, by God's blessing, in the soil he gives them."[66] Both the physical and "the social soil," said Ernestine Rose, "is waiting the plough wielded by woman's heart and head." Their ideas were like seeds, they argued. All they needed to do was to plant "the seed" in "good ground" in order that all might have "their own wine and fig tree."[67] "We draw the furrow through the waste fields of life," observed Lucy Stone; "our hands drop the seeds that spring up and bear fruit."[68] Their ideas and protests, like seeds, according to George William Curtis, were "planted alone in the soil, by a solitary husbandman; and the winds from heaven, the juices of earth, and the dews that fall by night fed it, and fed it, till it has grown to be a great crop, green to the harvest. . . ."[69]

Their crop had to be properly nurtured, however. Just as civilization was believed to destroy the beauty of nature, so social custom restricted and distorted woman's growth. "If you seize the young tree," observed C. C. Burleigh, "when it just begins to put forth to the air, and sunshine, and dews, and bend it in all directions, for fear it will not grow in proper shape, do not hold the tree responsible for its distortion."[70] A culture that made it impossible for women to develop their full potential was, according to Ann Preston, unnatural: "If the whole body is left without exercise, one arm does not become strong; if the tree is stunted in its growth, one branch does not shoot into surpassing luxuriance."[71]

Clearly, these metaphors reflected the influence of Romanticism on those who advocated woman's rights. Linguistically woman's rights activists rejected the trimmed and pruned plants of an earlier age and the gardens which, rationally planned and meticulously tended, reflected man's desire to control nature and by extension women. As we have seen, woman's rights advocates argued that conventional dress imprisoned women's bodies, damaged their health, restricted their physical movement, and contributed to their invisibility and inequality. Similarly, they argued that if women in general did not display the same aptitudes as men, it was because women's abilities, like the growth of a topiary, had been artificially shaped by those whose goal was to stifle natural development. Borrowing an analogy from Goethe, Wendell Phillips declared that women were like oaks planted in flower pots. When such a thing happens, he predicted, "either the oak will be dwarfed, or the flower-pot will break. So we have planted woman in a flower-pot, hemmed her in by restrictions, and when we move to enlarge her sphere, society cries out, 'Oh! you'll break the flower-pot!' Well, I say, let it break. . . . Let us see how broadly the branches will throw themselves, and how beautiful will be the shape, and how glorious against the moonlit sky, or glowing sunset, the foliage shall appear."[72] Given the right conditions, given freedom from the constraints placed on them by social conventions designed by men to stunt the development of women, they would, as Sarah Grimké put it, emerge like insects from their "chrysalis state . . . feeble" and "powerless." Eventually, she confidently predicted, women, like butterflies, would develop the confidence and strength to "visit the flowers which bloom around."[73]

From the seed that they were planting, then, they expected a "glorious harvest," but they were not sure that they would live to "reap the fruits" of their efforts.[74] Henry Ward Beecher admitted as much when he said to an audience that he hoped his words would serve as a "leaven" to his listeners rather than to "bear immediate fruits. But as the farmer sows seed in October that he does not expect to reap till July," he continued, "so we must sow, and wait patiently for the harvest." Change, he later observed somewhat more optimistically, was likely to come slowly. "Plants had three periods of growth," he explained. "The first and slowest was by the root, next by the stem, which was less slow, last and quickest by the blossom and fruit. The world," he predicted, "was entering on the period of blossom and fruit."[75]

Such optimism, however, was restrained by the realization that removing the obstacles that stood in the path of equal rights for women would be difficult. "We do not expect," stated Stanton at the Seneca Falls convention, "our path to be strewn with the flowers of popular applause, but over the thorns of bigotry will be our way."[76] In 1850 Jane Elizabeth Jones pointed out to the woman's rights convention in Salem, Ohio, that most reforms were not effective because they were inadequate: "Lopping the branches of the tree but causes the roots to strike deeper and cling more closely to the soil that sustains it."[77] Three years later at another convention, Lydia Jenkins observed that the tree could not "blossom till the cankering worm be removed from its root."[78]

Such metaphors reflected the hopefulness of woman's rights advocates that their goals would be achieved through nurture rather than the militant use of brute strength. They hoped that the force of their arguments would overcome resistance to their efforts. Their view of nature in this context was relatively benign. It was likely to place only thorns, worms, and stubborn overgrown roots in the way of growth and development. But they recognized that nature also had a more vicious side, one characterized by violent and destructive forces such as those to be found in the wind and the sea, forces that could destroy if not controlled. And woman's rights advocates placed their movement in this context as well. They described themselves as both struggling against the forces of nature and harnessing those very forces to destroy those who dared to oppose them. Elizabeth Cady Stanton, for example, began the debate over woman's rights at Seneca Falls by warning, "On our banners will beat the dark storm clouds of opposition from those who have entrenched themselves behind the stormy bulwarks of custom and authority." They would press on, she assured her audience. "Undauntedly we will unfurl it [their banner] to the gale, for we know that the storm cannot rend from it a shred, that the electric flash will but more clearly show to us the glorious words inscribed upon it, 'Equality of Rights.'"[79] Her warning contained two messages. Their task, she suggested, was to survive by waiting out the storm which, while it raged about them, would not significantly alter their course. Such patience and persistence, she implied, would allow them to control the destructive tendencies of nature by directing them toward their own ends.

For Jane Elizabeth Jones, however, the storm was not something that women had to fight against. The woman's rights movement *was* the storm, and its supporters were the agents of potential disorder, violence, and destruction. In 1852 she described the era as a "time of progress" and predicted that "man might sooner arrest the progress of lightning or the clouds, or stay the waves of the sea, than stay the onward march of truth with her hand on her sword and her banner unfurled."[80] For the Rev. A. D. Mayo, the struggle for woman's rights was a "volcano" whose eruption would awaken a slumbering society.[81] For Susan B. Anthony, the woman's rights movement was a tidal wave. In an attempt to sound an optimistic note at the 1860 National Woman's Rights Convention in New York, she noted that "the influence has gone forth, the great ocean has been moved, and those who watch e'en now may see the mighty waves of truth, slowly swelling on the shores of time."[82] Wendell Phillips agreed. At the same convention he told his audience that change had come slowly in the past but that in New York in the past year the "moral barometer" had risen "a full inch." He concluded that "It is a proof that the monsoon is coming that will lift the old conservative ship, carrying the idea that woman is a drudge and a slave, out of the waters, and dash her into fragments on the surface of our Democratic sea."[83]

Romantic references to the forces of nature were reassuring in the sense that they confirmed the role of women as creators and nurturers. But they also allowed woman's rights activists to serve notice that the power of woman, like that of nature, could easily be channeled into disrupting the order that men gave themselves credit for having imposed on nature. Women if thwarted, they warned, could destroy the status quo as well as preserve it. Those who led the struggle to gain more rights for women wanted to nurture change. But if the changes they called for were resisted, they were willing to destroy what stood in the way of their ability to achieve their goals.

That these literate reformers should have appropriated such a wide variety of metaphors to express their demands is predictable. What is striking is their propensity to use a combination of metaphors which projected such dissonant and incompatible images: natural and artificial, passive and combative, victim and aggressor, masculine and feminine, builder and destroyer, sacred and secular, weak and powerful. Their eclecticism certainly had a practical dimension in the sense that it illustrates the degree to which gauging their audience posed a problem for them. At any one time, in any one place, woman's rights advocates were compelled to try to speak to various kinds of listeners—the hostile, the sympathetic, the rowdy, the curious, the angry, the doubtful, the ambivalent, the aggrieved, the affronted. They learned from experience that their audiences would be composed of men as well as women, of the orderly as well as the disorderly, of the educated and the illiterate, of the influential and the uninfluential. Their language and public presence had to be powerful enough to manipulate their audiences, to convince as many as possible of the justice of their claims while at the same time shaming the hecklers and exhibitionists who through their hisses and stamping attempted to disrupt their meetings and prevent them from being heard. Every speech and essay had to be a tactical experiment, an exercise in improvisation. Without money, organization, an official newspaper, or a large base of popular support, language was one of their few weapons. They had to get the attention of those in their audience before they could explain their ideas effectively. Consistency was not their immediate aim. Effectiveness was.

But the language used by woman's rights advocates before the Civil War performed a number of other functions as well. Each metaphor served them in different ways. As we have already seen, the language of natural rights and liberal individualism provided them with an ideological framework which helped them to develop their own sense of history and legitimized their right to promote their own self-interests. References to slavery dramatized the victimization of women at the hands both of men and of the social conventions that proscribed their economic, social, and political life, leaving them psychologically incapable of understanding their own subjugation. Placing their movement in the context of architecture and engineering allowed them rhetorically to demand the right to join men in applying skill, intellect, and creativity to the artificial world of design, construction, and technology in order to mold American social, economic, and political life. References to the millennium brought with them the promise and vision of the possibility of establishing a heaven on earth for women and the men who were willing to grant equal economic, educational, and political opportunities to them. Men had traditionally used military language to marginalize women. Early feminists used it to make women central. Military metaphors enabled woman's rights advocates to appropriate the right to participate in political debate and by extension politics itself on the same basis as men. They challenged those in their audience, whether hostile or sympathetic, to respond as a first step in legitimizing the desire of women to share power equally with men. Moreover, by placing before their audiences the image of women as combatants, woman's rights advocates laid the groundwork for encouraging their listeners to reevaluate not only their ideas about traditional gender roles but also their ideas about power and the way that it should be distributed. On one hand references to nature in organic and biological metaphors, like a scrim on a stage, allowed those willing to speak out in favor of woman's rights to soften the edges of their militancy by reminding those in their audiences of woman's creative and nurturing roles. On the other, such references served as a warning to listeners that women, like nature, could be violent and destructive, and that when they were exhibiting those characteristics, resistance was both dangerous and useless.

The combination of metaphors and analogies used by woman's rights activists liberated women linguistically from the restrictions placed on them by the ideologies of republicanism, domesticity, and benevolence and provided them with a way of identifying themselves. It did not make them men. But like the metaphor of reform dress, it made them like men. Because this language was used by male and female reformers alike, it helped them to establish and maintain their group identity and to diminish gender distinctions among them by providing them with a practical example of the ability of men and women to work together to change society. In this way verbal language, like the visual language of clothes, took the place of formal organization as a way of establishing the bonds necessary to provide the kind of support and encouragement that the men and women who publicly supported woman's rights needed. Use of this particular set of metaphors testified to membership in the community of woman's rights reformers and the like-mindedness of its participants.

Like the ideology that it expressed, the language of the woman's rights movement was a hybrid. Dramatic and, to many, shocking and inflammatory, it was used by woman's rights advocates as a powerful weapon in order to attract attention to their cause and prompt public discussion of gender roles and relations and the position of women in American society. The debate that ensued over the goals of the woman's rights movement so eloquently enumerated in the Declaration of Sentiments and the public statements that followed were an important first step in transforming American society and creating a culture that would eventually provide women with expanded economic, social, and political opportunities.

IV

THE STRATEGY

The provocative combination of metaphors that woman's rights advocates used to express their ideology and demands was intended to place women side by side with men in public life and to attract the attention of the general public in order to develop grass-roots support for the reforms that they were proposing in the area of gender roles and relationships. Gaining a mass audience for their message was a major problem, however. Certainly conducting petition drives, publishing and distributing tracts, lobbying lawmakers, and giving public speeches and lectures were important ways to promote the cause. By the end of the 1850s thousands of individuals attended national woman's rights conventions. And those who read woman's rights literature or attended conventions or lectures, whether sympathetic or not, no doubt discussed the issue of woman's rights with their relatives, friends, and acquaintances and thereby helped to cultivate interest in the movement if not necessarily support for it. But relying solely on such activities was not likely to guarantee the kind of broad-based popular support needed to redefine gender roles and further expand woman's opportunities to participate as equals with men in public life.

Other factors also contributed to this problem. One was the fact that woman's rights activists lacked their own organization and had to work through personal networks and other reform groups in order to further their goals. Another was that they lacked independent sources of revenue with which to cover such things as travel expenses, rental fees, and printing costs. Still another was their sometimes intentional and sometimes inadvertent neglect of potential supporters. Woman's rights activists held out little hope that members of the upper class might be recruited to support their efforts and, therefore, spent very little time trying to attract them. Lucy Stone summarized her attitude toward the well born and wealthy when in 1855 she wrote to Antoinette Brown that she intended to spend only one day promoting the cause of woman's rights in the fashionable resort of Saratoga Springs, New York. "The people who congregate at Saratoga are not reformers," she observed. "The rich and fashionable, move only when the masses that are behind and under them move. So that our work is with the mass, who have no reputation to lose, no ambition to gratify, and who, as they do not depend upon the Public, need not smother their convictions for its favor." According to Stone, those who vacationed at Saratoga "always *follow*, and *never* lead Public opinion."[1]

The leaders of the woman's rights movement neglected the working class as well. They were concerned about improving employment and educational opportunities for working-class women and advocated the passage of property laws that would guarantee that a woman could control her own wages. But that did not stop those who planned public events from charging fees of as high as twenty-five cents a session to attend their conventions which were held during the work week and scheduling sessions at those conventions during the morning and afternoon.[2] The result was that those who actually sat in their audiences and heard their speeches tended to be those with discretionary time and money.

What they needed was to expose vast numbers of ordinary men and women to their message in order to provoke widespread discussion about the condition of women as a first step in bringing about the changes they wanted. Their primary strategy for guaranteeing that kind of national exposure was to supplement their petition drives, lobbying efforts, and speechmaking with efforts to cultivate the interest of journalists in their cause. They understood that managing the press well could provide them with an important conduit to the general public as well as special interest groups such as educators, employers, and lawmakers. Therefore, they went to great lengths to attract the attention of the reporters and editors of two kinds of periodicals: those representing the newspapers of the popular or "penny press" and those who edited reform journals. The former, while not necessarily sympathetic, provided them access to readers all over the country. The latter, who were more likely to be supportive but whose influence was more limited, helped to cultivate the support of those already interested in reform and to preserve the loyalty of their supporters.

From the very beginning, woman's rights advocates recognized the importance of focusing the attention of the popular press on their movement. "Imagine the publicity given to our ideas by thus appearing in a widely circulated sheet like the [New York] *Herald*," wrote Elizabeth Cady Stanton to Lucretia Mott shortly after the Seneca Falls convention. "It will start women thinking and men too, and when men and women think about a new question, the first step in progress is taken."[3] They never lost sight of the need to attract the attention of prominent newspaper editors to their cause. "Just so far as the newspapers go, opinion goes; just so far as they are read, ideas are recognized," said Wendell Phillips, referring to the importance of the press at the 1856 National Woman's Rights Convention in New York.[4] And in 1860 Susan B. Anthony wrote that if they could get the resolutions passed by the Albany convention published in the [New York] *Tribune*, they would be read by as many as 800,000 readers. "As much effect comes of *wisely publishing* our meetings as of holding them," she argued.[5]

The possibilities and rewards for attracting the attention of newspaper editors were expanding by the time woman's rights advocates began their campaign. Before the 1830s newspapers had been designed to serve the needs of politicians and businessmen. Frequently controlled by one political party or another, they were expensive and usually sold by subscription. The result was that their circulation was limited.[6] For all practical purposes, they contained little or nothing that bore directly upon the lives of most women.

The 1830s, however, marked the rise of what has been labeled the "penny press." These newspapers were cheap and hawked on city streets. They had daily, semi-weekly, and weekly editions. They still provided their readers with commercial information and discussions of political issues. But they also contained human interest stories.[7] Compared to their predecessors, they had large circulations. Their editors, all of whom were male, not only reflected public opinion, they made it and shared it. Penny press editors, particularly those in smaller towns and cities with limited budgets, shamelessly borrowed stories from each other, but particularly from editors in major metropolitan areas like New York, to fill the space between their advertising columns. Throughout the period in question, editors of papers like the St. Louis *Daily Missouri Republican* and the *Chicago Daily Tribune* clipped and republished stories from a wide variety of newspapers including the *New York Tribune*, the *New York Times*, and the *New York Herald* as well as smaller papers like the *Louisville Courier* and the *Albany [New York] Argus*. Sometimes they cited their sources. Sometimes they did not. But this practice combined with the use of telegraph technology allowed editors of papers like the *Republican* to provide their readers with up-to-date information from all over the country, including descriptions of woman's rights conventions held in faraway and relatively small places like Worcester, Massachusetts, and Syracuse, New York.

The three newspapers with the widest circulation during the antebellum period, and thus with the most potential for helping woman's rights advocates spread their ideology, were the *New York Herald*, the *New York Times*, and the *New York Tribune*. All of them were published daily in New York City but also had weekly, semi-weekly, California, or European editions. The most recent attempt to analyze the influence of these three major New York newspapers estimates that together their circulation in 1856 was about 397,000 copies. Priced at a few pennies an issue, they were intended to both inform and influence public opinion concerning the issues of the day.[8]

What the editors of these three papers thought about the woman's rights movement was important. New York City was not the center of the woman's rights movement, but five out of the eleven antebellum national woman's rights conventions were held there, and the editors of these papers had the means to send reporters to cover woman's rights activities held elsewhere. These New York editors had significant national influence because their papers were widely circulated and their articles were often republished by other papers.

Because newspaper editors had the potential for attracting the attention of a broad-based national audience to the issue of woman's rights by covering the activities of the movement and debating the merits of woman's rights demands in their columns, woman's rights advocates devoted a great deal of effort to manipulating the penny press in cities like New York to serve their own interests. It was, they hoped, through the editors of papers like these that they could spark a national reassessment of gender roles and relations, and influence not only ordinary men and women but also those in positions to change the status quo to support reforms that would expand social, economic, and political opportunities for women.

The oldest of the three most influential papers in New York was the *New York Herald*, founded in 1835 by its editor James Gordon Bennett, a Scotsman who was born in 1795 and educated at Blair's College in Aberdeen. At the age of twenty-five, Bennett landed in Boston where he got a job as a clerk and proofreader in a local publishing house. He spent some time in Charleston, South Carolina, and then in New York learning to be an editor and publisher.[9] In 1835 he began publishing the *New York Daily Herald* from an office on Wall Street hoping to appeal to a mass market composed of "merchant, mechanic, working people—the private family as well as the public hotel—the journeyman and his employer—the clerk and his principal." Viewing himself as independent of party, he straightforwardly announced that he intended to provide his readers with "facts on every public and proper subject." In his newspaper, he did not intend to distinguish clearly between news and editorial. When he thought it warranted, he warned his readers, he intended to sprinkle news stories with his opinions which he promised would be "independent, fearless, and good tempered."[10]

Bennett was first and foremost a businessman. He was not a reformer. That is not to say that he saw no way in which society could be improved, but that his sense of social responsibility was inhibited by his determined adherence to the principles of laissez-faire economics. As a result, he opposed abolition as well as the demands of woman's rights advocates. Yet he was perceptive enough to understand that there was money to be made from reform. The activities of abolitionists and woman's rights activists provided good news copy and the opportunity to emblazon his masthead with the kind of sensational headlines that were sure to sell newspapers.

The second newspaper was the *New York Daily Tribune*. Its editor was Horace Greeley. Born in 1811 on a farm near Amherst, Massachusetts, Greeley was a largely self-educated man. He learned the printing trade in Vermont and arrived in New York in 1831 to begin his career in journalism. Three years later he was the editor of a literary magazine.[11] In 1841 he began publishing the *Tribune*, a paper he hoped would promote the moral, social, and political well-being of the people. Greeley was interested in social reform of all sorts including woman's rights. He agreed that women were being denied equal rights and opportunities. One practical response to that belief was to hire Margaret Fuller and Jane Grey Swisshelm, both editors in their own right, as reporters for the *Tribune*. He also believed that women should have the right to vote if they wanted it and that politics would benefit from their participation.[12] Greeley was committed to providing a public forum for the serious discussion of controversial social issues.[13] Therefore, he was willing to support unpopular causes such as abolition and woman's rights in his newspaper. That did not make him less mercenary than Bennett. It simply meant that his motives for discussion of social issues went beyond his concern for profit.

The third paper was the *New York Daily Times*, edited by Henry J. Raymond, who was born on a farm in upstate New York in 1820. After he graduated from the University of Vermont in 1840, he went to work as an assistant to Greeley on the *Tribune*. A man with a penchant for politics, he served in the New York state legislature before he began publishing the *Times* in 1851.[14] His intent was "to promote the best interests of the society in which we live" and "the welfare of our fellow-men." He promised to remain open-minded in his editorial policy and predicted that "we shall be *Conservative*, in all cases where we think Conservatism essential to the public good; and we shall be *Radical* in everything which may seem to us to require radical treatment, and radical reform." He pledged to remain "temperate and measured" in his language and to discuss public affairs dispassionately.[15] Raymond tried to resist the kind of sensational journalism and vitriolic language that James Gordon Bennett found so appealing. In an editorial published shortly after the Civil War entitled "Good Manners in Journalism," he criticized Horace Greeley for calling the governor of the state of New York a "liar." "The fact that language of this sort is used only by the coarsest, lowest, and most ignorant people, is a sufficient reason why it should not be used by newspapers," he wrote.[16] But his commitment to the use of temperate language had its limits.

Raymond did not support the woman's rights movement, denounced women who spoke from the platform as "unsexed," and believed that only those in sympathy with "the insanest of the spouters at the Woman's Conventions" would argue for equality between men and women.[17] But that did not mean that he was totally unsympathetic to the plight of women. Indeed, in the name of fairness, justice, and expediency, he supported a number of reforms designed to improve their condition and provide them with some opportunities equal to those provided to men. In 1855, for example, his paper came out in favor of establishing a normal school and free academy for working-class women in New York City modeled after the one that had been established earlier for boys. His support of vocational education for women was occasioned by his awareness that technology had "stolen away the trade of thousands of females" whose families depended on them to earn a living. He not only argued that women should be placed in charge of teaching the young but also predicted that employment opportunities in retail sales and clerical work, if not already widely available, would soon open to them. A free academy would provide them with the skills that they would need to perform jobs in those areas and help to alleviate their economic plight.[18]

Three years later an editorial appeared in the *Times* supporting the idea of establishing a free library for working-class women which would do for them "what the Mercantile Library has done for the young men of the City, —afford them the means of acquiring knowledge which will enable them to fill higher positions of labor, and thus improve their own condition." The *Times* editorial acknowledged that many women were poorly paid for their work and that they lacked economic opportunity to earn a decent living partly because they were not qualified for better-paying jobs.[19] And in 1859 Raymond ran an editorial in support of a bill pending in the New York state legislature which would have amended the 1848 New York Married Woman's Property Act to allow married women the right to control and dispose of both their own property and their earnings. It characterized the bill as "simply *just* in its provisions."[20]

Despite his support for such reforms, however, Raymond did not subscribe to the belief that women were like men or should be treated as if they were equal to men. He supported the idea that "God created the sexes, like yet unlike, with the myriad diversities of moral influence that spring from their diversities of constitution."[21] He even believed that women's creative spirit differed in substantial ways from that of men. Men achieved great things when they had "obstacles to surmount," when their "fortitude" was tested, and when "dangers" called forth "their courage." Female "genius," he argued, manifested itself only in a social atmosphere which allowed "sensibilities" to inspire "intellect."[22] Women were simply more refined, sensitive, and moral than men, and therefore, should "be treated with greater delicacy and more respectful regard for appearance on account of their sex." An editorial in 1859 opposing capital punishment for women reflected these beliefs. The editorial was a response to the sentencing of Mary Hartung, a servant in New York City, to hang for having poisoned her mistress. An appeal was made to the governor, but he refused to commute her sentence. Raymond objected to the governor's decision and felt compelled publicly to justify his position when one of his readers wrote him a letter to protest that capital punishment was a necessary deterrent to crimes of this sort. "If every insubordinate servant might poison her mistress, to whom she takes a dislike" and "escape punishment—who would be safe?" the disturbed reader complained.

Despite this potential threat to public order in general and the safety of employers in particular, Raymond argued that a woman did not cease "to be a woman the moment she commits a crime" and denounced the practice of hanging women as uncivilized, "brutal and inhuman." He contended that "precisely the same differences, mental, moral, and physical, exist between men and women when they are criminals as when they are not" and wrote that he hoped New York would "never again exhibit to the world the abhorrent spectacle of hanging a woman."[23]

Raymond's concern for the condition of women was steeped in paternalism and self-interest. He supported limited reform, reform that would improve the condition of women while preserving the political prerogatives and power of men. "When men show themselves willing to extend to women the degree of legal protection and of fair play to which they are justly entitled, we shall hear less clamor about the claims to a share of political power which the extreme advocates of Women's Rights are fond of advancing," his editorial predicted.[24]

Understanding the value of harnessing the influence of the popular press to benefit their cause, woman's rights supporters began devising strategies to attract the attention of men like Bennett, Greeley, and Raymond as well as the editors of small-town newspapers in places like Rochester, New York; West Chester, Pennsylvania; and Providence, Rhode Island. One such strategy, suggested both by Ernestine Rose and Matilda Gage, was to hold conventions in cities like New York, which published the most newspapers with the largest circulation, so that their message would reach the largest number of people possible.[25] A second was to barrage newspaper editors with space to fill with information regarding their movement by providing them with notices, articles, and letters to the editors on the subject of woman's rights.[26] Getting notices about forthcoming conventions published was particularly important to the movement since, according to Anthony, it was believed that they would "draw out the *curious*, as well as all the friends interested to the *first* session, and when they have listened . . . [they will] become interested" and will continue to attend the rest of the sessions.[27] But while they could submit such material, there was no guarantee that it would be published. Such was the case in 1852 when the organizers of the Syracuse convention sent a copy of their call to Henry Raymond of the *Times*. In an editorial, Raymond apologized for not publishing their notice. "The rules of our business office," he explained, "oblige us to exclude all gratuitous services of the kind required." He then explained why he opposed the doctrines of the woman's rights movement. His refusal to publish their call was, no doubt, a disappointment to the organizers of the convention. But Raymond spent so much prominent space commenting upon the movement and warning his male readers to oppose this attempt to dispossess them of their rights and privileges that in the end everyone who read the paper was well aware that a convention was to be held at Syracuse.[28]

A third strategy used by woman's rights activists was carefully to analyze what kind of coverage they received in order to ensure that the information that they wanted to reach the public would do so. For example, at the 1851 Worcester woman's rights convention, Wendell Phillips pointed out that most newspapers limited their coverage of woman's rights conventions to publishing their resolutions. That being the case, he argued, they needed to construct their resolutions so that they contained both their demands and their arguments in support of those demands.[29] A fourth strategy involved doing and saying things that would be considered news. Shocking or even outraging public opinion was sure to attract the attention of the press and force people to give thought to the issues that they were raising. "It is public opinion that deprives woman of most of her rights," Wendell Phillips told the 1850 Worcester convention. Only when public opinion changed would the "barriers and restrictions thrown around woman . . . fall." In order to change public opinion woman's rights supporters might be required to martyr themselves and their reputations, he warned them. Five years later, he told an audience in Boston that the best way to change public opinion was to shock people "into reflection." "Never mind the press," he advised. "When it abuses you it's a good sign. If it laughs, it's a good sign. It's a sign it's alive."[30] It was also a sign that the woman's rights movement was not dead. Being alive meant that it could continue to attract the attention of the press. Failure to provide the press with what today would be called a media event could result in a report such as the one that appeared in the *Chenango Union* of Norwich, New York, in 1855. The newspaper reported that Susan B. Anthony had delivered an address in support of woman's rights. But, the newspaper said, "it was . . . just what has been said a thousand times before, on the same subject, and reported for the newspapers nearly as often. We shall, therefore, be excused for not attempting to give anything more than a meager outline of her remarks."[31] That kind of report clearly did little to advance their cause.

Their fifth strategy was to manipulate the press by shamelessly courting it, particularly that part of it represented by Bennett, Raymond, and Greeley since the influence of those three editors was unprecedented. Woman's rights advocates flattered. They teased. They criticized the papers and their editors. The results were predictable. None of the editors, concerned as they were about circulation, was likely to miss a chance to publish a story that mentioned them or their papers by name or one in which someone criticized one of their competitors. It was this strategy in combination with the others that gained for woman's rights advocates the national press coverage they so desperately needed.

In flattering the papers, woman's rights advocates publicly acknowledged the press as an agency of public opinion. But their compliments were also designed to use the press to mold public attitudes toward their movement. In 1852 Paulina Wright Davis wrote to Stanton "Our Prov-[idence] Journal in the first of the movement *claimed* jestingly to be our organ. A few days since I had occasion to say something to the public in reply to some remarks of the Editor on Bloomerism. Accordingly I commenced by acknowledging the journal to be the only organ of the Woman rights [movement]. I went with the article to the Editor and watched him while he read it and I assure you it was amusing, but he could do no less than give me a place" in his columns.[32] At the National Woman's Rights Convention in 1856, Wendell Phillips said of the press, "We live in a government where the *New York Herald* and the *New York Tribune*, thank God, are more really the government than Franklin Pierce and Caleb Cushing."[33] The compliment was noted by all three New York papers in their extensive coverage of the proceedings.[34] Lucy Stone closed the same convention in New York with a reference to Horace Greeley. "When he speaks," she declared, "the nation listens."[35] And two years later newspaper stories about the National Woman's Rights Convention in New York reported that William Lloyd Garrison had said that "he knew the Press of New-York represented public opinion, and he knew that those who were sent here would represent public opinion, or they would not be employed."[36]

Woman's rights advocates also teased newspaper editors about their treatment of the movement. At the 1856 convention Wendell Phillips, alluding to the demands being made by woman's rights advocates, said that in Athens wives were not allowed out of the house and that anyone who claimed that right for them would have been considered a fanatic. "I do not know," he continued, "but that the *Herald* of that day would have branded him as an infidel."[37] In 1860 Martha C. Wright made the *New York Observer* the target of her humor when she commented that when "all that we have been demanding has been granted, as it will be very soon, then the *New York Observer* will piously fold its hands and roll up its eyes, and say 'This beneficent movement we have always advocated.'"[38] At the same convention Stanton, speaking in favor of liberalizing divorce laws, said, "I know Horace Greeley has been most eloquent, for weeks past, on the holy sacrament of ill-assorted marriages; but let us hope that all wisdom does not live, and will not die, with Horace Greeley. I think if he had been married to the *New York Herald*, instead of the Republican party, he would have found out some Scriptural arguments against life-long unions, where great incompatibility of temper existed between the parties."[39] And Ernestine Rose could not resist taking her turn to tease Greeley when she pointedly identified him to the audience as "Horace Greeley, the editor of the *Tribune*" and then commented, "(I am particular to mention it, lest there should be another Greeley in the world.)" at which point the audience broke into laughter.[40]

Male woman's rights advocates tended to be somewhat more confrontational in their dealings with the press. But that technique was no less effective in attracting attention to their cause, as William Lloyd Garrison discovered in 1853. Furious at the treatment that temperance and anti–slavery reformers had received at the hands of the editors of the New York penny press earlier in the week, Garrison addressed the afternoon session on the first day of the National Woman's Rights Convention. They had assembled in New York, he observed, to contest the "hoary tyranny" of men who through the ages had continually "robbed" women of their rights. "The opposition to the movement is assuming a malignant and desperate satanic character. . . . The pulpit is excited, the press is aroused." He maintained that the press reflected "the state of public opinion" which, he argued, symbolized "the intellectual and moral condition of the nation." He characterized the large circulation papers in New York as "profligate and diabolical in spirit and purpose" and charged that they merely catered "to the popular appetite." At least in England, he observed, the press fairly reported the activities of reformers whatever the editorial opinions of the editors. He charged that it was impossible to get a fair report in this country. "Read the New York papers this morning, generally, and see how utterly lost to all decency, and animated by the very spirit of hell, these journals are." The reporters who came to their meetings were sent to "caricature, blackguard, defame, and misrepresent, as though they were doing something" heroic. Opposition from the press was better for the movement than its support, he argued. "Do you want the compliments of the satanic press, the New York Times, Express, and Herald? If you want the compliments of such journals, you will be bad enough to take a place among the very vilest and lowest of the human race. They are animated by a brutal, cowardly, and devilish spirit."

The rules of the convention forced Garrison to limit his speech to twenty minutes. Paulina Wright Davis spoke next never mentioning the press. But immediately after her speech, Garrison again gained the floor. Apparently fearing that he had perhaps gone a bit too far, he attempted to explain himself. While he refused to take back his words against the reporters who had attended the earlier temperance and abolitionist conventions, he assured his audience that he did not intend to insult the reporters attending the woman's rights convention and trusted that their reports would be "fair and accurate." After a short exchange between Garrison and Charles Burleigh concerning the *National Democrat* and its editor, Lucretia Mott attempted to smooth the waters by suggesting that they say no more about the newspapers and simply hope for fair coverage of their activities.[41] That seems to have settled the issue. No further public comment was directed toward the press during the convention though one can imagine what was said in private about Garrison's outburst.

On the surface, Garrison's attack on the New York press can be dismissed as a temper tantrum or merely another example of the kind of flamboyant rhetorical style that had once led him to call the Methodist Church "'a cage of unclean birds, and synagogue of Satan'."[42] But when the issue is Garrison's relationship with the press, a closer look is justified. It is clear that Garrison understood perfectly how important the press was to any reform movement and began attempting to exploit it early in his career as a reformer. In a visit to England in 1833, for example, he decided that one way to promote his brand of abolition was to debate an agent of the American Colonization Society, Elliott Cressen. When his opponents tried to substitute a conference for public debate, he went to the press. The *Times* of London repeated his challenge, and he proceeded to debate the issues in the columns of the newspapers instead of from the speakers' platform. On another trip to England in 1846, he spent much of his time cultivating the support of important journalists such as the editor of *Punch* and the editor of the *Daily News* instead of holding a large number of public meetings.[43]

By the time of his outburst at the woman's rights convention in New York in 1853, he was a seasoned speaker and an experienced performer. His impassioned rhetoric must be viewed within this context. Garrison was completely capable of displaying extraordinary composure under stress as his behavior during and after his 1835 confrontation with the Boston mob indicates. His restrained public response to the murder of fellow editor Elijah Lovejoy in Alton, Illinois, in 1837 also illustrates his ability to hold his tongue as well as his pen.[44] When, as a veteran reform activist, he stood on the platform of the New York woman's rights convention, he stood there as a public performer whose job it was to engage his audience and manipulate their emotions. The reporters who were taking down the proceedings for the next edition of their newspapers were a part of that audience, and they would hardly miss the chance to record dramatic and abusive rhetoric directed toward them and their employers. Some response from them was practically guaranteed and with that response could come more lines about the cause of woman's rights in the columns of their newspapers. If that was his goal, he succeeded. All three papers published reports of his diatribe.[45]

Thomas Wentworth Higginson launched an attack on the press similar to that of Garrison at the woman's rights convention in New York three years later. In this case Higginson was irritated by an article that Raymond had published the day before regarding the woman's rights movement. Higginson began his attack with the observation that in England woman's rights advocates "had to encounter all the thunders of *The Thunderer*—all the terrors of *The Times*—whilst here it had to undergo the very diluted thunders of *The Times the Little.*" A man in the audience, unfamiliar to reformers and reporters alike, identified only as a "gentleman from Virginia" rose to respond, noting that he felt compelled to speak because he found Higginson's remarks defamatory and without substance. He found it hypocritical, he said, to invite free discussion of the issue of more rights for women and then criticize Henry Raymond "because he took the liberty to discuss this question freely in his paper." Higginson responded that "there was not a man in New York who better understood on which side his bread is buttered than the editor of the *Daily Times*. That gentleman always wished people to understand that his journal was the *Times*, and not the *Tribune*, and never failed to avail himself of the Woman's Rights movement as giving him such an opportunity." He then compared Raymond to "a little boy running along the street, and carefully dodging between two big boys [Greeley and Bennett]." Then he continued with flattery laced with a heavy dose of sarcasm. "I will always say of it . . . that the reports in the *Times* are very perfect and very excellent. I do not mean any disrespect to the other reporters present when I say that the report of yesterday's proceedings of this Convention, published in this morning's *Times*, was fuller and far more perfect than the report of any other paper. And so it always is with the reports of the *Times*," reports that, he concluded, "are as full as its criticisms on moral subjects are empty." Lucy Stone rose to speak and quickly changed the subject.[46] Higginson's speech, like that of Garrison's three years before, was widely reported in the city's penny press.[47]

Cultivating the interest of the editors of large circulation newspapers like the *Herald* and the *Tribune* was an essential component in attempts on the part of woman's rights advocates to promote discussion of their ideas on a national basis. And they worked hard to do so. They had less trouble eliciting interest from the editors of the reform press who were predisposed to discuss a large variety of proposals designed to improve society. Among those who were most supportive of the various demands made by woman's rights advocates were the abolitionists William Lloyd Garrison of *The Liberator* and Frederick Douglass, editor of *The North Star*.[48] Garrison began his public, personal support of woman's rights as early as 1840 when he defended the right of female antislavery delegates to participate in the proceedings of the World Anti-Slavery Convention held in London. His willingness to champion the cause of woman's rights eventually contributed to the split in the abolitionist movement. He began his editorial support of the cause in 1848 when he devoted three columns in *The Liberator* to reports of the woman's rights conventions held in Seneca Falls and Rochester.[49] Thereafter, he faithfully published in his paper letters and essays written by woman's rights advocates as well as announcements and reports of their lectures and conventions. When he could not attend such public events himself, he excerpted descriptions of them from Greeley's *Tribune*.

Garrison's ability to cultivate a large audience sympathetic to woman's rights was limited by his subscription list, which was never very long. Support for his paper came primarily from the free black community, and he gave away more copies of *The Liberator* than he sold. Garrison compensated for this situation through his masterful use of the exchange system, a practice on the part of editors that involved sending complimentary copies of their newspapers to each other and then reprinting articles from other papers that they believed would be of interest to their readers. Garrison's self-described "harsh," "earnest," and "uncompromising" positions on the political and social questions of the day practically guaranteed that other editors, particularly those who were hostile to reform, would reprint his stories if only to respond to them. The public seemed to love controversy, and the editors understood that a good argument was sure to sell newspapers. In this way Garrison was able to spark and sustain public debate on controversial issues such as abolition and woman's rights in areas of the country like the conservative South where reform ideology was not welcome.[50]

Frederick Douglass was also an early advocate of woman's rights. He printed the call to the Seneca Falls convention in 1848 and during the convention argued in support of the demand that women be granted the right to vote.[51] Like Garrison, he published both firsthand and secondhand accounts of woman's rights conventions, the texts of lectures delivered by woman's rights advocates, letters to the editor debating the issue of woman's rights, and announcements supporting petition drives despite the fact that his primary interest was in abolition. He was convinced that women had the right to political, social, educational, and economic equality with men. "Nature," he wrote, "has given woman the same powers, and subjected her to the same conditions with man. She is on the same earth, breathes the same air, subsists on the same food, physical, moral, mental and spiritual. She has, therefore, an equal right with man, in all efforts to obtain and maintain a perfect existence."[52]

Among the most significant female reform editors were Amelia Bloomer of *The Lily*, Paulina Wright Davis, editor of *The Una*, Anna E. McDowell, who published *The Woman's Advocate*, and Lydia Sayer Hasbrouck of *The Sibyl*.[53] Bloomer began publishing *The Lily* in Seneca Falls, New York, several months after the first woman's rights convention was held in that city. Her monthly, which originally cost its subscribers fifty cents a year, was dedicated to the cause of temperance but by 1852 also advocated dress reform and equal rights for women. At its high point it may have had as many as 4,000 subscribers. In 1853, Bloomer began publishing her journal twice a month; but two years later, in anticipation of a move to Iowa, she sold it to Mary B. Birdsall of Richmond, Indiana, who edited it until its demise in 1858.[54] Like Garrison and Douglass, Bloomer published first- and secondhand accounts of woman's rights activities and wrote editorials endorsing the cause. She solicited and published a series of "Sun Flower" essays written by Elizabeth Cady Stanton.[55] In 1851 and 1852 she published two more series of essays on woman's position signed by the anonymous "Senex."[56]

Paulina Wright Davis of Providence, Rhode Island, began editing *The Una* in 1853. She had, however, exhibited an interest in founding a woman's rights journal a year earlier when she sent out a prospectus calling on woman's rights activists to support the publication of a periodical to be called *The Egeria*.[57] She believed that the movement needed its own journal because, she argued, women in general and the woman's movement in particular "must have some exponent more courageous, sincere and devoted than the ordinary newspapers of the day have hitherto been able to afford." The *Egeria* was to have been a weekly paper published in New York City and edited by Elizabeth Oakes Smith. It was to have cost its subscribers two dollars a year.[58] Unfortunately, the one thousand subscribers that were required to begin publication did not materialize.

But Davis did not give up. At the Syracuse convention held later that year she continued to argue for the publication of such a journal. Woman's rights advocates, she said, needed a paper "in which our views shall be fairly presented to the world. . . . We can do little or nothing without such an organ. We have no opportunity now to repel slander, and are restricted in disseminating the truth from the want of such an organ. The *Tribune* and some other papers in the country, have treated us generously; but a paper to represent us must be sustained by ourselves. We must look to our own salvation."[59] Susan B. Anthony objected to Davis's suggestion. While she acknowledged that the press was "the most efficient means of enlightening and elevating public sentiment," she argued that there were already several journals edited by women. She felt that the convention should vote to support them rather than sponsor a new periodical.[60]

When the convention refused to support her proposal, Davis decided to establish her own monthly paper which she called *The Una*. She charged her subscribers a dollar a year and promised them that she would "discuss with candor and earnestness the Rights, Relations, Duties, Destiny and Sphere of woman." She did not consider it a substitute for the paper she had previously proposed, but she felt that it would provide an appropriate avenue to report accurately the progress of the movement and could be counted on to "be a faithful exponent of its principles." To that end, she published stories, poems, essays, book reviews, and editorials as well as announcements and reports of various woman's rights activities.[61]

By 1854, however, Davis's editorial efforts had begun to affect her health and woman's rights advocates again brought up the issue of establishing an official woman's rights journal. At the National Woman's Rights Convention held in Philadelphia in 1854, one of the delegates again suggested that a paper be established in New York City. After considerable debate, the convention once more rejected the idea on the grounds that there was no money available to support its publication, that those editors in the reform press who advocated woman's rights should be given as much support as possible, and that, in any case, the issues raised by woman's rights advocates were well publicized in the popular press. "The time was when it may have been necessary to establish an organ," Lucy Stone argued. "But we now have access to the newspapers at large." Newspaper editors, she claimed, were now perfectly willing to "publish all that women wish" and had for some time demonstrated their good will by representing their principles fairly.[62] Davis continued to edit *The Una* but recruited Caroline Healey Dall of Boston to help her. The journal ceased publication in 1855.[63]

Anna E. McDowell of Philadelphia began publishing *The Woman's Advocate* in 1855 as a weekly paper dedicated to advancing the interests of working-class women. As a part of that effort, she published a classified ads section in her paper listing jobs available to unemployed females. She aspired to make the *Advocate* a national magazine, but on a practical level it remained at best regional in influence. While McDowell was willing to support the general goals of the woman's rights movement, her interest remained focused on improving job opportunities for working women. She, therefore, was not particularly interested in the issue of suffrage. Her political conservatism and the narrow focus of her efforts attracted subscribers like Stephen Douglas of Illinois, Charles Sumner of Massachusetts, and Sarah Josepha Hale, editor of *Godey's Lady's Book*, none of whom were strong supporters of the woman's rights movement. Her paper was also short-lived. In 1856, only a little over a year after it first appeared, it merged with a temperance paper.[64]

That same year Lydia Sayer Hasbrouck began publishing *The Sibyl* in Middletown, New York. Hasbrouck intended her journal to be a forum for the discussion of human rights and offered to publish the opinions of those who disagreed with her. She campaigned against woman's enslavement to fashion and supported suffrage as a part of her demand that woman be given rights "equal with her brother." Along with poems and historical essays, she ran announcements of local, state, and national woman's rights conventions and published lectures delivered by the advocates of woman's rights as well as original essays supporting the cause.[65]

Jane Swisshelm also supported some aspects of the woman's rights movement. She edited the *Pittsburgh Saturday Visiter* from 1848 to 1857. At its most popular, it reached a circulation of 6,000 subscriptions.[66] Swisshelm considered her weekly to be a "family newspaper" and printed fiction, historical and biographical essays, articles focusing on the arts, science, technology, and agriculture as well as general news stories. She was willing to defend the right of woman's rights advocates to speak out and denounced other editors who misrepresented the cause and its supporters. She reserved space in her paper to cover the activities of woman's rights advocates, taking her stories from other newspapers like the *Tribune* when necessary. But her personal advocacy of woman's rights issues was selective and, from the point of view of the leaders of the movement, somewhat erratic.

The support of reform editors like Garrison and Bloomer was important because their papers provided woman's rights advocates with a way of communicating with those who were particularly interested in social reform. But there were limits to the effectiveness of the reform press in promoting the ideas of the movement. First of all, only *The Una* was dedicated exclusively to woman's rights. The result was that most reform editors were not willing to provide as much space to the promotion of the cause as the leaders of the movement would have liked. Frederick Douglass, for example, in a piece about a woman's rights convention held in Rochester, noted that William H. Channing had read a very interesting letter to the audience. But he apologized for being unable to print it all and argued that to print only a portion of it "would destroy its force."[67] Another problem was that reform editors rarely had the financial ability to send their own reporters to woman's rights conventions and other public events. Sometimes, they went themselves. But if they did not, they had to depend upon published proceedings and tracts or descriptions of woman's rights activities published by sympathetic penny press editors like Greeley.

Compared to daily and weekly newspapers like those in New York, the circulation of the reform periodicals was limited. It is true that each copy of a reform newspaper might be read by more than one person. In 1861, Susan B. Anthony, for example, wrote to Wendell Phillips that "the only [*National Anti-Slavery*] *Standard* subscriber in Johnstown [New York] told" her that "his paper was actually worn out every week by being passed round from one to another to read" and that Stanton's copies of the *Standard* and *The Liberator* were "read by five different families."[68] The subscription price of reform newspapers was not particularly high, ranging from fifty cents to two dollars. But as Anthony pointed out in her letter, many who were interested in supporting reform were not willing to buy subscriptions since even the sympathetic read the reform press only as a supplement to "their county paper, the Weekly Tribune, and their religious paper."[69] Circulation figures for reform newspapers are imprecise where they exist at all, but they clearly do not begin to match the circulation figures of papers like either the *New York Herald* or *Tribune.*

Reform papers also tended to be short-lived compared to the penny press. While *The Liberator* and Frederick Douglass's newspaper lasted until the Civil War, some of the others had a shorter life span. The result was that reform papers had difficulty sustaining an audience. Moreover, they tended to preach to the converted, and while they may have preserved what support existed, it remains to be seen how instrumental they were in recruiting new adherents to the cause.[70] The end result was that while the support of reform editors was a valuable asset to the woman's rights movement, the attention of the penny press was more significant simply because it provided woman's rights advocates with access to a national mass audience.

The leaders of the woman's rights movement were generally satisfied with the amount, if not always the tone, of the response they got from the editors of the penny press. Manipulative techniques such as using provocative language, espousing unconventional ideas, providing the press with media events, cajoling editors into publishing their notices, articles, and letters, and mentioning Bennett, Raymond, or Greeley or their papers by name in public meetings usually assured space for stories on woman's rights issues in the papers of the day. As early as 1848, Stanton wrote that there was "no danger of the Woman Question dying for want of notice. Every paper you take up has something to say about."[71] And two years later she wrote to Anne W. Johnson of Salem, Ohio, that the press was continuing to pay a great deal of attention to their efforts. Before they had organized themselves at Seneca Falls, she observed, newspapers had given little space to the issue of women and their place in American society. But since then, she reported, "you seldom take up a paper that has not something about women."[72] Paulina Wright Davis agreed, noting in 1851 at the Worcester convention that a wide variety of periodicals had been giving the ideas of woman's rights advocates "effective publication."[73] Two years after that at the woman's rights convention in New York, she declared that "never in the history of public opinion" had "propagandism been more successful."[74]

The leaders of the woman's rights movement understood the importance of using both the penny press and reform journals to promote their cause. And they were shrewd and quite successful in their efforts to do so. They manipulated the media in order to provoke and sustain widespread debate over gender roles and relations, to recruit new supporters, and to maintain the commitment of those already convinced that their cause was a just one. Whether or not individual newspaper editors supported the goals of the woman's rights movement was less important than their willingness to participate in the debate over the issues raised by woman's rights supporters. By responding to the demands of the woman's rights movement and engaging in public discourse with woman's rights advocates, they acknowledged women's political competency and allowed women to move beyond the restrictions that social convention placed on their public activities. The response that woman's rights advocates elicited and the discourse that resulted had the effect of expanding woman's position in the world outside the home.

The media, of course, also benefited from the relationship they established with the movement. The demands of woman's rights supporters and their activities were news. Reporting those activities was good for circulation, and increased circulation guaranteed an increase in profits. Thus, in their attempts to attract a national audience for their message, woman's rights activists formed a symbiotic relationship with the press, a relationship based on the principle of mutual exploitation but one that also carried with it mutual benefits.

V

THE RESPONSES

Throughout the woman's rights campaign before the Civil War, reform advocates addressed their demands for equality to anyone who would listen: lawmakers, the general public, and newspaper editors. With the exception of their willingness to begin to modify property rights to benefit women, state legislators and those whose task it was to revise state constitutions remained largely unresponsive to demands that women's interests be the focus of reform. As a result, there was little change in woman's legal status before 1860.

It is difficult to systematically assess the impact of woman's rights advocacy on the hundreds of anonymous individuals who sat in convention or lecture audiences or who read essays advocating woman's rights. A few wrote letters to be read at woman's rights conventions. Some wrote letters to editors of their local newspapers. But most of them remained largely inarticulate.

Occasionally, someone in the audience spoke from the floor or gallery at conventions and engaged those on the podium in debate over the issues being raised there. The leaders of the woman's rights movement originally intended their meetings to be forums for open discussion of the issues. They were prepared to spar with anyone bold enough to engage them in public discourse. And in the early years, they did discuss issues on the floor. It soon became clear, however, that providing the opportunity for open debate at their conventions did not necessarily help to advance their cause.

What occurred on the third day of the National Woman's Rights Convention held in Cleveland, Ohio, in 1853 illustrates the point. In the morning session a man in the audience named Joseph Barker, speaking at great length from the floor, argued that among other things whatever rights Eve had originally had, she had "forfeited" them for herself and her posterity when she tempted Adam. When he asked to be recognized again a short time later, some in the audience objected. Caroline Severence, a supporter of both woman's rights and free speech, objected to attempts to gag him, and he again took the floor to tell the audience that he had

374   YANKEE NOTIONS.

EXPENSIVE LUXURIES.

Violence erupted at the National Woman's Rights Convention held
in Cleveland in 1853 when a minister responded to an outburst
from William Lloyd Garrison by pulling his nose. *Yankee Notions*,
December 1853, p. 374. Courtesy of the Library of Congress.

nothing further to say but that he was determined to maintain his right to
continue if he so chose. By the time he had finished defending his right to
speak, it was nearly time to adjourn the session. When the afternoon
session opened, Antoinette Brown responded to Barker at length, and a Dr.
Nevin asked for the opportunity to do the same. Ernestine Rose, tired of
theological "quibbling" and concerned about wasting precious time, objected to his request on the grounds that they had other business to
conduct. Mott, like Severence, committed to the principles of free debate,
moved that Nevin be allowed to speak, only to find herself sitting through
a personal diatribe directed against Barker in which Nevin addressed
neither the issue of woman's rights nor the theological issues raised earlier
in the day. The discussion deteriorated further when William Lloyd
Garrison, irritated by the irrelevance of Nevin's discourse, began insulting
him from the floor and calling him names.[1] Nevin responded by physically
attacking Garrison after the session and pulling his nose.[2]

   Given experiences like this, it is not surprising that, as time passed, the
agenda of woman's rights conventions became more rigid and debate

involving those on the platform and those in the audience became less frequent. Woman's rights advocates came to understand that their ability to get their message across depended upon their ability to control their audience and that open debates which invited audience participation could hinder such efforts.

Conscientiously adhering to their agenda did not solve all of their problems with crowd control, however. Their conventions were also disturbed by rowdies whose indecorous behavior included hissing, booing, and stamping their feet, thus making it impossible for many in the audience to hear what was being said. In 1853 during the National Woman's Rights Convention held in New York, heckling took on a new dimension. The two-day meeting convened at 10 A.M. on Tuesday, September 6, in the Broadway Tabernacle. Lucretia Mott presided. The organizers had scheduled three sessions per day. There appear to have been no disturbances during the morning and afternoon sessions of the first day. The problems started at the evening session when someone in the audience began hissing during a speech by William H. Channing. The meeting was interrupted by yells and other disruptions before Mott adjourned the meeting at 9:30.

Only an occasional interruption marred the proceedings of the morning and afternoon sessions on Wednesday. The real trouble began almost immediately after Mott called the evening session to order at 7:30 when screeches and general confusion ensued, making it impossible for most of the audience to hear the speakers who valiantly tried to talk over the noise of the crowd. Amidst "shouting, yelling, screaming, bellowing, laughing, stamping, cries of 'Burleigh,' 'Root,' 'Truth,' 'shut up,' 'take a drink,' 'go to bed,' 'Greeley,' 'go it, Lucy,'" Ernestine Rose moved to adjourn the meeting, and the convention ended in what could only be described as complete chaos.[3]

The disturbances appear to have been premeditated and were certainly not unprecedented. A few days earlier, the World's Temperance Convention had been disrupted when female delegates attempted to assert their right to participate in the affairs of the conference. As the New York *Evening Post* pointed out, New York was "infested by gangs of blackguards, who take pleasure in attempts to disorganize the conventions of antislavery, woman's rights, and temperance ultraists." But what was shocking about the temperance disturbance is that it was perpetrated by ministers and gentlemen who were themselves delegates and participants in the convention.[4]

According to the editor of *The Una*, however, those responsible for the disturbance at the woman's rights convention were not members of the same group. They were instead part of a group of "genteel vagabonds," local New Yorkers who were noted for this sort of thing.[5] That view was confirmed in both the New York *Express* and the New York *Home Journal*.

Before the assembly even convened that evening, according to the *Express*, there had been signs of trouble as a crowd gathered outside the doors and in the hall of the Broadway Tabernacle under the watchful eye of the local police. After jockeying for positions likely to guarantee them the best seats, the crowd rushed through the open doors at 7:15. Within minutes every seat was taken and the gallery was filled with "a large number of gentlemen who had come there specially to inspirit in their own way, the proceedings." Down below on the platform the officers assembled and the speakers prepared themselves for the proceedings to begin. "The floor of the house," according to the *Home Journal*, "was occupied by a most respectable and rather rustic-looking audience" who were prepared to behave themselves and listen to the proceedings. But above them, "in the gallery were stationed about fifty of those excruciating bipeds, who are called 'men-about-town'—creatures who wear extremely white and fine Panama hats, with wrinkles in them, exceedingly thick gold chains, astonishing pantaloons, and most glossy boots." Such men, the paper asserted, spent their afternoons in Broadway bars rather than at respectable places of employment. In any case, the writer continued, "these erect beasts of prey had evidently formed the great design of silencing the ladies, and they did it."[6] Having succeeded once, a similar group disrupted the National Woman's Rights Convention held in New York in 1859.[7] The only positive thing to come out of such incidents was that they helped to attract the attention of the press.

The assessment of historians has been that with the exception of Greeley's *Tribune*, the popular press either ignored the woman's rights movement or regarded it negatively and did little or nothing to promote the cause.[8] But a survey of major American daily newspapers in cities like New York, Philadelphia, and Boston in the Northeast and St. Louis, Chicago, and Cleveland in the middle of the country indicates that the attitudes of their editors toward the issue of woman's rights were anything but uniform. Whatever their position on the issue, editors usually did not ignore the movement and rarely missed opportunities to publish news about and comment upon its campaign. They lifted a movement with little money, no permanent organization, and no official newspaper of its own out of obscurity by bringing it to the attention of a national audience and thereby inadvertently helped to incorporate women more completely into public life.

The *New York Herald*, the *New York Tribune*, and the *New York Times* devoted an impressive amount of space to woman's rights activities and, not surprisingly given the fact that five of the eleven national conventions were held in New York, also covered woman's rights activities with more regularity than newspapers in other parts of the country. The editorial policy of the *Tribune* was the most sympathetic. Those of the *Times* and the *Herald* were not. The result was that the way their editors treated the movement and its advocates differed. Headlines of news stories, for example, ranged from sensational to factual, following the general editorial style of each paper. The *Herald* tended to alternate straightforward informational headlines with sensational ones. In the beginning it found the activities of woman's rights reformers merely "curious," implying in a left-handed way that they were worthy of notice and investigation. But rather than providing its readers with a discussion of the condition of women, it tended to dwell on the disruptions that plagued woman's rights conventions.[9] By 1853 the rhetoric of its headlines had become more dramatic as well as more patronizing. It announced the convening of woman's rights meetings in New York as a "Grand Rally of Bloomers" and described the organizers of the convention as "strong minded women" who were "getting their pluck up."[10] But it dismissed them as a source of entertainment by referring to their convention as a "bloomer comedy."[11] By 1856 its headlines can only be described as sensational, characterized by rhetoric that questioned the integrity, sexual identity, and sexual behavior of the participants in woman's rights conventions. Headlines described their convention as a "Grand Rally at the Tabernacle of Women of all Ages and Sexes," dubbed their speeches "Rich, Rare and Racy," and charged that "free love" was a part of the woman's rights platform.[12]

Unlike the headlines of the news stories that emblazoned the masthead of the *Herald*, those appearing in the *Tribune* and the *Times* usually lacked any sort of editorial comment. Throughout the period, they merely announced that woman's rights advocates were holding conventions.[13]

Starting in 1852 all three New York newspapers devoted an impressive amount of news and editorial space to the activities of the woman's rights advocates. All three covered the proceedings of the National Woman's Rights Convention held in Syracuse in September of that year, for example. The *Herald* ran five stories. Two were a full column long, one was three-and-a-half columns long, and two were four-and-a-half columns long—columns that ran the full length of the page. The *Tribune* ran four news stories covering the event. Two were half a column each, one was two columns long, and one was four-and-a-half columns long. The *Times* gave the convention considerably less space than its competitors. It ran three stories of a half column each.[14] From that point on, all of the national woman's rights conventions held in New York City were covered in all three papers. The New York convention of 1853, also known as the "mob convention," generated a total of six separate news stories in the three papers.[15] The 1856 national convention held in New York City warranted five.[16] And between 1858 and 1860, the three papers ran at least thirteen stories reporting upon annual national convention proceedings.[17]

Although it is possible to follow the general pattern of woman's rights activism throughout the country by the attention it received in the New York penny press, the three papers, not surprisingly, paid less attention to national conventions held in other states and New York state woman's rights conventions than they did to those that were held in New York City. The early national conventions held in Worcester, Massachusetts, in 1850 and 1851 were both reported by the *Tribune*.[18] The national convention in Cleveland in October of 1853 following the mob convention in New York City and the Philadelphia national convention in 1854 were reported and commented upon by both the *Tribune* and the *Times*.[19]

The only national convention that was completely ignored by the New York press represented by the *Herald*, *Tribune*, and *Times* was the Cincinnati national convention held on Oct. 17 and 18, 1855. Apparently none of the editors sent reporters to cover the event. In any case, however, a public disturbance in New York City involving local free love advocates distracted them at the very time that the convention was being held and claimed the space that might have otherwise been devoted to woman's rights.[20] Such goings on had more appeal to both New York journalists and their readers than a national woman's rights convention being held hundreds of miles away. Editors closer to Cincinnati followed the lead of their colleagues in New York. The *Daily Missouri Republican* in St. Louis and the *Cleveland Daily Plain Dealer*, for example, ignored the woman's rights convention held in Cincinnati. Both published instead Greeley's account of free love activities.[21]

When they were mentioned at all, state conventions in New York were more likely to gain attention from New York editors than those held in other parts of the country. New York state conventions in Albany and Saratoga occasionally merited a notice in the New York City press.[22] Greeley and Raymond sometimes also paid attention to conventions held in New England, Pennsylvania, or Ohio, but their coverage was sporadic.[23]

The length of news stories concerning the convention activities of woman's rights advocates varied in all three papers. When they covered out-of-town conventions, the editors sometimes published only short notices of a few lines which at most listed the names of the most prominent speakers. But stories reporting the proceedings of national conventions, particularly those held in New York, were long and detailed. They provided readers with the texts of speeches as well as descriptions of the participants and their audiences interspersed with occasional editorial comment. The five-and-a-half-column article covering the 1850 Worcester convention that appeared in the *Tribune*, for example, provided texts of the speeches of Paulina Wright Davis, Lucretia Mott, William H. Channing, Wendell Phillips, and Ernestine Rose. Rose was described as having spoken "with great eloquence." The reporter assigned to cover the convention found that "Her French [she was Polish] accent and extemporaneous manner, added quite a charm to her animated and forcible style."[24]

Editorial comment on the demands of woman's rights advocates and their activities reflected the attitudes of each editor toward reform combined with their view of woman's proper place in society. James Gordon Bennett began his editorial coverage of the woman's rights movement when it surfaced in 1848. Given his later attacks on the movement, it seems clear that the Seneca Falls convention caught him off guard, unprepared to take a strong position either for or against the reforms that woman's rights advocates were proposing. The first editorial described their meeting as a logical if unexpected extension of what it called the "age of revolutions" and characterized their Declaration of Sentiments as "interesting" and "amusing" but "defective." At the time the paper claimed to be unwilling to play the role of the "despot" and "define the duties of women" even though, as it turned out, it did not hesitate to do so in the years that followed once Bennett had given the issue some thought. The tone of this first editorial was condescending yet playful. It complimented the ladies on having among them a woman such as Lucretia Mott who it maintained would "make a better President than some of those who have lately tenanted the White House."[25] But it did not address the issues at stake. It argued neither that women had no basis for their complaints nor that their right to try to improve their situation was inappropriate. Bennett simply used their cause to have some fun.

The tone of *Herald* editorials changed soon thereafter. By the early 1850s, they tended to describe woman's rights advocates in terms of their appearance, sexual identities, and mental stability (or lack thereof). There was little in *Herald* editorials that distinguished them from its headlines and news stories. For example, in a scathing editorial commenting on the first National Woman's Rights Convention held in October 1850, in Worcester, Massachusetts, it dubbed the organizers and participants as a "motley gathering of fanatical mongrels" and "fugitive lunatics."[26] Similarly two years later it dismissed the convention in Syracuse as a "farce" and characterized female woman's rights advocates as "flimsy, flippant, and superficial," unattractive, and ill-tempered man-haters. They were, it charged, women of "boundless vanity and egotism, who believe they are superior in intellectual ability" to everyone else. Men who participated in woman's rights conventions were "hen-pecked husbands" who should be wearing "petticoats." Supporters in general were a "class of wild enthusiasts and visionaries—very sincere, but very mad."[27]

The *Herald*'s vicious attacks on woman's rights advocates continued thereafter unabated. In response to the woman's rights convention held in New York in the fall of 1853, it charged that the women who led the movement were "entirely devoid of personal attractions," and described them as "thin maiden ladies" who, having been rejected as potential brides, "are now endeavoring to revenge themselves upon the sex who have slighted them." It ended by characterizing the "results of all their labors" as "gas, twaddle, nonsense."[28]

The *Herald* editorial policy remained consistent throughout the 1850s.

In response to the 1856 National Woman's Rights Convention held in New York, it characterized the movement as "the greatest absurdity in the world. Its conventions are the gatherings of an insane asylum—the patients not yet . . . brought down by that physician, public opinion, to a low diet of common sense and a medical regimen of ordinary insanity." And it continued to attack reformers as "male, female and hybrid."[29]

Bennett was particularly disturbed by the militancy of the early woman's rights advocates, which clearly struck a nerve. It posed two problems for editors like him. First, the military rhetoric of the woman's rights supporters was a linguistic claim to political competency. It was their way of demanding that women be allowed to participate in public discourse with men in pursuit of goals that were designed to both preserve republican principles and serve the interests of women as a group. By describing their activities as military campaigns, they placed their political claims side by side with those advocated by men through their political parties.

Two responses to those claims were possible. One was to totally ignore them and in so doing refuse to acknowledge the right of women to participate in contemporary political discourse and by extension to participate in the kind of political activity that resulted from that discourse. Such a response would have made woman's rights advocates for all practical purposes invisible as well as politically impotent. Fortunately for them, this did not happen.

The second possible response was to acknowledge the right of women to participate in political discourse (and by extension politics) by responding to them in the traditional male language of war. This did happen when newspaper editors reported the activities of woman's rights supporters and responded in editorials to their demands. In his comments on the Seneca Falls convention, for example, Bennett announced to the reading public that the woman's rights "standard is now unfurled by their own hands."[30] In 1852 when the primary topic of the National Woman's Rights Convention at Syracuse was whether or not to establish a permanent organization, the *Herald* described their debate as a "muster" and predicted that there would be considerable "sharp shooting" between the two factions discussing the issue.[31] And an editorial in the same issue called female speakers "aggressors" and criticized a male speaker for crossing "swords" with them.[32] A month before, Bennett's competitor Raymond had warned his brethren that they would be judged harshly by future generations if, "through misguided kindness or gallantry" they opened "the smallest postern gate" in the male fortification system "to admit the foe."[33] Raymond continued to discuss the woman's rights movement in a military context. Eight years later he wrote that even when they gained the legal right to pursue careers as ministers, doctors, and merchants, women would still face prejudices that would place them at a disadvantage. The need to deal with that prejudice, he argued, was merely a "fortune of war."

If they were going to fight, he concluded, they would simply have to put up with it.[34]

Similarly, though somewhat more sympathetically, a contributor to the *Pennsylvania Farmer*, commenting on the 1852 West Chester woman's rights convention, noted that the woman's rights movement was not "an idle joke, but a formidable assault by calm and intelligent minds, upon old ideas and institutions."[35] At the same time the editor of the West Chester *Jeffersonian* warned that "an army with bayonets is less to be feared than the tongues" of female woman's rights activists. He promised that his "blood and ink" would "be fearlessly shed in their defense" against the "cruel assault" of those who opposed them.[36]

Throughout the 1850s American newspaper editors, among them the most powerful in the country, responded to discussions concerning the political claims of women in military terms even when they found those claims inappropriate. During the 1858 national convention in New York, for example, Mr. P. D. Moore from New Jersey declared that "the cause of woman's rights could only secure immediate recognition through a display of Sharpe's rifles and a woman's insurrection." In his response to that comment in his editorial the next day, Raymond described "Sharpe's rifles" as a "most unfeminine instrument." Implying that the private power of women was potentially as dangerous as the public power that they sought, he suggested that poison would be a more appropriate weapon. "With a small quantity of Prussic acid or strychnine, a strong-minded lady might very easily dispatch all the male members of her family" without the benefit "of an awkward rifle," he wrote.[37] Bennett had responded much the same way two years before when in an editorial he argued that women should "not . . . mingle in the fight." Their place was, he suggested, well behind the front lines where it was their "duty . . . to pick up the killed and wounded" and "dress the wounds" of the combatants.[38] Thus, whether they supported or opposed the movement, the editors of the popular press throughout the period publicly acknowledged and testified to the competency of women to participate in politics by carrying on a discourse with them expressed in military language. By doing so, they unwittingly aided and abetted women in their efforts to expand their opportunities to participate in public life.

The second problem posed by the use of military rhetoric by women was that it was difficult for men like Bennett to take up their gauntlet in anything approaching an appropriate or socially acceptable way. Woman's rights advocates placed their male adversaries in the position of having to choose between one set of social conventions that encouraged them to affirm their masculinity by protecting themselves and their prerogatives from attack and another set that prohibited them from engaging in public combat, verbal or literal, with women of their own social class. Men were supposed to protect such women, not fight with them. To engage even in rhetorical combat with women threatened the very definition of what it meant to be male.

In order to solve this problem, they simply defined the foe as something other than a group of women. As long as the women who challenged them remained women, they found themselves impotent. Their hands were tied. But if they could convince themselves and the public that these women were either figuratively or literally something else, they could legitimately take action. They could defend themselves and the exclusive power and privileges that affirmed their claim to being men.

Female assertiveness and activism both before and after the Civil War typically elicited responses that addressed the nature of women in general and focused on the issue of female sexuality in particular. In her study of the antislavery feminists, Jean Fagan Yellin has noted that women who first spoke in public were accused of being sexually promiscuous. The Grimké sisters were particularly susceptible to such attacks in the late 1830s and early 1840s. And Abby Kelley remembered the sting of being referred to as a "harlot" and a "Jezebel" years after a minister made her the focus of one of his sermons.[39] Women like the Grimkés, Lucy Stone, and Frances Wright were vulnerable to such charges partly because they were unmarried and partly because they happened to live in circumstances that made it difficult or impossible for an adult male, either husband or father, to monitor and control their behavior sexual or otherwise. It was their circumstances—which theoretically provided the *opportunity* for promiscuity—rather than their actual sexual behavior that gave credibility to the charge. Single, well-educated, economically independent, and socially influential women in the late nineteenth century and early twentieth century were similarly suspect. Public concern about their sexual behavior was the same, though the charge was slightly different. In their case, as both Nancy Sahli and Carroll Smith-Rosenberg have pointed out, male members of the medical, psychological, and educational communities labeled them sexually deviant and called them lesbians.[40]

A third response, however, was more typical of the period immediately following the Seneca Falls convention. Led by Bennett, those who opposed the woman's rights movement were more likely to question the sexual identity of its advocates than they were to speculate about their sexual behavior or criticize their sexual preferences. Most of the more outspoken woman's rights activists were, after all, middle class and respectably if not necessarily happily married. Charges of sexual promiscuity were not consistent with the reality of their social class and marital status. Therefore, before the Civil War, it was their gender rather than the sexual behavior of those who supported woman's rights that was at issue.

In the eyes of journalists like Bennett, women who supported the cause of woman's rights became people who were "supposed to be women" but clearly were not. They were described as lacking the physical attractive-

The New York Pictorial Picayune.

WE ARE EQUAL TO MEN, BECAUSE WE ARE THEIR WIVES

WE ARE GREATER THAN MEN, BECAUSE WE ARE THEIR MOTHERS.

FEMALE EMANCIPATION.

OHIO WOMEN'S RIGHTS CONVENTION,
HELD AT AKRON, MAY 28TH AND 29TH, 1851.

Holding conventions provided woman's rights advocates with an opportunity to expose the general public to their demand for equal rights. Newspaper and magazine editors often responded by publishing negative images of both male and female participants. *New York Pictorial Picayune*, January 1, 1852, p. 4. Courtesy of the Library of Congress.

ness and good temper generally expected from members of the female sex. The *Herald* accused them not only of preferring to wear men's clothes, but also of sporting "long shaggy beards" as well as "a wonderful development of forehead, absence of hair above it, and a general squareness of face, set off by singular determination and heaviness of the jaw" that was distinctively masculine. It described them as a kind of "hybrid," a third sex, as "mannish women like hens that crow." Their sex was "not accurately defined by exterior developments."[41] These women who, while championing one sex, sought victory over the other were accused of being "viragos" and "Amazons" who "reverse the law of nature."[42]

Journalists also cast similar aspersions on male supporters of the movement, picturing any man who spoke in support of the cause as a kind of "she-male." Bennett described male woman's rights supporters as effeminate "husbands, mild and broken in spirit."[43] Charles Burleigh was described by a representative of the New York press as "a woman down to his shoulderblades, but a man if pantaloons be the insigne below."[44] And the Syracuse *Star* labeled all male feminists "Aunt Nancy men."[45]

The fact that both male and female feminists were charged with having taken on the physical characteristics of the opposite gender illustrates, as did the controversy over dress reform, the degree to which access to the rights of citizenship and its prerogatives were associated with the possession of male bodies in the American mind.[46] Suggesting that men who supported woman's rights were in reality partly female was a rhetorical way of denying them their manhood and thus emasculating them, or, to put it less strongly, of depriving them of the rights and privileges that their bodies entitled them to. In this way Bennett and some of his colleagues attempted to discredit them, obscure their message, and deny them the kind of public influence that being male should have given them.

Dealing with female woman's rights advocates was a different matter. Belligerent and combative, they could not be easily dismissed, particularly when they publicly challenged men to a fight. In the process of demanding equal rights, women claimed the right to describe, discuss, and act out human experiences that were generally understood to be exclusively reserved for members of the male gender. Merely denying them their femininity did not have the same affect as denying men their masculinity because femininity did not carry with it access to public life and political power. The best that Bennett and other journalists could do was to accuse them of being Amazons.

In doing so, they drew upon an image that had long been important to the imagination of Western manhood. As Abby Wettan Kleinbaum has pointed out, by the nineteenth century the Amazon had a long history as an important component of Western European male fantasy life. Whether based in historical fact or not, the myth of the Amazon was used by men to flatter and glorify themselves, to testify to their own heroism, worth, and historical significance. To engage in combat with an Amazon served as the greatest trial of male strength and courage. To conquer one was a physical and sexual act that transcended all others.

To defeat an Amazon was a worthy test of manhood because she was the ultimate hero(ine)—a ferocious warrior, strong, brave and competent; a builder of culture and civilization; an autonomous and independent being; the possessor of great wealth and physical beauty; a creature whose expression of sexuality was essentially exploitative. Amazons were invaders. They represented the ultimate threat to male transcendence. Capable of great rage, bold and vengeful, fierce and formidable, Amazons were intent upon the defeat, humiliation, and destruction of men and all that they had built.[47]

The evidence that Kleinbaum provides supports her contention that the myth of the Amazon was designed by men not to "enhance" the image of women but to document man's struggle against them.[48] Nevertheless, that image was in some ways a very positive one and provided female woman's rights advocates with a powerful role model image to carry with them in their struggle for equal rights. Women who were Amazons were acknowledged as worthy and competent opponents. They were dangerous and to be feared. They were difficult to subdue. And they had the ability to get what they wanted.

Thus, when editors of the penny press used the term Amazon (or virago or she-male) to describe female woman's rights advocates, they were paying them the compliment of ascribing to them characteristics that they admired in those of their own gender and acknowledging the seriousness of woman's threat to male political, economic, and social hegemony. As products of Western culture, they sought an appropriate context for understanding female woman's rights advocates and devising an appropriate strategy for effectively dealing with them. The Amazon ideal gave them that context and strategy. While men who considered themselves gentlemen might hesitate to physically harm an ordinary woman, the Amazon image allowed them to imagine successfully defending themselves against and subduing an extraordinary one.[49]

The image of woman's rights advocates as Amazons allowed newspaper editors like Bennett to put the demand for gender equality into a perspective that justified and confirmed their opposition to a change in gender roles and relations. Woman's rights supporters threatened men in the same ways that their Amazon forebears had threatened men in ages past: militarily, socially, politically, and economically as well as sexually. Woman's rights advocates defined their movement as a war designed to defeat those who opposed them. Failure to defeat the Amazon in battle brought with it pain and humiliation, even mutilation and death. There was no reason to think that failure to stop woman's invasion of male public space and appropriation of male prerogatives would not have similar consequences in a figurative if not literal sense. Amazons built their own civilizations and accumulated and controlled all the wealth therein, excluding men from positions of power and authority. The thought of American women doing anything similar was a frightening prospect to men who were in such positions. Like the Amazons, American women might no longer be so dependent upon men. Amazon women captured and subjugated men sexually in order to satisfy their own lust and need to reproduce. Acknowledging women's rights to equality in other areas of life was likely to bring in its wake the need to redefine their sexual nature. The idea that a woman might have a right to her self both within and outside the marriage relation was a prospect fraught with anxiety for men whose double standard of sexuality served their needs and allowed them to ignore those of their sexual partners. Clearly, failure to defeat attempts of militant American women to redress the grievances so clearly articulated in print and from podium and platform had potentially dire consequences for men.

It was useful, then, for some male newspaper editors to apply this old and powerful metaphor to the challenge that woman's rights advocates posed to male dominance. An Amazon victory here on American soil, they warned, would result in the death and destruction of civilization as they knew it. It was a possibility they did not want to contemplate. In a war with the Amazons, they suggested, the stakes were high and the outcome was anything but certain.

Throughout the period before the Civil War, Bennett and others like him used powerful martial metaphors to respond to the demands of woman's rights advocates. Such a response, however, was largely rhetorical and symbolic. It was a response designed more to sell newspapers and engage the imagination of their readers than it was an attempt to participate in meaningful public discourse about the actual condition of women or the merits of their complaints. Bennett devoted considerable space to the cause but in the process held most woman's rights supporters up to ridicule and expressed contempt for their campaign. He did not even attempt to argue that woman's rights supporters misrepresented the past. He did not try to refute the charges that they had been denied their rights and that social custom deprived them of equal opportunities in education and employment. Nor did he attempt to justify traditional subjugation of women. Bennett did not take the opportunity to use his editorial column to discuss in any substantive way the social, political, and economic issues raised by woman's rights advocates. Even so, the public attention that he directed toward the movement encouraged discussion of woman's role in society, gave legitimacy to their participation in public debate, and thereby helped to advance the cause.

The *Tribune*'s editorial position was different and consistent with Horace Greeley's desire to insure that social issues, however controversial, were freely debated. It asked its readers to approach the issue of woman's rights with an open mind. It advised them to resist the temptation to "condemn or laugh" until they had considered what the goals of the movement really were.[50] Greeley's support of the original goals of woman's rights advocates was sincere. While he did not view men and women as equal either in intelligence or in physiology, he was willing to support the ideas that women should have equal rights before the law and that women should have access to better jobs and equal pay.[51] He also supported the right of women to the vote.

In the early years of the movement, Greeley could be more than generous in his willingness to support their cause, publish notices of their meetings, and report their activities. In 1855, for example, he wrote to Susan B. Anthony that he had received her letter and an announcement for the upcoming campaign to hold local woman's rights meetings throughout the state of New York. "I will publish the latter in all our editions," he promised, but told her that he was returning the money she had sent to pay for the publication of the call. "To charge you full price would be too hard and I prefer not to take anything," he wrote.[52] He was as good as his word and published the announcement frequently during the first few months of 1855.[53]

There was a limit to his support, however. He was under tremendous pressure from his competitors, and though he did not mind bearing the stigma of supporting reform causes, by 1856 he was becoming more sensitive to the criticism directed at him by those who opposed his editorial positions in such matters. That year Anthony again asked him to print notices of their upcoming convention in New York. This time Greeley refused to publish the notices as news. His excuse was that his "political antagonists take advantage of such publications to make the Tribune responsible for the anti-Bible, anti-Union, etc., doctrines, which your conventions generally put forth. I do not desire to interfere with your 'free speech,'" he assured her. "I desire only to secure for myself the liberty of treating public questions in accordance with my own convictions, and not being made responsible for the adverse convictions of others. I can not, therefore, print this programme without being held responsible for it." He advised Anthony, therefore, to place the notices in the advertising columns of his paper. "If you advertise it," he explained, "that is not in my department, nor under my control."[54]

By the end of the 1850s, Greeley's paper had become more reserved in its support of the movement. In 1858 it informed its readers that the movement had been infiltrated by "weak-minded fanatics" who were distracting attention from the legitimate grievances originally expressed in the Declaration of Sentiments. In a fit of impatience with their program and disappointment in their achievements, it declared that the efforts of woman's rights advocates in the past ten years had not accomplished much.[55]

And when Elizabeth Cady Stanton brought up the issue of divorce at the 1860 National Woman's Rights Convention in New York, Greeley opposed the ideal of liberalizing divorce law. He wrote that while he was a great supporter of woman's rights, he found the argument that marriage was a mere contract "shocking," "pernicious," "debasing," "objectionable," and "dangerous." He was convinced that marriage was an "indissoluble union" that was necessary to preserve "pure paternity, public morality, and social well-being." Essentially, he believed that divorce was an excuse to pursue self-interest and personal comfort at the expense of the public good.[56]

Because he had been so generally supportive, woman's rights leaders were sensitive to the effect that the divorce issue had on him. Parker Pillsbury wrote to Stanton shortly after the convention, "What a pretty kettle of hot water you tumbled into at New York! . . . You broke the very heart of the portly Evening Post and nearly drove the Tribune to the grave." But Lydia Mott saw a silver lining in the debate that ensued over the issue. "One good thing you have done," she observed to Stanton, is to have "driven the New York *Tribune* to that very absurd position that divorce is wrong in *any case*."[57] Such a rigid position could only work to make people consider the issue seriously and thus work in their favor, she believed.

Greeley's counterpart at the *Times*, Henry Raymond, established his editorial policy toward woman's rights during his first year of publication in 1851 when he playfully announced that American women were "bent on appropriating more than their fair share of Constitutional privileges." Their efforts, Raymond wrote, were "the reaffirmation of certain arrant heresies," and he demanded that woman's rights advocates be "severely rebuked" and "speedily repressed." He also called for "the organization of a 'Rights of Man Association' to withstand the greedy appropriativeness of woman-kind." If that did not work, he advocated that men turn to "dissolution or secession." In any case, he insisted, "anti-masculine agitation must be stayed by some means."[58]

But his sense of humor wore thin when the woman's rights activists persisted in their agitation. Two years into his editorial career at the *Times*, Raymond began to view woman's rights advocates as irritating, tiresome, and disruptive. In contrast to his straightforward news head-lines, he ran editorial headlines calling woman's rights advocates "Female Pests" and "Riotous Women Clamoring for their Rights" and character-ized the female leaders of the woman's rights movement as "tonguey" and "coarse grained" "she-males," "unwomanlike women," an "Amazonian troupe" who were attempting to "secure the abolition of all distinction in gender."[59]

His editorial rhetoric may have been an echo of Bennett's, but Raymond, unlike his competitor, was willing to discuss seriously some of the issues raised by woman's rights advocates. As we have already seen, he supported the right of women to control their own inherited and earned property, but he opposed giving women the right to vote. He opposed woman's suffrage for both philosophical and practical reasons. First he denied that the vote was some sort of abstract right that could be claimed by any group, including women. He felt that the decision to give any constituency the right to vote was a matter of "expediency" determined by the degree to which extending the privilege would produce or preserve social and political stability. As a practical matter, he believed that "women, *as they are*, are not fit to vote" and advised reformers to direct their efforts away from earning the franchise and toward giving women "the rudiments of political training." He also felt that there was danger in giving women the vote because respectable women would stay home and the less respectable would gain more influence in politics.[60]

Whatever their position on the issues raised by the woman's rights movement, both Greeley and Raymond were prepared to defend the right of woman's rights supporters to speak out on the issues. Editorial response to the activities of the mob that disrupted the 1853 national convention in New York reflected a combination of a commitment to the principles of free speech, a sense of moral outrage, injured civic pride, and a determination to censure unacceptable social behavior. Raymond of the *Times* used the incident to make fun of the reformers, calling it a "jolly affair," but also scolded the "villains" who had been responsible for the premature adjournment of the meeting. "They did wrong," he wrote. "Let anybody who can hire a house and pay for it have his way, and let none be disturbed."[61] Greeley's response was predictable given his general support of the movement at the time. He denounced the small group who had purchased tickets for the sole purpose of preventing the majority from hearing the speakers. He thanked "the disturbers for so stirring the souls of the speakers that their words came gushing forth from their lips with exceeding fluency and power." Two days later he again spoke out against the "folly" of those who hoped to weaken the movement by preventing those who supported it from speaking freely. "Nothing is so good for a weak and unpopular movement as this sort of opposition," he pointed out. "There is in the public mind of this country an intuitive love of fair play and free speech, and those who outrage it for any purpose of their own merely reinforce their opponents, and bestow a mighty power on the ideas they hate and fain would suppress."[62] Bennett neglected to criticize the rowdies but grudgingly complimented the leaders of the woman's rights convention for their ability to handle the affair. "The strong-minded women came out in full force," he wrote, "and appeared undaunted by the attempt at the last meeting to disturb its proceedings. They have proved, if they have not the right on their side, that they are not wanting in coolness and self-possession."[63]

The incident brought editorial comment from other newspapers as well. The thrust of the *Christian Inquirer* editorial was similar to that of the *Tribune* and the *Times*. Labeling the riot a disgraceful exhibition "of the vilest rowdyism in this city" it asserted that the women who assembled in the Tabernacle had "a perfect legal and moral right to express their views in public upon questions of human welfare" in a hall that they had reserved and paid for. "Ruffian persecution is sure to add power to the very extravagance which it assails," it continued, and those who participated in the disturbance "should be visited at once with legal punishment and public reprobation."[64] William Lloyd Garrison, editor of *The Liberator* in Boston, predictably blamed the disturbances on "well-dressed rowdies and 'certain lewd fellows of the baser sort' stimulated to make their assaults by the Satanic press" of New York City.[65] The New York *Sun* cautioned its readers to forbear viewing the riot as "very amusing, very funny, and all that." Even though its editorial policy was to oppose the cause of woman's rights, the paper denounced the actions of the mob. Such events hindered "moderate and substantial reforms" by discouraging respectable citizens, wishing to protect their reputations, from supporting worthy causes for fear that the public meetings that they attended might be "converted into disgraceful farces" and that they might thereby be subject to "contempt and ridicule."[66] The *Home Journal* objected to the disturbance because it reflected badly on the whole city. As the editor put it—"the wretches triumphed, and the city was again disgraced."[67]

Time did not diminish the outrage with which some editors like Raymond responded to attempts by trouble-makers to disrupt the meetings of woman's rights reformers. When a similar event occurred at the National Woman's Rights Convention held in 1859, Raymond described the scene as "disgraceful and mortifying to the last degree" but acknowledged that through it all, the presiding officers "preserved a remarkably good temper." He then protested that "no possible reform" should have to go through such an "ordeal" and charged the proprietor of the hall and the police with dereliction of duty.[68]

In order to provide their readers with national news, representatives of the penny press in other parts of the country were largely dependent upon the news gathering efforts of editors like Bennett, Greeley, and Raymond and telegraph technology. The amount of attention that could be devoted to issues like woman's rights was limited by a number of factors in such periodicals. Most papers during the period before the Civil War comprised only four pages, most of which carried advertising, local and business news, and political commentary. When editors of dailies had extra space to fill, they clipped and republished stories from other newspapers, sometimes citing the origins of the stories, sometimes not. Media events planned and promoted by woman's rights advocates had to compete for attention with everything else reported by other newspaper editors. Considering all this, the amount of space devoted to woman's rights in papers like the *St. Louis Daily Missouri Republican*, the *Cleveland Daily Plain Dealer*, and the *Daily Chicago Tribune* was substantial. The *Republican* was a Whig paper with daily, tri-weekly, and weekly editions in a slave state whose general editorial attitude toward social reform was, not surprisingly, unenthusiastic. When it ran articles concerning the activities of temperance reformers, abolitionists, or free love advocates, the sources of those articles were usually New York papers and the tone was more often than not critical unless the source was Greeley's *New York Tribune*.[69] Despite its lack of sympathy with social reform and its distance from the center of woman's rights activities, however, the *Republican* carried stories on 5 of the 11 national woman's rights conventions held between 1850 and 1860 ranging in length from a half column to a short announcement. The tone of those stories, like that of the *Tribune*, tended to be straightforward and informational rather than negative.[70]

The *Cleveland Daily Plain Dealer* was a Democratic paper. Advertisements dominated its columns, and it published only three to five columns of news a day. Its editor J. W. Gray ignored the 1848 conventions. In 1850 he reprinted what he described as a "diatribe" from the *New York Mirror* poking fun at the demands that woman's rights advocates made at their convention in Worcester, Massachusetts. A few days later he published a short article rather straightforwardly describing the proceedings of the convention there. The *Plain Dealer* did not cover the second convention in Worcester but did run three commentaries on the Bloomer costume, one written by a correspondent in Philadelphia. It sent a reporter to the Massilon, Ohio, woman's rights convention held in May of 1852 and devoted four columns to reporting and discussing its proceedings. It also published announcements and reviews of Elizabeth Oakes Smith's lectures on "Mankind" and "Womankind" held in Cleveland right after the Massilon convention, ran an article on the Syracuse convention held in the fall of that year relayed by telegraph, and published a call for the Cleveland convention to be held the next year. Following the mob convention in New York in 1853, Gray published an editorial critical of the woman's rights movement entitled "The Humbug of Woman's Rights." A few weeks later he announced that "male females and female males" along with "battalions of bloomers" and "armies of sympathizers in breeches and standing collars" were about to descend on Cleveland to hold yet another woman's rights convention. Despite his skeptical stance, Gray published ten columns worth of news and editorial comment on the convention held in his city. While the paper did not come out with an endorsement of the movement, it did encourage discussion of the issues that it raised and published descriptions of woman's rights advocates which were generally flattering and complimentary. Apparently having said all he had to say on the matter, Gray devoted very little space to the issue thereafter.[71]

The *Daily Chicago Tribune*, like the *Republican*, was largely dependent upon editors in New York for its news of woman's rights activities. It is difficult to assess the total amount of space that the *Tribune* devoted to the cause since many of its issues are no longer extant. What is available, however, indicates that the paper carried stories clipped from both the *New York Herald* and the *New York Tribune* and by 1853 took the position that the issues being raised by woman's rights advocates deserved a fairer hearing than they seemed to be getting and offered the Chicago lyceum series as an ideal place to provide Chicagoans with firsthand information about the movement. It republished a lengthy story from the *Cleveland Plain Dealer* as well as an editorial from the *New York Herald* about the 1853 Cleveland convention. By 1858 it came out in support of woman's rights, arguing that the cause was a just one and suggesting that the most serious obstacle to equal rights was the resistance of women rather than the opposition of men.[72]

Midwesterners were not the only ones to spread news of the movement. Newspapers published in the East but outside of New York also served as important conduits for news of the woman's rights movement. The *Philadelphia Public Ledger and Daily Transcript*, for example, supported the cause from the beginning and ran stories on both the Seneca Falls and Rochester conventions held in the late summer of 1848, republishing a story from the *Rochester Advertiser* that took an entire column of space. Two years later, it published a short notice, a long story, and an editorial on the first national convention held in Worcester. Its position was that American womanhood had not attained "the full measure of social equality for which she was manifestly created" and asked its readers to give serious consideration to their movement and to consider the benefits of allowing women to do anything they could do well. While the paper carried only a short article on the second convention held in Worcester, it carried two on the Syracuse convention in 1852 along with a scathing editorial criticizing those who, like Bennett, misrepresented its "objectives and proceedings" and demanding that the public take seriously the demands of woman's rights advocates.[73] In 1853, the paper published another strongly worded editorial deploring attempts of rowdies to interrupt the proceedings of the woman's rights convention held in New York. No matter how objectionable the sentiments of public speakers, it argued, "attempts to put down any discussion by mob violence, cannot be regarded as anything else than a gross public outrage and an invasion of the sacred right of freedom of speech."[74] And although the length of its stories usually did not compare with those published in the *Herald, Tribune,* and *Times* in New York, the *Public Ledger* published reports of every national woman's rights convention held for the rest of the decade except the one held in New York in 1859.[75]

The editor of the *Boston Daily Advertiser* began the paper's coverage of the woman's rights movement by clipping and republishing a long article from the *Rochester Democrat* describing the woman's rights meeting held there shortly after the Seneca Falls convention. Its content was largely factual but included editorial comment at the end which described some of the demands being made as "impractical, absurd, and ridiculous" and woman's rights advocates as bent on revolution. Thereafter, the paper included descriptions of various lengths of every national woman's rights convention held before the Civil War except those held in Syracuse, Cleveland, and Cincinnati. By the mid-1850s its editorial tone could best be described as neutral.[76]

Woman's rights advocates were justified in the pride they took in their efforts to attract the attention of the press to the cause of woman's rights. By providing the press with media events and courting the interest of editors like Greeley and Bennett, they assured that their reform would receive newspaper coverage not only in the Northeast but also in the Midwest. And whatever the nature of that coverage, the space that was devoted to the cause and its goals assured that the general public was kept relatively well informed about the activities of woman's rights supporters.

As we have seen, they were not always happy about the tone and content of articles describing them and their activities. They were often frustrated by what they considered to be inaccurate representations of their position and goals. They complained both in public and in private about the matter and used every opportunity to correct misunderstandings promulgated by the press. As early as 1848, Elizabeth Cady Stanton grumbled that "one might suppose from the articles that you find in some papers, that there are editors so ignorant as to believe that the chief object of these recent conventions was to seat every lord at the foot of a cradle, and to clothe every woman in her lord's attire."[77] Stanton was still fretting when she wrote to Elizabeth Smith Miller five years later, "I send you the Rochester *Journal*. Well, doesn't the editor pitch into me without mercy? I would answer him, but he wouldn't publish what I say, so there is no use. For the present we must let these narrow-minded and unfair critics rage. They cannot put down our ideas and we will have our day in the end."[78]

Both Antoinette Brown and Ernestine Rose used the platform of the state woman's rights convention in Albany, New York, in 1854 to charge that goals of the convention "had been greatly misrepresented by the misunderstanding of the reporters from the public press."[79] Martha C. Wright echoed the complaints of her friends, but she did it privately. Angry about the inaccuracy of newspaper reports concerning woman's rights activities, she wrote to Susan B. Anthony in 1856, "Isn't it wonderful how those *Tribune* Reporters can sit there, looking so pious, and pretending to report fairly, and then pervert and misrepresent as they do, giving just enough truth to serve their purpose." She had not been able to attend the national convention and was frustrated because she could not tell from the newspaper reports what had transpired there. "The worst of it is," she continued, "there are so many who are glad to take all that such papers say, for gospel."[80] Things had not improved much four years later when she wrote to Stanton, "Even the saintly and dignified *Evening Post* maligns us, as you will see—asserts that the resolution[s] were adopted wh[en] they never were and makes various false charges."[81]

A perfect example of journalistic misrepresentation and of the ability of newspaper editors literally to make news as well as report it is to be found in the response of the *New York Times* to Higginson's attack on it in 1856. The *Times* reported Higginson's attack but added something extra to the story. It reported that after Higginson's speech, Henry Blackwell had come to the defense of the *Times* and its editor from the convention floor. According to the story, Blackwell noted that the *Times* "was but a young journal" and that "its growth, popularity and influence were wholly without a precedent in the newspaper literature of the country. He regarded it," continued the report, "as one of the best, most reliable and influential papers in America. So greatly superior in all respects to the *Herald*, that they should never be mentioned in the same breath. The *Times* has given the *best reports* on every possible subject, of any paper he knew of," Blackwell is alleged to have said. He is reported as having compared the *Times* to the *Herald* and the presumably more sympathetic *Tribune* in their coverage of the convention. "The *Times*' report is twice as long and much more authentic than that of the *Tribune*, which was only a synopsis. The account in the *Herald* was a contemptuous burlesque. Far from blaming the Editor of the *Times*, he considered that he was to be honored, because although he condemns the woman's rights movement, he is not afraid to place the facts before the public, that they may judge for themselves. The *Times* in regard to this Convention, so far, has been the only paper which has been entirely satisfactory, and the course of its Editor is the more to be honored, as he is opposed to our principles."[82]

Higginson's speech appeared in the official proceedings of the convention and in the accounts that appeared in all three prominent New York newspapers. Blackwell's alleged response appeared only in the *Times*. It is possible that Blackwell did defend Raymond and his newspaper at the convention. But it is not likely. If he did not, the *Times* insertion illustrates the kind of misstatement that woman's rights advocates complained about.

To some extent woman's rights advocates could depend upon the editors of the reform press not only to support their efforts but also to correct misrepresentations and to protest the insults directed against the reformers by their less sympathetic colleagues. In 1850, for example, Jane Swisshelm felt compelled to correct what she dubbed "a bit of spleen" which had appeared in the *Commercial Journal*. The *Journal* had referred to Elizabeth Wilson of Ohio as "miss" and had accused her of saying that Jenny Lind had exhibited indelicate and improper behavior "in consenting to sing for the pleasure of these male tyrants." Swisshelm wrote that she normally considered such reports "too silly to excite anger" but in this case deemed it necessary to respond. "This *Miss* Wilson is a married woman," she wrote. "The report that speeches and resolutions were made or passed condemning Jenny Lind is evidently a falsehood cut out of the whole cloth—the manufacture of some ninny who mistakes lying for wit."[83]

Other reform journals also dedicated themselves to defending the reformers. In 1853 the *National Anti-Slavery Standard* responded to an article appearing in the *Hartford Republican* which described the adjournment of the Cleveland woman's rights convention as a "row, under the auspices of the insane virago Abby Kelley." "This disgraceful allusion to Abby Kelley Foster . . . is our only apology for noticing it," wrote the editor. "If we had found it in Bennett's *Herald*, the fit channel for such vituperation, we should have passed it in silence; but its appearance in a paper so respectable and generally so informed as our Free Democratic contemporary of Hartford surprises us not a little."[84]

Woman's rights advocates appreciated the help of the reform press in such matters. But they discovered that even reform editors were not always as consistently supportive as the leaders of the woman's rights movement might have liked. Jane Swisshelm is a case in point. Swisshelm was a maverick, an outsider who did not fraternize with the leaders of the movement. Although she was genuinely sympathetic with efforts to improve the status of women in American society, she frequently infuriated woman's rights advocates by her independence and propensity to criticize their policies and activities. She insisted, for example, that questions concerning the kinds of clothes that women wore and the issue of slavery were extraneous to the issue of woman's rights. She felt that the Bloomer costume that Stanton, Anthony, and Bloomer insisted on promoting was not only unflattering but also subjected its "wearer to indelicate exposure." She dismissed the arguments of both those who supported and those who opposed the costume as "sheer nonsense, with a large spice of impertinence."[85] And despite her abolitionist sympathies, she also felt that associating the cause of women with that of slaves was bad policy. Comparing the woman's rights movement to "a little boat launched upon a tempestuous river," she argued that it was "not strong enough to bear the additional weight of all the colored men in creation."[86]

Opposition to their reform strategies was no doubt frustrating to the leaders of the movement. But in some ways, it worked to their advantage. First, it played a role in helping them to strengthen the commitment of those who supported their cause. In a sense, criticism helped to unify the movement by giving woman's rights sympathizers an enemy to focus on. Criticism, even by those who were generally supportive like Swisshelm and Greeley, isolated woman's rights advocates from nonreformers and provided an opportunity to solidify their group. Poor treatment made them martyrs and encouraged them to develop an aggressive, martial spirit by giving them an enemy to fight. Their willingness to suffer martyrdom in the form of personal attacks was a measure of their steadfastness as well as their dedication and commitment to the group. Newspaper editors also served as barometers. Opposition provided a way of measuring the revolutionary implications of their demands. It was a way of confirming that their vision of gender equality represented a dramatic break with the past.

Monitoring changes in the response of the editors of the popular press also gave them a way of evaluating the degree to which they were succeeding in influencing public opinion and a reason to be optimistic about the possibilities for change. In the early years of the movement, according to Stanton, "all the journals from Maine to Texas seemed to strive with each other to see which could make our movement appear the most ridiculous."[87] But by 1850, she began to notice a change. "Ridicule," she reported, was "giving way to reason. Our papers begin to see that this is no subject for mirth, but one for serious consideration."[88] Paulina Wright Davis agreed. In 1851 she told those who attended the Worcester convention that "the general tone of public sentiment, as manifested by the leading papers of the day is undergoing rapid change for the better."[89] At the 1853 convention she continued her optimistic tone. "The criticism of first impressions has entirely exhausted itself," she said, "the stage of serious investigation has fairly set in; the 'movement' has a recognized existence and a standing among the things that *are*, and are *to be*; and the argument is narrowed down already to certain differences about points and policies, means and measures."[90] Such assessments gave the leaders of the movement a way of measuring progress and of boosting the morale of their followers.

In the end, however, because the press was the principal conduit through which woman's rights activists communicated with the general public, the way that newspaper editors responded was less important than the fact that they responded at all. What they said and how they said it was less important than how much they said and how often. Editors like Bennett, Greeley, and Raymond provided woman's rights advocates with an unprecedented degree of public exposure both because the circulation of their papers was so large and because what they reported was republished by editors in other parts of the country. Reform editors served the cause by attempting to correct misstatements made by others concerning the movement, defending individual woman's rights supporters, and supplementing the exposure that the movement received from the penny press. The exposure that they jointly provided encouraged debate about the role of women in American society all over the country. Discussion about woman's proper role had to take place before significant reform was possible. So the discourse that journalists prompted helped in and of itself to legitimize their claims and added a new dimension to female presence in public life.

The cause of woman's rights made some headway before the Civil War. Married women in states like New York gained more control over their property, educational opportunities for women were opening up, and their participation in reform activities was increasingly valued by their male colleagues. But most women still suffered from gender-specific legal, political, social, and economic disabilities. The success of woman's rights activists in manipulating the press guaranteed that their protests were not ignored. And they found that situation encouraging. But their efforts were overwhelmed in 1861 when the country turned its attention to war. Those who were also abolitionists welcomed whatever opportunity the war might bring to destroy the institution of slavery. As feminists they anticipated improved opportunities for women to participate more fully in public life through the war effort. They entered the period of the Civil War relatively united. But when the war was over, that unity would be decimated by a factionalism that would continue to plague the movement into the twentieth century.

CONCLUSION

James Gordon Bennett of the *New York Herald* was a skilled journalist. He was successful partly because he understood the power of words and how to combine them in ways that could stimulate the imagination and fantasies of his readers. When he called female woman's rights advocates "hens that crow," he meant to insult and publicly humiliate them as women and to belittle their efforts to expand woman's right to participate more fully in public life. His tactic was not entirely successful. By using this metaphor, Bennett also in a very graphic way presented the ideas of the woman's rights movement to the reading public in terms they could not help but understand and unintentionally gave support to the very movement he sought to ridicule.

The "hens that crow" metaphor suggested that what women wanted was not to *be* roosters but the opportunity to be *like* roosters. Before the Civil War, male access to economic and educational opportunities as well as their ability to accumulate social and political power and privilege may have been limited by circumstances such as their social class, physical or intellectual ability, or condition of servitude, but it was not usually limited by their gender. Woman's rights supporters wanted that principle to apply to women as well as men. Female woman's rights advocates did not want to change their gender, they merely wanted to make gender an irrelevant factor in the pursuit of social, economic, and political life both inside and outside the home. They wanted the opportunity, like roosters, to crow if they could.

Bennett's reference to hens that crow also acknowledged that women were capable of fulfilling the enhanced roles that they were demanding. He did not write that women were *trying* to crow and were failing. He wrote that women *were* crowing. In doing so, he publicly acknowledged that in fact their gender did not necessarily inhibit their ability to do the kinds of things previously done exclusively by men. In that sense he metaphorically recognized women's ability to free themselves from the restrictions that their possession of female bodies placed on them. He admitted that at least some women were competent to participate more fully in public life and suggested that when women started crowing like roosters they could not be ignored. Thus, his epithet illustrates the degree to which women working in reform in general and woman's rights in particular had already imposed themselves on the public consciousness as public figures.

Bennett's metaphoric response to the demands of woman's rights advocates stands as testimony to their accomplishments in the antebellum period. By 1860, a small cadre of woman's rights advocates had collectively created an ideology that justified efforts on the part of American women to move beyond the roles delegated to them by Republican Motherhood and the cult of domesticity and to pursue their own self-interest in public as well as private life. To express that ideology, they had also developed a reform idiom that crossed gender boundaries and implicitly rejected the private sphere as the most appropriate context within which women could carry out their social, economic, and political roles. Eschewing familiar references to the domestic duties and the selflessness of traditional female activities, they relied on metaphors that linguistically thrust women out of the world of the home and placed them in a context that allowed them to pursue their own interests as architects, engineers, warriors, and farmers. Those metaphors were one of their most powerful weapons. They helped the leaders of the movement to express their feminist ideology and provided them with a public presence by provoking the public imagination and helping to attract attention to their cause. In the absence of a formal organizational structure, their ideology and the verbal and nonverbal techniques they used to express it served as the framework within which they could work to enhance woman's opportunities to participate more fully in all aspects of public life.

The vanguard of the woman's rights movement understood that their biggest enemy was not necessarily opposition but ignorance, disinterest, and apathy. In order to establish the political competency of women, they had to force the American public to think consciously in terms of gender and its relationship to the distribution of social, economic, and political power, and to accept the idea that women had as much right as men to the exercise of that power.

Laying claim to the kind of public space previously dominated by men, they held conventions, conducted petition drives, gave speeches, wrote letters to editors, testified before state legislatures and constitutional conventions, and distributed pamphlets. During the 1850s thousands of ordinary people heard their message. But many thousands more, who had never seen a woman's rights advocate or heard one speak and were not likely to ever avail themselves of the opportunity to do so, read about the woman's rights campaign in the newspapers. Newspapers, then, were woman's rights advocates' most important public forum and their conduit to the general public. In that sense, newspaper editors were the most important audience for woman's rights advocates.

Without a widely circulated official newspaper of their own, woman's rights supporters were dependent upon the popular press to report their activities and disseminate their ideas. They therefore consciously and systematically devised strategies and performed public political rituals designed to elicit responses from the press. Their strategies worked. Even though advertising sometimes claimed more space than news or human-interest stories, penny press editors in both the Northeast and Midwest gave the campaign for woman's rights extensive if not always sympathetic coverage throughout the period. In one sense, the kind of attention that woman's rights issues received from newspapers was less important than the fact that they received any attention at all. Whether they supported the cause or not, penny press editors acknowledged woman's rights advocates and their demands as worthy of attention and discussion and defended their right to speak out. In doing so, they helped to establish the competency of women to contribute to public discourse and to discuss social and political issues from the perspective of their own ideology in the antebellum period. They also helped to create a culture that would begin more completely to incorporate, in theory if not always in fact, the social, economic, and political interests of women.

Before the Civil War, the leaders of the antebellum woman's rights movement established the intellectual, rhetorical, and public relations foundations upon which modern American feminism could be built. Their accomplishments illustrate both the possibilities and the limits imposed on them by the context in which they found themselves. They framed their demands within the parameters provided them by the prevailing belief systems and behavior patterns developed by men to serve male interests, and by the economic, social, and political realities of their day. Their arguments, rhetoric, and strategies were also framed by the tensions inherent in attempts to balance individual interests with those of the community, as well as those that accompanied the belief that all people were essentially the same and that factors like gender, ethnicity, or race only made them *appear* to be different.

By the end of the antebellum period, the leaders of the woman's rights movement had developed a way of addressing those tensions as they applied to gender. In private they struggled as individuals to define their own position on woman's rights issues. And they bickered with each other over the finer points of philosophy and strategy. But as a group, they generally agreed in public that for women to pursue their own self-interest would pose no threat to the welfare of society as a whole. They held that men and women were more alike than they were different and that many of the differences that appeared to separate them were culturally rather than biologically determined. They were sure that enhancing opportunities for women to participate on an equal basis with men in public life would not diminish their desire or ability to carry out their domestic responsibilities and were convinced that as long as women faced discrimination based on gender, the promise of equality in America would remain unfulfilled and the tyranny of one gender over another would continue.

But just as the leaders of the woman's rights movement worked out a coherent way of expressing their demands and pursuing their fulfillment, the social, economic, political, and intellectual basis of American life began to change dramatically. And the struggle for woman's rights entered a new phase. Woman's rights advocates found it necessary to adapt themselves, as well as their ideology, rhetoric, and strategies, to those changes. After the Civil War, the kind of unity and camaraderie that characterized the antebellum period began to dissolve amidst disagreement over whether or not to insist that the issue of gender be addressed in the Fourteenth and Fifteenth Amendments. Those interested in suffrage split into two groups one of which had a more ambitious social reform agenda than the other.[1] As the century progressed the kind of individualism that encouraged competitiveness, acquisitiveness, and selfishness in the pursuit of wealth—accompanied by increasing urbanization, class conflict, and ethnic diversity—began to be perceived as an immediate threat to the kind of society that many of those in the white middle class wanted to create. As William Leach has pointed out, some feminists in the 1870s, many of whom had helped to found the woman's rights movement in the 1850s, grew increasingly uncomfortable with their adherence to liberalism and its corollary "possessive individualism" and felt compelled to develop a new social vision to assuage their discomfort. They began to modify their social ideology by de-emphasizing conflict and stressing the need for co-operation, social harmony, and the integration of private and public life. In the process, they began to stress the importance of women's unique attributes and their role in humanizing and harmonizing the public realm.[2]

Emphasis on the differences between men and women was further encouraged during this period by the increasing influence of science on social thought. The Anglo-American scientific community changed the perspective previously used to study human beings in general and gender differences in particular. It discounted the significance of culture in determining gender characteristics and emphasized instead the importance of physical characteristics in an attempt to discover why various groups of people differed from each other. Physiologists, physical anthropologists, and evolutionary biologists confidently and authoritatively declared that women were not equal to men but were in fact inherently different, developmentally arrested, and intellectually inferior. These ideas, of course, were not new. But despite the fact that they were based more on the conventional wisdom than on empirical evidence, they were, Cynthia Russett argues, convincing because science as a discipline was so highly regarded and these particular scientific theories were so specific and inclusive.[3] In any case, they not only explained and justified the preservation of women's traditional and unequal social, economic, and political roles and the wisdom of preventing them from making further inroads into public life but also established the basis for believing that women who ventured into the public sphere needed special protection.

The significance of this shift for woman's rights advocates was profound. Their ideological rug, so to speak, was pulled out from under them. They had no way effectively to modify the impact of "possessive individualism" and were in no position of authority to challenge the validity of scientific pronouncements about gender differences. So by the end of the nineteenth century, they found themselves working within a new cultural milieu in which science, massive immigration, and the rise of the industrial working class were leading white, native-born Protestants to rethink their commitment to the ideals of equality and natural rights. They responded by refining, modifying, and reformulating their ideology and strategies as circumstance demanded. The result, as Aileen Kraditor has illustrated, was that many of those interested in promoting the cause of women within the suffrage movement abandoned their demand for equal rights and moved from a justice argument to one based on expediency and posited that women's special virtues should be used in public as well as private for the benefit of American society as a whole.[4] At the same time, they made further intrusions into public space by expanding their repertoire of strategies to include rallies and parades.[5] Others attempted to preserve and enhance women's domestic roles as mothers and lobbied for special protection for women through legislation designed to compensate for gender differences. They invaded legislative offices and the halls of Congress with increasing regularity. Whether feminist or not, in the early years of the twentieth century, their rhetoric was likely to be the rhetoric of motherhood rather than that of equal rights.[6] Only a few, such as those who eventually formed the National Woman's Party under the leadership of Alice Paul, continued to argue in public for gender equality.[7]

And still the context in which the "woman question" was debated continued to change. Suffrage ceased to be an issue in the 1920s, and feminists concerned themselves with other social, political, and economic issues.[8] The Depression and then World War II had profound effects on the economic and social lives of most Americans and wrought changes which both enhanced and inhibited women's opportunities.[9] Female social scientists like Helen Thompson and Jessie Taft, encouraged by their mentors at places like the University of Chicago and Columbia University, began using scientific methods to challenge prevailing scientific and social scientific theories about gender. The empirical data that they collected promoted interest in the influence of culture on determining gender characteristics and provided the basis for again arguing that women and men should have equal opportunities to pursue their interests.[10]

By the 1960s the feminist claims that culture rather than biology was responsible for perceived gender differences and that women had an obligation to fulfill themselves as individuals had come full circle. Women both publicly and privately renewed their efforts to move beyond the promise of equal opportunity to the fulfillment of that promise. More and more of them began to break free from the psychological and social chains that kept them from fulfilling their potential. They continued to confront gender-based discrimination. And like those who had come before them, they struggled to balance their obligations to others with their need to fulfill themselves. Nevertheless, as the leaders of the woman's rights movement had predicted a century before, they became in fact the architects, engineers, and warriors whose role it was to design, build, and defend a society in which social, economic, educational, and political opportunities were more equitably distributed between men and women.

NOTES

Introduction

1. Attributed to Lillie Devereux Blake, "Women's Rights Fables" (n.p.: n.p., n.d. [nineteenth century]) by Cheris Kramarae and Mercilee M. Jenkins, "Women Take Back Talk," in *Women and Language in Transition*, ed. Joyce Penfield (Albany: State University of New York Press, 1987), 147–48.

2. Eleanor Flexner, *Century of Struggle: The Woman's Rights Movement in the United States* (New York: Atheneum, 1972), 71–101; Keith E. Melder, *Beginnings of Sisterhood: The American Woman's Rights Movement, 1800–1850* (New York: Schocken, 1977), 143–59; Ellen Carol DuBois, *Feminism and Suffrage: The Emergence of an Independent Women's Movement in America, 1848–1869* (Ithaca: Cornell University Press, 1978), 21–52.

3. Elisabeth Griffith, *In Her Own Right: The Life of Elizabeth Cady Stanton* (New York: Oxford University Press, 1984); Lois Banner, *Elizabeth Cady Stanton: A Radical for Woman's Rights* (Boston: Little, Brown, 1980), 69–89; Kathleen Barry, *Susan B. Anthony: A Biography of a Singular Feminist* (New York: New York University Press, 1988); Andrea Moore Kerr, *Lucy Stone: Speaking Out for Equality* (New Brunswick, N.J.: Rutgers University Press, 1992).

4. Elizabeth Cady Stanton, Susan B. Anthony, and Matilda Joslyn Gage, eds., *History of Woman Suffrage*, 2 vols. (New York: Fowler and Wells, 1881), 1:67–74; Griffith, 51–59.

5. As a number of scholars have pointed out, those who struggled to improve the status of women in the nineteenth century called themselves and were known as woman's rights advocates. They did not call themselves *feminists. Feminism* is a twentieth-century term. See Nancy F. Cott, *The Grounding of Modern Feminism* (New Haven: Yale University Press, 1987), 3. When I occasionally use the term, I use it to mean anyone who advocates the kind of changes necessary to bring about social, economic, and political equality between men and women.

6. Hilda L. Smith, *Reason's Disciples: Seventeenth-Century English Feminists* (Urbana: University of Illinois Press, 1982), xiv, 4, 9, 15, 207.

7. Katharine M. Rogers, *Feminism in Eighteenth-Century England* (Urbana: University of Illinois Press, 1982), 81, 143.

8. Stanton, Anthony, and Gage, eds., 1:51–52; see also Norma Basch, "Equity vs. Equality: Emerging Concepts of Women's Political Status in the Age of Jackson," *Journal of the Early Republic* 3 (Fall 1983), 297–318.

9. Stanton, Anthony, and Gage, eds., 1:73–75.

10. See, for example, J. G. A. Pocock, "Introduction: The State of the Art," in *Virtue, Commerce, and History: Essays on Political Thought and History, Chiefly in the Eighteenth Century* (Cambridge: Cambridge University Press, 1985), 1–6; David Hollinger, "American Intellectual History: Issues for the 1980s," in *In the American Province: Studies in the History and Historiography of Ideas* (Bloomington: Indiana University Press, 1985), 186–88; David Hollinger, "Historians and the Discourse of Intellectuals," in *In the American Province*, 131–51; William J. Bouwsma, "Intellectual History in the 1980s: From History of Ideas to History of Meaning," *Journal of Interdisciplinary History* 12 (Autumn 1981), 289; John E. Toews, "Intellectual History After the Linguistic Turn: The Autonomy of Meaning

and the Irreducibility of Experience," *American Historical Review* 92 (October 1987), 882; J. G. A. Pocock, "Languages and Their Implications," in *Politics, Language, and Time: Essays in Political Thought and History* (New York: Atheneum, 1971), 3–41.

11. For discussions of the significance of poststructuralism for the historian, see David Harlan, "Intellectual History and the Return of Literature," *American Historical Review* 94 (June 1989), 581–609; David A. Hollinger, "The Return of the Prodigal: The Persistence of Historical Knowing," ibid., 610–21; David Harlan, "Reply to David Hollinger, ibid., 622–26; Joyce Appleby, "One Good Turn Deserves Another: Moving Beyond the Linguistic; A Response to David Harlan," ibid. (December 1989), 1326–1332; for an excellent summary of the concepts used by poststructuralists and their application to women, see Joan W. Scott, "Deconstructing Equality-Versus-Difference: Or, the Uses of Poststructuralist Theory for Feminism," *Feminist Studies* 14 (Spring 1988), 34–38.

12. For a good example of this sensitivity, see Mary Kupiec Cayton, "The Making of an American Prophet: Emerson, His Audiences, and the Rise of the Culture Industry in Nineteenth-Century America," *American Historical Review* 92 (June 1987), 597–620.

13. Edward Sapir, "Language and Environment," in *Selected Writings of Edward Sapir in Language, Culture, and Personality*, ed. David G. Mandelbaum (Berkeley: University of California Press, 1963), 89–103. This essay was first published in 1912.

14. Casey Miller and Kate Swift, *Words and Women* (Garden City, N.Y.: Anchor Books, 1976), 137; for a general introduction to the field of sociolinguistics, see Dell Hymes, *Foundations in Sociolinguistics* (Philadelphia: University of Pennsylvania Press, 1974).

15. Susan J. Wolfe, "The Rhetoric of Heterosexism," in *Gender and Discourse: The Power of Talk*, ed. Alexandra Dundas Todd and Sue Fisher (Norwood, N.J.: Ablex Publishers, 1988), 201; Miller and Swift, 138; Gillian Sankoff, *The Social Life of Language* (Philadelphia: University of Pennsylvania Press, 1980), xxi.

16. Ruth Borker, "Anthropology: Social and Cultural Perspectives," in *Women and Language in Literature and Society*, ed. Sally McConnell-Ginet, Ruth Borker, and Nelly Furman (New York: Praeger, 1980), 31.

17. As Anne Boylan has pointed out, while women could not vote in the early nineteenth century, they did participate in politics through such activities as boycotts, petitions, and lobbying. See Anne M. Boylan, "Women and Politics in the Era Before Seneca Falls," *Journal of the Early Republic* 10 (Fall 1990), 363–82.

18. Sankoff, 13–14; see also McConnell-Ginet, Borker, and Furman, eds., 55.

19. See Ward H. Goodenough, *Culture, Language, and Society* (Menlo Park, Calif.: Benjamin/Cummings Publisher, 1981), 30–36.

20. Carroll Smith-Rosenberg, "Hearing Women's Words: A Feminist Reconstruction of History," in *Disorderly Conduct: Visions of Gender in Victorian America* (New York: Oxford University Press, 1985), 11–52, esp. 26–47, quotation on page 42.

21. The literature which discusses these issues is vast. What follows are suggestions as to where to begin. Barbara Welter was the first to discuss the cult of domesticity in "The Cult of True Womanhood: 1820–1860," *American Quarterly* 18 (Summer 1966), 151–74. Shirley J. Yee suggests in *Black Women Abolitionists: A Study in Activism, 1828–1860* (Knoxville: University of Tennessee Press, 1992), 40–59, that black journalists, teachers, and ministers subjected women in their communities to many of the same expectations. For a discussion of changing attitudes toward housework, see Jeanne Boydston, *Home and Work: Housework, Wages, and the Ideology of Labor in the Early Republic* (New York: Oxford

University Press, 1990). For commentary on the cult of domesticity and the degree to which women were isolated in a sphere separate from men, see Linda K. Kerber, "Separate Spheres, Female Worlds, Woman's Place: The Rhetoric of Women's History," *Journal of American History* 75 (June 1988), 9–39.

22. For descriptions of women's domestic culture in the North, see Nancy F. Cott, *The Bonds of Womanhood: "Woman's Sphere" in New England, 1780–1835* (New Haven: Yale University Press, 1977); Carroll Smith-Rosenberg, "The Female World of Love and Ritual: Relations between Women in Nineteenth-Century America," *Signs* 1 (Autumn 1975), 1–29. For discussions of Southern women's culture, see Suzanne Lebsock, *The Free Women of Petersburg: Status and Culture in a Southern Town, 1784–1860* (New York: Norton, 1985) and Elizabeth Fox-Genovese, *Within the Plantation Household: Black and White Women of the Old South* (Chapel Hill: University of North Carolina Press, 1988).

23. Gerda Lerner discusses the ways that industrialization affected women in different classes in "The Lady and the Mill Girl: Changes in the Status of Women in the Age of Jackson," *Midcontinent American Studies Journal* 10 (Spring 1969), 5–15. Christine Stansell describes the world of working-class women in New York City. See Christine Stansell, *City of Women: Sex and Class in New York, 1789–1860* (Urbana: University of Illinois Press, 1987).

24. For discussions of the New York Married Women's Property Act, see Norma Basch, *In the Eyes of the Law: Women, Marriage, and Property in Nineteenth-Century New York* (Ithaca: Cornell University Press, 1982) and Peggy A. Rabkin, *Fathers to Daughters: The Legal Foundations of Female Emancipation* (Westport, Conn.: Greenwood, 1980).

25. Barbara J. Berg argues that urbanization was a necessary precondition for the rise of American feminism in *The Remembered Gate: Origins of American Feminism: The Woman and the City, 1800–1860* (New York: Oxford University Press, 1978). See Cott, *Bonds*, 70–71, for a discussion of disinterestedness as the basis for woman's reputation as a morally superior being. For discussions of women and benevolence, see Lori D. Ginzberg, *Women and the Work of Benevolence: Morality, Politics, and Class in the Nineteenth-Century United States* (New Haven: Yale University Press, 1990); Nancy A. Hewitt, *Women's Activism and Social Change: Rochester, New York, 1822–1872* (Ithaca: Cornell University Press, 1984); Anne Firor Scott, *Natural Allies: Women's Associations in American History* (Urbana: University of Illinois Press, 1992).

26. Many of the early woman's rights activists were Quakers. For background on the influence of the principle of egalitarianism on Quaker women, their lives, and their social activism, see Mary Maples Dunn, "Saints and Sisters: Congregational and Quaker Women in the Early Colonial Period," *American Quarterly* 30 (Winter 1978), 582–601; Jean R. Soderland, "Women's Authority in Pennsylvania and New Jersey Quaker Meetings, 1680–1760," *William and Mary Quarterly* 44 (October 1987), 722–49; Nancy A. Hewitt, "Feminist Friends: Agrarian Quakers and the Emergence of Woman's Rights in America," *Feminist Studies* 12 (Spring 1986), 27–49; Joan M. Jensen, *Loosening the Bonds: Mid-Atlantic Farm Women, 1750–1850* (New Haven: Yale University Press, 1986). For one discussion of the influence of religious revivals on women, see Mary P. Ryan, *Cradle of the Middle Class: The Family in Oneida County, New York, 1790–1865* (New York: Cambridge University Press, 1981).

27. Blanche Glassman Hersh, *The Slavery of Sex: Feminist-Abolitionists in America* (Urbana: University of Illinois Press, 1978), 20–28; for another discussion of the connection between abolitionism and the rise of the woman's rights movement, see DuBois, *Feminism and Suffrage*.

28. Ginzberg, 98–132.

29. Linda Kerber, *Women of the Republic: Intellect and Ideology in Revolutionary America* (Chapel Hill: University of North Carolina Press, 1980), 269–88; Linda Kerber, "Daughters of Columbia: Educating Women for the Republic, 1787–1805," in *The Hofstadter Aegis: A Memorial*, ed. Stanley Elkins and Eric McKitrick (New York: Knopf, 1974), 36–59; Kathryn Kish Sklar, *Catharine Beecher: A Study in American Domesticity* (New Haven: Yale University Press, 1973).

30. For discussions of political culture and the rise of male suffrage, see Chilton Williamson, *American Suffrage: From Property to Democracy, 1760–1860* (Princeton: Princeton University Press, 1960).

31. Griffith, 9, 11, 49–50.

32. Katharine Anthony, *Susan B. Anthony: Her Personal History and Her Era* (Garden City, N.Y.: Doubleday, 1954), 102.

33. Otelia Cromwell, *Lucretia Mott* (Cambridge: Harvard University Press, 1958), 18–19.

34. Alice Stone Blackwell, *Lucy Stone: Pioneer of Woman's Rights* (Boston: Little, Brown, 1930), 22–23, 25.

35. Hersh, 220–29.

36. See, for example, Flexner, *Century of Struggle*; William L. O'Neill, ed., *The Woman Movement: Feminism in the United States and England* (Chicago: Quadrangle, 1969); Anne F. Scott and Andrew M. Scott, *One Half the People: The Fight for Woman Suffrage* (Philadelphia: J. B. Lippincott, 1975); Ross Evans Paulson, *Women's Suffrage and Prohibition: A Comparative Study of Equality and Social Control* (Glenview, Ill.: Scott, Foresman, 1973); and William O'Neill, *Everyone Was Brave: The Rise and Fall of Feminism in America* (Chicago: Quadrangle, 1969).

37. See, for example, Robert E. Riegel, *American Feminists* (Lawrence: University of Kansas Press, 1963), preface; Hersh, 41, 191, 193; Olive Banks, *Faces of Feminism: A Study of Feminism as a Social Movement* (New York: St. Martin's Press, 1981), 7–8; James L. Cooper and Sheila McIsaac Cooper, *The Roots of American Feminist Thought* (Boston: Allyn and Bacon, 1973), 6–7; Cott, *Grounding*, 16–17; Josephine Donovan, *Feminist Theory: The Intellectual Traditions of American Feminism* (New York: Frederick Ungar, 1985), 1–36.

38. Kerber, *Women of the Republic*, 15–32; Jane Rendall, *The Origins of Modern Feminism: Women in Britain, France, and the United States, 1780–1860* (London: Macmillan, 1985), 7–32, quotation on page 7.

39. Rosemarie Zagarri, "Morals, Manners, and the Republican Mother," *American Quarterly* 44 (June 1992), 192–215.

40. For general discussions of journalism in this period, see Frank Luther Mott, *American Journalism, A History: 1690–1960* (New York: Macmillan, 1962); Donald Lewis Shaw, "At the Crossroads: Change and Continuity in American Press News, 1820–1860," *Journalism History* 8 (Summer 1981), 38–50; John C. Nerone, "The Mythology of the Penny Press," *Critical Studies in Mass Communication* 4 (December 1987), 376–404.

41. See, for example, Flexner, 81–82; Melder, 148, 151; E. Claire Jerry, "The Role of Newspapers in the Nineteenth-Century Woman's Movement," in *A Voice of Their Own: The Woman's Suffrage Press, 1840–1910*, ed. Martha M. Solomon (Tuscaloosa: University of Alabama Press, 1991), 19; Lynne Masel-Walters, "To Hustle with the Rowdies: The Organization and Functions of the American Woman Suffrage Press," *Journal of American Culture* 3 (Spring 1980), 168.

42. I began my analysis of penny press response to the issue of woman's rights by determining which papers had the largest circulation, the assumption being that those papers with the largest circulation probably had the most influence nationally. The *New York Daily Herald*, the *New York Daily Tribune*, and the *New York Daily Times* had the largest circulations during the period in question. For circulation

figures, see Douglas Fermer, *James Gordon Bennett and the* New York Herald: *A Study of Editorial Opinion in the Civil War Era, 1854–1867* (New York: St. Martin's Press, 1986), 323–27. I read daily issues of each of these three papers for one month preceding and two weeks after every known state and national convention held between 1848 and 1860. In order to assess the degree to which these three newspapers contributed to the diffusion of information about the movement and to survey the attitude of editors in other parts of the country to woman's rights, I read each issue of the *Chicago Daily Tribune*, the *Boston Daily Advertiser*, and the *St. Louis Daily Republican* from the first day of national woman's rights conventions to up to ten days after. In the case of Cleveland and Philadelphia, each of which served as host to a national convention, I read the *Cleveland Daily Plain Dealer* and the *Philadelphia Public Ledger and Daily Transcript* for one week before and two weeks after the convention that they hosted and from the first day of other national conventions to up to ten days after.

43. See, for example, Ann Russo and Cheris Kramarae, *The Radical Women's Press of the 1850s* (New York: Routledge, 1991), 1–17; Bertha-Monica Stearns, "Reform Periodicals and Female Reformers, 1830–1860," *American Historical Review* 37 (July 1932), 678–99; Martha M. Solomon, "The Role of the Suffrage Press in the Woman's Rights Movement," in *A Voice of Their Own*, 1–16.

44. For a general discussion of these developments, see DuBois, *Feminism and Suffrage*; Wendy Hamand Venet, *Neither Ballots nor Bullets: Women Abolitionists and the Civil War* (Charlottesville: University Press of Virginia, 1991).

1. The Advocates

1. *New York Daily Herald*, September 14, 1852, p. 4.

2. The kind of networks I am referring to are those like the ones analyzed in Judith Wellman, "The Seneca Falls Women's Rights Convention: A Study of Social Networks," *Journal of Women's History* 3 (Spring 1991), 9–37.

3. Before the Civil War national woman's rights conventions met in Worcester, Mass. (1850), Worcester, Mass. (1851), Syracuse, N.Y. (1852), New York, N.Y. (1853), Cleveland, Ohio (1853), Philadelphia, Pennsylvania (1854), Cincinnati, Ohio (1855), and New York, N.Y. (1856, 1858, 1859, 1860). There was no national convention in 1857.

4. For discussions of the men who participated in the woman's rights movement, see William Leach, *True Love and Perfect Union: The Feminist Reform of Sex and Society* (Middletown, Conn.: Wesleyan University Press, 1989), 300–16; Blanche Glassman Hersh, *The Slavery of Sex: Feminist-Abolitionists in America* (Urbana: University of Illinois Press, 1978), 218–251.

5. For the influence of the Quaker religion on the early woman's rights movement, see Nancy A. Hewitt, "Feminist Friends: Agrarian Quakers and the Emergence of Woman's Rights in America," *Feminist Studies* 12 (Spring 1986), 27–49. While woman's rights advocates were often involved simultaneously in a number of reform movements, abolition and temperance seem to have been the most important in forming the woman's rights movement. See Naomi Rosenthal, Meryl Fingrutd, Michele Ethier, Roberta Karant, and David McDonald, "Social Movements and Networks Analysis: A Case Study of Nineteenth-Century Women's Reform in New York State," *American Journal of Sociology* 90 (March 1985), 1043.

6. Ellen Carol DuBois, *Feminism and Suffrage: The Emergence of an Independent Women's Movement in America, 1848–1869* (Ithaca: Cornell University Press, 1978), 21–52.

7. Brief biographies of most of these early woman's rights advocates may be found in the *Dictionary of American Biography*, 22 vols. (New York: Scribner, 1928–

1958) and Edward T. James, ed., *Notable American Women: A Biographical Dictionary, 1607–1950*, 3 vols. (Cambridge: Harvard University Press, 1971). For a discussion of the networks formed by the signers of the Declaration of Sentiments, see Judith Wellman, "Woman and Radical Reform in Upstate New York: A Profile of Grassroots Female Abolitionists," in *Clio Was a Woman: Studies in the History of American Women*, ed. Mabel E. Deutrich and Virginia C. Purdy (Washington, D.C.: Howard University Press, 1980), 113–27.

8. Elizabeth Cady Stanton, Susan B. Anthony, and Matilda Joslyn Gage, eds., *History of Woman Suffrage*, 2 vols. (New York: Fowler and Wells, 1881), 1:528.

9. Paulina Wright Davis to Elizabeth Cady Stanton, September 1, 1852, Elizabeth Cady Stanton Papers, Library of Congress, Washington, D.C., in *Papers of Elizabeth Cady Stanton and Susan B. Anthony*, ed. Patricia G. Holland and Ann D. Gordon (Wilmington, Del.: Scholarly Resources, 1991, microfilm, series 3), reel 7, frames 320 and 321.

10. Elisabeth Griffith, *In Her Own Right: The Life of Elizabeth Cady Stanton* (New York: Oxford University Press, 1984), 72–73.

11. One hundred men and women signed the Declaration of Sentiments at the Seneca Falls convention in 1848. See Stanton, Anthony, and Gage, eds., 1:73. According to the official history of the suffrage movement, the Tabernacle in New York was "packed" with three thousand people during the first session of the 1853 national convention. See ibid., 1:548.

12. Ibid., 1:91–92.

13. Davis to Stanton, December 12 [1851], Elizabeth Cady Stanton Papers, Theodore Stanton Collection, Mable Smith Douglass Library, Rutgers University, New Brunswick, N.J., in *Papers*, ed. Holland and Gordon, reel 7, frames 133 and 134.

14. Carol Lasser and Marlene Deahl Merrill, *Friends and Sisters: Letters between Lucy Stone and Antoinette Brown Blackwell, 1846–93* (Urbana: University of Illinois Press, 1987), 114–15.

15. *Proceedings of the Woman's Rights Convention Held at Syracuse, September 8th, 9th, and 10th, 1852* (Syracuse: J. E. Masters, 1852), 78–85; see also Angelina Grimké Weld, *Letter from Angelina Grimké Weld, To the Woman's Rights Convention Held at Syracuse, September, 1852* (Syracuse: Malcolm Block, n.d.).

16. *Proceedings . . . Syracuse . . . 1852*, 85–88.

17. Harriot K. Hunt quoted in *The Liberator*, XXII (October 8, 1852), p. 164.

18. Ernestine Rose quoted in ibid.

19. Lucy Stone quoted in ibid.

20. See, for example, Elizabeth Oakes Smith quoted in ibid.

21. *Proceedings . . . Syracuse . . . 1852*, 85–88. For another description of the debate over whether or not to organize, see Stanton, Anthony, and Gage, eds., 1:540–42.

22. Stanton, Anthony, and Gage, eds., 1:476, 484–86.

23. Ibid., 1:152–58, 161.

24. Elizabeth Oakes Smith in *The Liberator*, XXII (October 8, 1852), p. 164.

25. This would continue to be true for those women who attempted to step outside the bounds that traditionally had confined women to the home. For a discussion of the attention that early female doctors, students, and social workers paid to their clothes and public appearance, see Regina Markell Morantz-Sanchez, *Sympathy and Science: Women Physicians in American Medicine* (New York: Oxford University Press, 1985), 120–21; Rosalind Rosenberg, *Beyond Separate Spheres: Intellectual Roots of Modern Feminism* (New Haven: Yale University Press, 1982), 189; Linda Gordon, *Heroes of Their Own Lives: The Politics and History of Family Violence, Boston: 1880–1960* (New York: Viking Press, 1988), 66–67.

26. For an excellent summary of the kinds of messages that can be communicated by clothes, see Patricia C. Cunningham and Susan Vaso Lab, "Understanding Dress and Popular Culture," in *Dress and Popular Culture* (Bowling Green, Ohio: Bowling Green State Popular Press, 1991), 5–18.

27. Lucretia Mott to Stanton, October 3, 1848, Stanton Papers, Library of Congress, in *Papers*, ed. Holland and Gordon, reel 6, frame 822.

28. Griffith, 71; *The Lily*, III (July 1851), p. 53 (September 1851), p. 69, IV (January 1852), p. 1.

29. Stanton to Elizabeth Smith Miller, June 4, 1851, in *Elizabeth Cady Stanton as Revealed in Her Letters, Diary, and Reminiscences*, ed. Theodore Stanton and Harriot Stanton Blatch, 2 vols. (New York: Harper, 1922), 2:31; Davis to Stanton, September 1, 1852, Stanton Papers, Library of Congress, in *Papers*, ed. Holland and Gordon, reel 7, frame 320.

30. *Pittsburgh Saturday Visiter*, September 20, 1851, p. 138. Swisshelm was selective in her support of the various demands of the woman's rights movement. She considered dress reform a distraction from more important issues.

31. *New York Daily Times*, February 8, 1853, p. 8.

32. Philadelphia *Evening Bulletin*, October 18, 1854, in *Papers*, ed. Holland and Gordon, reel 8, frame 68.

33. Susan B. Anthony to Lucy Stone, May 25, 1852 [1853], Blackwell Family Papers, Schlesinger Library, Radcliffe College, Cambridge, Mass., in *Papers*, ed. Holland and Gordon, reel 7, frames 710 and 711; Stanton to Elizabeth Smith Miller, June 30, 1853, Elizabeth Cady Stanton Papers, Theodore Stanton Collection, in ibid., reel 7, frame 769.

34. Elizabeth Cady Stanton to Henry Stanton, April 11, 1851, in Stanton and Blatch, eds., 2:27.

35. Ida Husted Harper, *The Life and Work of Susan B. Anthony*, 3 vols. (Indianapolis: Hollenbeck Press, 1898 and 1908), 1:72; see also *Proceedings . . . Syracuse . . . 1852*.

36. Elizabeth Cady Stanton to Anthony, March 1, [1853], Stanton Papers, Library of Congress, in *Papers*, ed. Holland and Gordon, reel 7, frame 571.

37. Davis to Elizabeth Cady Stanton, [July] 20, [1852], ibid., reel 7, frame 309.

38. Elizabeth Cady Stanton to Miller, June 4, 1851, in Stanton and Blatch, eds., 2:28–31.

39. Stone to Anthony, February 13, 1854, Blackwell Family Papers, Library of Congress in *Papers*, ed. Holland and Gordon, reel 7, frames 962 and 963.

40. Anthony to Stone, February 9, 1854, ibid., reel 7, frames 960 and 961.

41. Stone to Anthony, February 13, 1854, ibid., reel 7, frame 962; Elizabeth Cady Stanton to Anthony, February 19, 1854, Stanton Papers, Library of Congress, in ibid., reel 7, frame 998.

42. Anthony to Gerrit Smith, December 25, 1855, Gerrit Smith Papers, Special Collections Department, Syracuse University Library, Syracuse, New York, in ibid., reel 8, frame 335.

43. Smith to Elizabeth Cady Stanton, December 1, 1855, in Stanton, Anthony, and Gage, eds., 1: 836–39.

44. Ibid., 1:842; "Gerrit Smith on Woman's Rights," *The Sibyl*, I (August 15, 1856), pp. 26–27 and (September 1, 1856), pp. 38–39; Broadside in Gerrit Smith Papers, *Papers*, ed. Holland and Gordon, reel 8, frames 323–26.

45. Elizabeth Cady Stanton to Martha Coffin Pelham Wright [December 17, 1855], Garrison Family Papers, Sophia Smith Collection, Smith College, Northampton, Mass., in *Papers*, ed. Holland and Gordon, reel 8, frame 327; Elizabeth Cady Stanton to Smith, December 21, 1855, in Stanton, Anthony, and Gage, eds., 1:839–42; Anthony to Smith, December 25, 1855, Gerrit Smith Papers, in *Papers*, ed. Holland and Gordon,

reel 8, frame 334; "Woman's Rights," *The Lily,* VIII (February 15, 1856), 31–32; Broadside, "A Letter from Mrs. Stanton to Gerrit Smith," 1855, in Susan B. Anthony Scrapbook 1, Susan B. Anthony Papers, Rare Books Division, Library of Congress, Washington, D.C., in *Papers,* ed. Holland and Gordon, reel 8, frames 330–331.

46. Smith to Elizabeth Cady Stanton, December 19, 1855, Stanton Scrapbook 1, Elizabeth Cady Stanton Papers, Special Collections, Vassar College Library, Poughkeepsie, New York, in *Papers,* ed. Holland and Gordon, reel 8, frames 328 and 329.

47. Stanton, Anthony, and Gage, eds., 1:842–44.

48. "Letter from Sarah M. Grimké to Her Friend Gerrit Smith," in *The Lily,* VIII (October 1, 1856), pp. 130–31.

49. See, for example, *Harper's Weekly Magazine,* I (October 10, 1857), p. 656 and II (August 14, 1858), p. 528; *Frank Leslie's Illustrated Newspaper,* IV (October 31, 1857), p. 352 and VII (August 6, 1859), p. 158; Leach, 244; for a discussion of Bloomer caricature, see Gary L. Bunker, "Antebellum Caricature and Woman's Sphere," *Journal of Women's History* 3 (Winter 1992), 23–29.

50. *New York Daily Herald,* May 13, 1859, p. 4; for a discussion of dress reform after the Civil War, see Robert E. Riegel, "Women's Clothes and Women's Rights," *American Quarterly* 15 (Fall 1963), 395–401.

51. Joan Wallach Scott, "French Feminists Claim the Rights of 'Man:' Olympe de Gouges in the French Revolution," Lecture delivered on April 2, 1991, Washington University, St. Louis, Missouri.

52. Smith to Elizabeth Cady Stanton, December 1, 1855, in Stanton, Anthony and Gage, eds., 1:837.

2. The Ideology

1. Elizabeth Cady Stanton, Susan B. Anthony, and Matilda Joslyn Gage, eds., *History of Woman Suffrage,* 2 vols. (New York: Fowler and Wells, 1881), 1:51.

2. References to these sources appear in Ellen Carol DuBois, *Feminism and Suffrage: The Emergence of an Independent Women's Movement in America, 1848–1869* (Ithaca: Cornell University Press, 1978), 31–47; Robert E. Riegel, *American Feminists* (Lawrence: University of Kansas Press, 1963), preface; Blanche Glassman Hersh, *The Slavery of Sex: Feminist-Abolitionists in America* (Urbana: University of Illinois Press, 1978), 41, 191, 193; Olive Banks, *Faces of Feminism: A Study of Feminism as a Social Movement* (New York: St. Martin's Press, 1981), 7–8; James L. Cooper and Sheila McIsaac Cooper, *The Roots of American Feminist Thought* (Boston: Allyn and Bacon, 1973), 6–7; Nancy Cott, *The Grounding of Modern Feminism* (New Haven: Yale University Press, 1987), 16–17; Josephine Donovan, *Feminist Theory: The Intellectual Traditions of American Feminism* (New York: Frederick Ungar, 1985), 1–63; Susan P. Conrad, *Perish the Thought: Intellectual Women in Romantic America, 1830–1860* (New York: Oxford University Press, 1976), 141–57; Elisabeth Griffith, *In Her Own Right: The Life of Elizabeth Cady Stanton* (New York: Oxford University Press, 1984), 54; Linda Kerber, *Women of the Republic: Intellect and Ideology in Revolutionary America* (Chapel Hill: University of North Carolina Press, 1980), 15–32; Jane Rendall, *The Origins of Modern Feminism: Women in Britain, France, and the United States, 1780–1860* (London: Macmillan, 1985), 7–107.

3. Kerber, 269–88. See also Mary Beth Norton, *Liberty's Daughters: The Revolutionary Experience of American Women, 1750–1800* (Boston: Little, Brown, 1980), 228–99; Jan Lewis, "The Republican Wife," *William and Mary Quarterly* 44 (October 1987), 689–721; Lester H. Cohen, "Mercy Otis Warren: The Politics of Language and the Aesthetics of Self," *American Quarterly* 35 (Winter 1983), 481–

98; Linda Kerber, "The Republican Ideology of the Revolutionary Generation," *American Quarterly* 37 (Fall 1985), 485, 488.

4. Barbara Welter, "The Cult of True Womanhood, 1820–1860," *American Quarterly* 18 (Summer 1966), 151–74; Nancy F. Cott, *The Bonds of Womanhood: "Woman's Sphere" in New England, 1780–1835* (New Haven: Yale University Press, 1977); Carroll Smith- Rosenberg, "The Female World of Love and Ritual: Relations between Women in Nineteenth-Century America," *Signs* 1 (Autumn 1975), 1–29; Kathryn Kish Sklar, *Catharine Beecher: A Study in American Domesticity* (New Haven: Yale University Press, 1973). For a reassessment of the idea of "woman's sphere" informed by the most recent literature, see Linda K. Kerber, "Separate Spheres, Female Worlds, Woman's Place: The Rhetoric of Women's History," *Journal of American History* 75 (June 1988), 9–39.

5. Lori D. Ginzberg, *Women and the Work of Benevolence: Morality, Politics, and Class in the Nineteenth-Century United States* (New Haven: Yale University Press, 1990); Barbara Leslie Epstein, *The Politics of Domesticity: Women, Evangelism, and Temperance in Nineteenth-Century America* (Middletown, Conn.: Wesleyan University Press, 1981); Mary P. Ryan, *Cradle of the Middle Class: The Family in Oneida County, New York, 1790–1865* (New York: Cambridge University Press, 1981); Nancy A. Hewitt, *Women's Activism and Social Change: Rochester, New York, 1822–1872* (Ithaca: Cornell University Press, 1984).

6. Griffith, 8; Alma Lutz, *Created Equal: A Biography of Elizabeth Cady Stanton, 1815–1902* (New York: John Day, 1940), 7–8; Lois Banner, *Elizabeth Cady Stanton: A Radical for Woman's Rights* (Boston: Little, Brown, 1980), 6.

7. Elizabeth Cady Stanton, *Eighty Years and More (1815–1897): Reminiscences of Elizabeth Cady Stanton* (New York: European Publishing Co., 1898), 46.

8. Theodore Stanton and Harriot Stanton Blatch, eds., *Elizabeth Cady Stanton as Revealed in Her Letters, Diary, and Reminiscences*, 2 vols. (New York: Harper, 1922), 1:52.

9. Ibid., 1:38.

10. Stanton, 43–44; Stanton and Blatch, eds., 1:51; Griffith, 19–23; Banner, 13–14.

11. Griffith, 24–32; Ellen DuBois, "The Limitations of Sisterhood: Elizabeth Cady Stanton and Division in the American Suffrage Movement, 1875–1902," in *Women and the Structure of Society: Selected Research From the Fifth Berkshire Conference on the History of Women*, ed. Barbara J. Harris and JoAnn K. McNamara (Durham: Duke University Press, 1984), 161; see also Lutz, 30.

12. Griffith, 39.

13. Stanton recalled hearing the Declaration of Independence read on such occasions. See Stanton, 18; Philip F. Detweiler, "The Changing Reputation of the Declaration of Independence: The First Fifty Years," *William and Mary Quarterly* 19 (October 1962), 566; Peter Simon Newman, "American Popular Political Culture in the Age of the French Revolution" (Ph.D. diss., Princeton University, 1991), 122–83.

14. Horace Greeley, "The Rights of Woman," *Pittsburgh Saturday Visiter*, May 11, 1850, p. 66.

15. Antoinette Brown, *Albany Evening Journal*, February 15, 1854, p. 2.

16. Woman's Rights Resolution reported in *The Sibyl*, IV (May 15, 1860), p. 758; for similar statements, see William H. Channing, *Frederick Douglass's Paper*, December 23, 1853, p. 2; Resolution of the Syracuse Woman's Rights Convention, *National Anti-Slavery Standard*, XIII (September 16, 1852), p. 68.

17. *New York Daily Times*, August 2, 1852, p. 2.

18. Stanton, Anthony, and Gage, eds., 1:705.

19. Lucy Stone in *Proceedings of the Woman's Rights Convention, Held at the Broadway Tabernacle in the City of New York, Tuesday and Wednesday, September*

6 & 7, *1853* (New York: Fowler and Wells, 1853), 34–35. Wendell Phillips also advocated this strategy. See Wendell Phillips, "Freedom for Women," *Series of Woman's Rights Tracts* (Rochester: Curtis, Butts, and Co., n.d.), 13. "I say, take your rights."

20. Paulina Wright Davis quoted in the *New York Daily Tribune*, October 28, 1850, p. 6.

21. Antoinette Brown in *Proceedings . . . New York . . . 1853*, 40.

22. Stanton, Anthony, and Gage, eds., 1:680.

23. Clarina I. H. Nichols, "The Responsibilities of Woman," *Series of Woman's Rights Tracts*, 11.

24. John Locke, *Second Treatise of Government*, ed. C. B. Macpherson (Indianapolis: Hackett Publishing Co., 1980), 8, 30, 43.

25. Carole Pateman, *The Sexual Contract* (Stanford: Stanford University Press, 1988).

26. "The Declaration of Independence as Adopted by Congress," *The Papers of Thomas Jefferson Vol. I: 1760–1776*, ed. Julian P. Boyd (Princeton: Princeton University Press, 1950), 429; for a discussion of the Lockean origins of the Declaration of Independence, see Carl Becker, *The Declaration of Independence: A Study in the History of Political Ideas* (New York: Vintage, 1942); for a discussion of the Scottish moral sense origins of the document, see Garry Wills, *Inventing America: Jefferson's Declaration of Independence* (New York: Vintage, 1979); for a critique and refutation of Wills's interpretation, see Ronald Hamowy, "Jefferson and the Scottish Enlightenment: A Critique of Garry Wills's *Inventing America: Jefferson's Declaration of Independence*," *William and Mary Quarterly* 36 (October 1979), 503–23.

27. James Otis, *The Rights of the British Colonies Asserted and Proved* (Boston, 1764), in *Pamphlets of the American Revolution, 1750–1776*, ed. Bernard Bailyn, 4 vols. (Cambridge: Harvard University Press, 1965), 1:420, 421–22.

28. Abigail Adams to John Adams, March 31, 1776 and John Adams to Abigail Adams, April 14, 1776, *Adams Family Correspondence*, ed. H. L. Butterfield, 4 vols. (Cambridge: Harvard University Press, 1963–73), 1:370, 382.

29. John Adams to James Sullivan, May 26, 1776, *The Works of John Adams*, ed. Charles Francis Adams, 10 vols. (Boston: Little, Brown, 1850–56), 9:375–76.

30. Richard Henry Lee to Mrs. Hannah Corbin, March 17, 1778, *The Letters of Richard Henry Lee*, ed. James C. Ballagh, 2 vols. (New York: Macmillan, 1911–14), 1:392.

31. Judith Apter Klinghoffer and Lois Elkis, "'The Petticoat Electors': Women's Suffrage in New Jersey," *Journal of the Early Republic* 12 (Summer 1992), 159–93; Edward Raymond Turner, "Women's Suffrage in New Jersey: 1790–1807," *Smith College Studies in History* 1 (July 1916), 165–87; William A. Whitehead, "The Origin, Practice, and Prohibition of Female Suffrage in New Jersey," in Stanton, Anthony, and Gage, eds., 1:447–51; Gregory Evans Dowd, "Declarations of Dependence: War and Inequality in Revolutionary New Jersey, 1776–1815," *New Jersey History* 103 (1985), 53–58.

32. For other discussions of the implications of Locke's ideas and political philosophy for women, see Melissa A. Butler, "Early Liberal Roots of Feminism: John Locke and the Attack on Patriarchy," *American Political Science Review* 72 (March 1978), 135–50; Lorenne M. G. Clark, "Women and Locke: Who Owns the Apples in the Garden of Eden?" in *The Sexism of Social and Political Theory: Women and Reproduction from Plato to Nietzsche*, ed. Lorenne M. G. Clark and Lydia Lange (Toronto: University of Toronto Press, 1979), 16–40; Sheryl O'Donnell, "Mr. Locke and the Ladies: The Indelible Words on the *Tabula Rasa*," *Studies in*

Eighteenth-Century Culture 8 (1979), 151–64; Teresa Brennan and Carole Pateman, "'Mere Auxiliaries to the Commonwealth': Women and the Origins of Liberalism," *Political Studies* 27 (June 1979), 191–95.

33. Karlyn Kohrs Campbell, *Man Cannot Speak for Her: A Critical Study of Early Feminist Rhetoric*, 2 vols. (New York: Greenwood, 1989), 1:52.

34. See Declaration of Sentiments in Stanton, Anthony, Gage, eds., 1:70.

35. Elizabeth Cady Stanton, "Address to the New York State Legislature," in ibid., 1:679.

36. Lester H. Cohen, "The American Revolution and Natural Law Theory," *Journal of the History of Ideas* 39 (July–September 1978), 491–502.

37. There is an extensive literature on the ideological causes for the American Revolution. See, for example, Bernard Bailyn, *The Ideological Origins of the American Revolution* (Cambridge: Harvard University Press, 1967); Pauline Maier, *From Resistance to Revolution: Colonial Radicals and the Development of American Opposition to Britain, 1765–1776* (New York: Alfred A. Knopf, 1972), 27–48.

38. Declaration of Sentiments in Stanton, Anthony, and Gage, eds., 1:70.

39. Gerrit Smith to Elizabeth Cady Stanton, December 1, 1855, in Stanton, Anthony, and Gage, eds., 1:836. See also Harriet Taylor Mill, "The Enfranchisement of Women," *Series of Woman's Rights Tracts*, 6. "Women have never had equal rights with men. The claim in their behalf, of the common rights of mankind, is looked upon as barred by universal practice."

40. Susan B. Anthony, "The True Woman," 1859, Susan Brownell Anthony Papers, Schlesinger Library, Radcliffe College, Cambridge, Mass., in *The Papers of Elizabeth Cady Stanton and Susan B. Anthony*, ed. Patricia G. Holland and Ann D. Gordon (Wilmington, Del.: Scholarly Resources, 1991, microfilm, series 3), reel 9, frames 441 and 442.

41. For examples of speeches citing their achievements, see Rebecca Sanford in *Proceedings of the Woman's Rights Convention, Held at the Unitarian Church, Rochester, N.Y., August 2, 1848* (New York: Robert J. Johnston, 1870), 6; H. H. Van Amringe in *Proceedings of the Woman's Rights Convention, Held at Worcester, October 23 & 24, 1850* (Boston: Prentiss and Sawyer, 1851), 39; Ernestine Rose in *Proceedings of the Woman's Rights Convention, Held at Worcester, October 15th & 16th, 1851* (New York: Fowler and Wells, 1852), 44; B. Rush Plumbly in *Proceedings of the Woman's Rights Convention Held at West Chester, Pa. June 2d and 3d, 1852* (Philadelphia: Merrihew & Thompson, 1852), 35; Ernestine Rose, *Speech of Mrs. E. L. Rose, At the Woman's Rights Convention, Held at Syracuse, September 1852* (Syracuse: Malcolm Block, n.d.), 2–3; Lydia Jenkins in *Proceedings of the National Women's Rights Convention, Held at Cleveland, Ohio, on Wednesday, Thursday, and Friday, October 5th, 6th, and 7th, 1853* (Cleveland: Gray, Beardsley, Spear, & Co., 1854), 13; Henry Blackwell in ibid., 46–48; Wendell Phillips in *Proceedings of the Ninth Woman's Rights Convention Held in New York City, Thursday, May 12, 1859* (Rochester: A. Strong, 1859), 12. The quotation is from Rose in *Proceedings . . . Worcester . . . 1851*, 44.

42. Clarina I. H. Nichols in *Proceedings . . . Worcester . . . 1851*, 70, 71–72; Antoinette Brown in *Proceedings . . . New York . . . 1853*, 94–95; Frances Gage in *Proceedings . . . Cleveland . . . 1853*, 105. For other examples, see H. H. Van Amringe in *Proceedings . . . Worcester . . . 1850*, 41; Matilda Gage, *Speech of Mrs. M. E. J. Gage, at the Woman's Rights Convention, Held at Syracuse, September 1852* (Syracuse: Malcolm Block, n.d.), 6–7; E. D. Culver in *Proceedings of the Tenth National Woman's Rights Convention, Held at the Cooper Institute, New York City, May 10th and 11th, 1860* (Boston: Yerrinton & Garrison, 1860), 55–56.

43. John Robertson, "The Scottish Enlightenment at the Limits of the Civic

Tradition," in *Wealth and Virtue: The Shaping of Political Economy in the Scottish Enlightenment*, ed. Istvan Hont and Michael Ignatieff (Cambridge: Cambridge University Press, 1983), 137–78.

44. Ibid., 151.

45. This was particularly true of John Millar. See William C. Lehmann, *John Millar of Glasgow, 1735–1801: His Life and Thought and His Contributions to Sociological Analysis* (Cambridge: Cambridge University Press, 1960), 142. See also Rendall, 23–28.

46. See, for example, Rosemarie Zagarri, "Morals, Manners, and the Republican Mother," *American Quarterly* 44 (June 1992), 192–215.

47. Charles Camic, *Experience and Enlightenment: Socialization for Cultural Change in Eighteenth-Century Scotland* (Chicago: University of Chicago Press, 1983), 56, 66–67; John Dwyer, *Virtuous Discourse: Sensibility and Community in Late Eighteenth-Century Scotland* (Edinburgh: John Donald, 1987), 53–54.

48. Genevieve Lloyd, *The Man of Reason: "Male" and "Female" in Western Philosophy* (Minneapolis: University of Minnesota Press, 1984); quotation on page 104.

49. Arthur M. Wilson, "'Treated Like Imbecile Children' (Diderot): The Enlightenment and the Status of Women," in *Women in the Eighteenth Century and Other Essays*, ed. Paul Fritz and Richard Morton (Toronto: Samuel Stevens Hakkert, 1976), 100–101; Blandine L. McLaughlin, "Diderot and Women," in *French Women and the Age of Enlightenment*, ed. Samia I. Spencer (Bloomington: Indiana University Press, 1984), 299; Elizabeth J. Gardner, "The *Philosophes* and Women: Sensationalism and Sentiment" in *Women and Society in Eighteenth Century France*, ed. Eva Jacobs (London: Athlone Press, 1979), 23.

50. Dwyer, 52–65.

51. Ruth H. Bloch, "The Gendered Meanings of Virtue in Revolutionary America," *Signs* 13 (Autumn 1987), 49–53, quotation on page 57.

52. Leslie Stephen and Sidney Lee, eds. *Dictionary of National Biography*, 22 vols. (London: Oxford University Press, 1949–1950), 15:101–103.

53. D. H. Meyer, *The Instructed Conscience: The Shaping of the American National Ethic* (Philadelphia: University of Pennsylvania Press, 1972), 7; Wendell Glick, "Bishop Paley in America," *New England Quarterly* 27 (September 1954), 347–49.

54. Julia Ward Howe, *Reminiscences, 1819–1899* (Boston: Houghton, Mifflin, 1899), 13; Carol Lasser and Marlene Deahl Merrill, *Friends and Sisters: Letters between Lucy Stone and Antoinette Brown Blackwell, 1846–93* (Urbana: University of Illinois Press, 1987), 17.

55. William Paley, *The Principles of Moral and Political Philosophy* (Boston: Joshua Belcher, 1811), 51, 70, 62.

56. Ibid., 339, 80.

57. Ibid., 206–207.

58. Ibid., 234–35.

59. Ibid., 36.

60. Stephen and Lee, eds., 18:1169–73.

61. Meyer, 37–39.

62. Terence Martin, *The Instructed Vision: Scottish Common Sense Philosophy and the Origins of American Fiction* (Bloomington: Indiana University Press, 1961), vii–viii; Douglas Sloan, *The Scottish Enlightenment and the American College Ideal* (New York: Teachers College Press, 1971), 241; S. A. Grave, *The Scottish Philosophy of Common Sense* (Oxford: Clarenden Press, 1960), 4.

63. Benjamin Wisner, ed., *Memoirs of the Late Mrs. Susan Huntington, of Boston Massachusetts* (York, Eng.: W. Alexander and Son, 1828), 106.

64. Martin, 4; see also Meyer, 42; Sidney E. Ahlstrom, "The Scottish Philosophers and American Theology," *Church History* 24 (September 1955), 268.

65. Dugald Stewart, *General View of the Progress of Metaphysical, Ethical, and Political Philosophy Since the Revival of Letters in Europe* (Boston: Wells and Lilly, 1822), 309–12.

66. Dugald Stewart, *Outlines of Moral Philosophy* (Edinburgh: Cadell and Co., 1829), 246, 114–15, quotation on page 273.

67. Mary Wollstonecraft, *A Vindication of the Rights of Woman* (New York: Norton, 1967), 218.

68. R. M. Janes, "On the Reception of Mary Wollstonecraft's *A Vindication of the Rights of Woman*," *Journal of the History of Ideas* 39 (April–June 1978), 293–302. For Silliman's comments, see Benjamin Silliman, *Letters of Shahcoolen* (Boston: Russell and Cutler, 1802), 21–63.

69. [Jane Haldimand Marcet], *Conversations on Political Economy; In Which the Elements of That Science Are Familiarly Explained* (Philadelphia: Moses Thomas, 1817).

70. Harriet Martineau, *Illustrations of Political Economy*, 9 vols. (London: Charles Fox, 1832–34).

71. See *National Union Catalog*, 685 vols. (London: Mansell Publishing, 1968–80), 360:613–14 for a listing of editions for Marcet and ibid., 365:128–29 for those for Martineau. In their history of the suffrage movement, Stanton, Anthony, and Gage credited Marcet and Martineau with making the subject of political economy comprehensible to ordinary people. See Stanton, Anthony, and Gage, eds., 1:34.

72. Stanton also gave George Combe and Spurzheim credit for popularizing the importance of "feelings, sentiments and affections." See Stanton, Anthony and Gage, eds., 1:51.

73. Bloch, 56.

74. For other discussions of Scottish Enlightenment philosophy and women, see Jane Rendall, "Virtue and Commerce: Women in the Making of Adam Smith's Political Economy," in *Women in Western Political Philosophy: Kant to Nietzsche*, ed. Ellen Kennedy and Susan Mendus (Brighton: Wheatsheaf Books, 1987), 44–77; Louise Marcil Lacoste, "The Consistency of Hume's Position Concerning Women," *Dialogue* 15 (September 1976), 425–40; Carol Kay, "Sympathy, Sex, and Authority in Richardson and Hume," *Studies in Eighteenth-Century Culture* 12 (1983), 77–92; Steven Burns, "The Humean Female," *Dialogue* 15 (September 1976), 415–24.

75. Declaration of Sentiments in Stanton, Anthony, and Gage, eds., 1:72.

76. Lucretia Mott to Elizabeth Cady Stanton, March 16, 1855, Box 54, Folder 1563, William Lloyd Garrison Papers, Sophia Smith Collection, Smith College, Northampton, Massachusetts.

77. Elizabeth Cady Stanton letter in *Proceedings . . . Worcester . . . 1850*, 53.

78. Declaration of Sentiments in Stanton, Anthony, and Gage, eds., 1:72.

79. Elizabeth Cady Stanton in *Report of the Woman's Rights Convention Held at Seneca Falls, N.Y., July 19th and 20th, 1848* (Rochester: J. Dick, 1848), 16.

80. Abby H. Price in *Proceedings . . . Worcester . . . 1850*, 21.

81. Antoinette Brown Blackwell in *Proceedings . . . New York City . . . 1860*, 74–75; see also Emma Willard, *Letter to Dupont De L'Eure on the Political Position of Women* (Albany: Joel Munsell, 1848), 7.

82. Theodore Parker, "A Sermon of the Public Function of Woman, Preached at the Music Hall, Boston, March 27, 1853," *Series of Woman's Rights Tracts*, 12.

83. Paulina Wright Davis in *Proceedings . . . Worcester . . . 1850*, 7, 13.

84. Ernestine Rose, *Speech*, 2–3, 4.

85. Elizabeth Cady Stanton in *Proceedings . . . New York City . . . 1860*, 67.

86. Lucy Stone in *Proceedings . . . New York . . . 1853*, 18; see also Theodore Parker sermon, March, 1853, in Stanton, Anthony, and Gage, eds., 1:277.

87. For discussions of that law, see Norma Basch, *In the Eyes of the Law: Women, Marriage, and Property in Nineteenth-Century New York* (Ithaca: Cornell University Press, 1982) and Peggy A. Rabkin, *Fathers to Daughters: The Legal Foundations of Female Emancipation* (Westport, Conn.: Greenwood, 1980).

3. The Language

1. George Lakoff and Mark Johnson have argued that the use of metaphor is fundamental to both everyday thought and behavior. See George Lakoff and Mark Johnson, *Metaphors We Live By* (Chicago: University of Chicago Press, 1980); George Lakoff and Mark Johnson, "Conceptual Metaphor in Everyday Language," *Journal of Philosophy* 77 (August 1980), 453–86.

2. Lucretia Mott, *New York Daily Herald*, September 7, 1853, p. 1.

3. Helen Hazelwood, "Woman," *The Lily*, VI (October 16, 1854), 147.

4. Ernestine Rose in *Proceedings of the Woman's Rights Convention Held at Syracuse, September 8th, 9th, and 10th, 1852* (Syracuse: J. E. Masters, 1852), 64.

5. Quoted in Carole Pateman, *The Sexual Contract* (Stanford: Stanford University Press, 1988), 90, 120.

6. Mary Wollstonecraft, *A Vindication of the Rights of Woman* (New York: Norton, 1967), passim.

7. For a discussion of the influence of abolitionism and its language on woman's rights advocates, see Jean Fagan Yellin, *Women and Sisters: The Antislavery Feminists in American Culture* (New Haven: Yale University Press, 1989), 3–52; see also Blanche Glassman Hersh, *The Slavery of Sex: Feminist-Abolitionists in America* (Urbana: University of Illinois Press, 1978), 189–200, and Ellen Carol DuBois, *Feminism and Suffrage: The Emergence of an Independent Women's Movement in America, 1848–1869* (Ithaca: Cornell University Press, 1978), 31–39.

8. Lucretia Mott in *Proceedings of the Woman's Rights Convention Held at the Broadway Tabernacle in the City of New York, Tuesday and Wednesday, September 6 & 7, 1853* (New York: Fowler and Wells, 1853), 5.

9. See, for example, speeches such as "Discourse on Women," "The Argument that Women Do Not Want to Vote," "Luther's Will," "The Laws in Relation to Women," in *Lucretia Mott: Her Complete Speeches and Sermons*, ed. Dana Greene (New York: Edwin Mellen Press, 1980).

10. Paulina Wright Davis in *Proceedings . . . New York . . . 1853*, 30.

11. Elizabeth Cady Stanton, Susan B. Anthony, and Matilda Joslyn Gage, eds., *History of Woman Suffrage*, 2 vols. (New York: Fowler and Wells, 1881), 1:104–105.

12. Emma Willard, "Letter to DuPont De L'eure on the Political Position of Women," *American Literary Magazine* 2 (April 1848), 250.

13. Lydia Jane Pierson in *Proceedings of the Woman's Rights Convention Held at Akron, Ohio, May 28 and 29, 1851* (Cincinnati: Ben Franklin, 1851), 37.

14. Abby Price in *Proceedings of the Woman's Rights Convention, Held at Worcester, October 23 & 24, 1850* (Boston: Prentiss & Sawyer, 1851), 33.

15. Paulina Wright Davis in *Proceedings of the Woman's Rights Convention, Held at Worcester, October 15th & 16th, 1851* (New York: Fowler and Wells, 1852), 7.

16. Ernestine Rose in *Proceedings of the Seventh National Woman's Rights Convention Held in New York City, November 25 and 26, 1856* (New York: n.p., 1856), 77.

17. Elizabeth Oakes Smith, *New York Daily Herald*, September 10, 1852, p. 8; see also *Proceedings . . . Syracuse . . . 1852*, 19.

18. Mrs. Birdsall speech quoted in "Presentation of the Woman's Rights Petition," *The Sibyl*, III (March 18, 1859), 523.

19. Lucy Stone, *New York Daily Herald*, September 14, 1852, p. 3.

20. Elizabeth Cady Stanton in *Proceedings of the Tenth National Woman's Rights Convention, Held at the Cooper Institute, New York City, May 10th and 11th, 1860* (Boston: Yerrinton and Garrison, 1860), 46; Ernestine Rose in ibid., 54.

21. Lucretia Mott in *Proceedings of the National Women's Rights Convention Held at Cleveland, Ohio, on Wednesday, Thursday, and Friday, October 5th, 6th, and 7th, 1853* (Cleveland: Gray, Beardsley, Spear and Co., 1854), 60–62.

22. Abby H. Price in *Proceedings . . . Worcester . . . 1850*, 35.

23. Mrs. E. Robinson, "Report on Education," in *Proceedings . . . Akron . . . 1851*, p. 25; see also Samuel Longfellow in Stanton, Anthony, and Gage, eds., 1:715–16.

24. See Elizabeth Oakes Smith, *New York Daily Herald*, September 10, 1852, p. 8; see also *Proceedings . . . Syracuse . . . 1852*, 18–19.

25. H. H. Van Amringe in *Proceedings . . . Worcester . . . 1850*, 44.

26. Willard, "Letter," 247.

27. Paulina Wright Davis, *New York Daily Tribune*, October 20, 1851, p. 7; see also Paulina Wright Davis, "On the Education of Females," *Woman's Rights Tracts* (Syracuse: N. M. P. Lathrop, 1853), p. 4.

28. Paula Baker, "The Domestication of Politics: Women and American Political Society, 1780–1920," *American Historical Review* 89 (June 1984), 628.

29. William Leach, *True Love and Perfect Union: The Feminist Reform of Sex and Society* (Middletown, Conn.: Wesleyan University Press, 1989), 14.

30. Nancy Baird in *Proceedings . . . Worcester . . . 1850*, 68.

31. Elizabeth Cady Stanton and Elizabeth Wilson McClintock to the Editors, Seneca County *Semi-Weekly Courier*, n.d. [September 1848], Elizabeth Cady Stanton Papers, Library of Congress, Washington, D.C. in *The Papers of Elizabeth Cady Stanton and Susan B. Anthony*, ed. Patricia G. Holland and Ann D. Gordon (Wilmington, Del.: Scholarly Resources, 1991, microfilm, series 3), reel 6, frame 779; Wendell Phillips in *Proceedings . . . Worcester . . . 1851*, 58.

32. Elizabeth Cady Stanton, *Address of Mrs. Elizabeth Cady Stanton, Delivered at Seneca Falls & Rochester, N.Y. July 19th and August 2d, 1848* (New York: Robert J. Johnston, 1870), 19.

33. Lucretia Mott to Mary Anne W. Johnson of Salem, Ohio, president *pro tem* of the Salem Woman's Rights Convention, April 19, 1850, in *The Liberator*, XX (May 17, 1850), 80.

34. Ernestine Rose, *An Address on Woman's Rights, Delivered Before the People's Sunday Meeting, in Cochituate Hall, on Sunday Afternoon, October 19th, 1851* (Boston: J. P. Mendum, 1851), 19.

35. Lucy Stone, *New York Daily Tribune*, September 8, 1853, p. 6.

36. Elizabeth Oakes Smith to Elizabeth Cady Stanton, March 2, 1852, Stanton Papers, Library of Congress, in *Papers*, ed. Holland and Gordon, reel 7, frame 173.

37. *Boston Weekly Telegraph*, n.d. [September 19–20, 1855], C. H. Dall Collection, Massachusetts Historical Society, Boston, Mass., in ibid., reel 8, frame 283.

38. Elizabeth Cady Stanton to Mary Anne W. Johnson, *The Liberator*, XX (May 17, 1850), 80.

39. Rev. A. D. Mayo letter, *New York Daily Herald*, September 12, 1852, p. 1.

40. Paulina Wright Davis in *Proceedings . . . New York . . . 1853*, 30.

41. *Pittsburgh Saturday Visiter*, September 20, 1851, p. 138.

42. Abby Price, *New York Daily Tribune*, October 17, 1851, p. 8.

43. [Lydia] Jenkins, *New York Daily Herald*, September 7, 1853, p. 2.

44. A. D. Mayo in *Proceedings . . . Syracuse . . . 1852*, 48.

45. Elizabeth Wilson to the Worcester convention, *The Liberator,* XX (November 15, 1850), 181.

46. "Woman's Rights," *The Lily,* II (March 1850), 22.

47. Senex, "Equality of Rights to Woman," *The Lily,* III (October 1851), 76.

48. Paulina Wright Davis, *New York Daily Tribune,* October 17, 1851, p. 7.

49. Matilda Gage, *Speech of Mrs. M. E. J. Gage, at the Woman's Rights Convention, Held at Syracuse, September 1852* (Syracuse, Malcolm Block, n.d. [1852]), 8.

50. Elizabeth Oakes Smith, *New York Daily Tribune,* September 9, 1852, p. 5; see also *Proceedings . . . Syracuse . . . 1852,* 17.

51. Paulina Wright Davis in *Proceedings . . . New York . . . 1853,* 25.

52. Ernestine Rose in *Proceedings . . . New York . . . 1856,* 77; Lucy Stone, *New York Daily Herald,* September 8, 1853, p. 2; Matilda Gage, *Speech,* 8.

53. Quoted in Robert W. Johannsen, *To the Halls of the Montezumas: The Mexican War and the American Imagination* (New York: Oxford University Press, 1985), 138.

54. Ibid., 137, 138–39.

55. "Editor's Table," *Godey's Lady's Book,* XXXIV (March 1847), 173. For details on Ann Chase, see Johannsen, 138–39.

56. Mrs. E. F. Ellet, "American Heroines," *Godey's Lady's Book,* XXXVI (January 1848), 11–14, (February 1848), 77–79, (March 1848), 145–48 (April 1848), 240–42 (May 1848), 300–302 (June 1848), 321–24, XXXVII (July 1848), 6–9, (August 1848), 68–70, (September 1848), 167–68, (October 1848), 201–202 (November 1848), 263–66, (December 1848), 373–75.

57. For examples of how evangelicals used military rhetoric, see E. Anthony Rotundo, "Body and Soul: Changing Ideals of American Middle-Class Manhood, 1770–1920," *Journal of Social History* 16 (Summer 1983), 26.

58. Sandra S. Sizer, *Gospel Hymns and Social Religion: The Rhetoric of Nineteenth-Century Revivalism* (Philadelphia: Temple University Press, 1978), 41–42.

59. One of the major principles of socio-linguistics is that populations have their own languages and that communication is possible within a group only if every member has "competency" in its language. See Ward H. Goodenough, *Culture, Language, and Society* (Menlo Park, Calif.: Benjamin/Cummings Publisher, 1981), 30–36.

60. E. Anthony Rotundo, "Manhood in America: The Northern Middle Class, 1770–1920" (Ph.D. diss., Brandeis, 1982), 25.

61. For a discussion of this idea as applied to gender roles in the late nineteenth century, see Peter G. Filene, *Him/Her/Self: Sex Roles in Modern America* (Baltimore: Johns Hopkins University Press, 1986), 93.

62. David G. Pugh, *Sons of Liberty: The Masculine Mind in Nineteenth-Century America* (Westport, Conn: Greenwood, 1983), 31–32.

63. Rotundo, 181.

64. Sandra M. Gilbert has discussed these themes as they are found in the literature of World War I in "Soldier's Heart: Literary Men, Literary Women, and the Great War," in *Speaking of Gender,* ed. Elaine Showalter (New York: Routledge, 1989), 282–309; Janna Thompson, "Women and War," *Women's Studies International Forum* 14 (1991), 64, 65. See also Jean Bethke Elshtain, *Women and War* (New York: Basic Books, 1987); Genevieve Lloyd, "Selfhood, War, and Masculinity," in *Feminist Challenges: Social and Political Theory,* ed. Carole Pateman and Elizabeth Gross (London: Allen and Unwin, 1986), 63–76.

65. Paulina Wright Davis in *Proceedings . . . Worcester . . . 1850,* 7–8.

66. Wendell Phillips in *Proceedings . . . New York . . . 1856,* 50.

67. Ernestine Rose in *Proceedings . . . New York . . . 1860,* 11–12; Antoinette Brown, *New York Daily Tribune,* December 3, 1853, p. 8.

68. Lucy Stone speech, clipping, *New York Tribune*, 1852, Blackwell Papers, Library of Congress, Washington, D.C.

69. George William Curtis, *An Address Vindicating the Right of Woman to the Elective Franchise* (New York: S. T. Munson, 1858), 12–13; see also Samuel J. May in *Proceedings . . . Syracuse . . . 1852*, 87–88. For similar sentiments in somewhat different language, see Mrs. S. T. Martyn, "The Right of Woman to Elective Franchise," *The Una*, II (February 1854), 216.

70. C. C. Burleigh in *Proceedings . . . Cleveland . . . 1853*, 181–82.

71. Ann Preston in *Proceedings of the Woman's Rights Convention Held at West Chester, Pa. June 2d and 3d, 1852* (Philadelphia: Merrihew & Thompson, 1852), 25.

72. Wendell Phillips in *Proceedings . . . New York City . . . 1856*, 50–51.

73. Sarah Grimké in *Proceedings . . . West Chester, Pa. . . . 1852*, 10. For a similar reference, see Henry Blackwell in *Proceedings . . . Cleveland . . . 1853*, 53.

74. Elizabeth Oakes Smith, *New York Daily Herald*, September 10, 1852, p. 7.

75. Henry Ward Beecher, *Woman's Influence in Politics: An Address Delivered By Henry Ward Beecher at the Cooper Institute, New York, Thursday Evening, February 2, 1860* (Boston: C. K. Whipple, 1870), 16; see also *New York Daily Herald*, February 4, 1860, p. 2. For a similar comment by Paulina Wright Davis, see *Proceedings . . . Syracuse . . . 1852*, 56.

76. Stanton, *Address . . . Seneca Falls and Rochester*, 19.

77. Stanton, Anthony, and Gage, eds., 1:106.

78. Lydia Jenkins in *Proceedings . . . New York City . . . 1853*, 14.

79. Stanton, *Address . . . Seneca Falls and Rochester*, 19.

80. J. Elizabeth Jones, *New York Daily Herald*, September 12, 1852, p. 1.

81. Rev. A. D. Mayo, "Womanhood," *The Sibyl*, I (April 1, 1857), 151.

82. Susan B. Anthony in *Proceedings . . . New York . . . 1860*, 7.

83. Wendell Phillips in ibid., 87.

4. The Strategy

1. Lucy Stone to Antoinette Brown, July 11, 1855, in Carol Lasser and Marlene Deahl Merrill, *Friends and Sisters: Letters between Lucy Stone and Antoinette Brown Blackwell, 1846–93* (Urbana: University of Illinois Press, 1987), 144.

2. Elizabeth Cady Stanton, Susan B. Anthony, and Matilda Joslyn Gage, eds., *History of Woman Suffrage*, 2 vols. (New York: Fowler and Wells, 1881), 1:386.

3. Elizabeth Cady Stanton to Lucretia Mott, September 30, 1848, in *Elizabeth Cady Stanton as Revealed in Her Letters, Diary, and Reminiscences*, ed. Theodore Stanton and Harriot Stanton Blatch, 2 vols. (New York: Harper, 1922), 2:20–21.

4. Wendell Phillips in *Proceedings of the Seventh National Woman's Rights Convention Held in New York City, November 25 and 26, 1856* (New York: n.p., 1856), 25.

5. Susan B. Anthony to William Lloyd Garrison, December 14, 1860, William Lloyd Garrison Papers, Department of Rare Books and Manuscripts, Boston Public Library, Boston, Mass., in *The Papers of Elizabeth Cady Stanton and Susan B. Anthony*, ed. Patricia G. Holland and Ann D. Gordon (Wilmington, Del.: Scholarly Resources, 1991, microfilm, series 3), reel 9, frame 962.

6. George Henry Payne, *History of Journalism in the United States* (Westport, Conn.: Greenwood, 1970), 241.

7. John C. Nerone, "The Mythology of the Penny Press," *Critical Studies in Mass Communication* 4 (December 1987), 376–404; Frank Luther Mott, *American Journalism, A History: 1690–1960* (New York: Macmillan, 1962), 243; Donald L. Shaw, "At the Crossroads: Change and Continuity in American Press News, 1820–1860," *Journalism History* 8 (Summer 1981), 39–41.

8. The *New York Herald* sold 93,340 copies. The *New York Tribune* sold 214,250 copies, and the *New York Times* sold 89,000. See Douglas Fermer, *James Gordon Bennett and the* New York Herald: *A Study of Editorial Opinion in the Civil War Era, 1854–1867* (New York: St. Martin's Press, 1986), 326.

9. For background on Bennett, see James L. Crouthamel, *Bennett's* New York Herald *and the Rise of the Popular Press* (Syracuse: Syracuse University Press, 1989), 1–18.

10. Frederic Hudson, *Journalism in the U.S., 1690–1872* (New York: Harper, 1968), 429, 433.

11. Glyndon Van Deusen, *Horace Greeley, Nineteenth-Century Crusader* (Philadelphia: University of Pennsylvania Press, 1953), 5–51.

12. Horace Greeley to Susan B. Anthony, February 8, 1855, Park Benjamin Papers, Rare Book and Manuscript Library, Columbia University, New York, N.Y., in *Papers*, ed. Holland and Gordon, reel 8, frame 132; "Letter of Horace Greeley" in *Proceedings . . . New York . . . 1856*, 55–57.

13. Warren G. Bovée, "Horace Greeley and Social Responsibility," *Journalism Quarterly* 63 (Summer 1986), 251–59; Hudson, 523–35.

14. Augustus Maverick, *Henry J. Raymond and the New York Press for Thirty Years* (Hartford, Conn.: A. S. Hale, 1870), 13–102; Francis Brown, *Raymond of the Times* (New York: Norton, 1951), 7–102.

15. Quoted in Maverick, 96–98.

16. Quoted in Hudson, 636.

17. "The Hanging of Women," *New York Times*, April 15, 1859, p. 4.

18. "A Free Academy for Women," *New York Daily Times*, February 13, 1855, p. 4.

19. "Employment for Women," *New York Daily Times*, November 11, 1858, p. 4. He also sat on the board of trustees of Elizabeth Blackwell's New York Infirmary for Indigent Women and Children. See Brown, 163.

20. "Property of Married Women," *New York Times*, April 8, 1859, p. 4; see also "Female Emancipation," ibid., February 6, 1860, p. 4; "Impracticable Rights," ibid., February 10, 1860, p. 4.

21. "The Hanging of Women," *New York Times*, April 15, 1859, p. 4.

22. "American Female Literature," *New York Daily Times*, June 5, 1854, p. 4.

23. "Capital Punishment of Women," *New York Times*, April 26, 1859, p. 4; "The Hanging of Women," ibid., April 15, 1859, p. 4.

24. "Property of Married Women," ibid., April 8, 1859, p. 4.

25. Ernestine Rose in *Proceedings of the Woman's Rights Convention Held at Syracuse, September 8th, 9th, and 10th, 1852* (Syracuse: J. E. Masters, 1852), 93. Matilda Gage reported in the *New York Daily Times*, September 8, 1853, p. 1; see also *New York Daily Tribune*, September 8, 1853, p. 5. For a comment by Susan B. Anthony on the importance of the press, see *New York Daily Times*, November 26, 1856, p. 1.

26. See, for example, Elizabeth Cady Stanton to Susan B. Anthony, September 10, 1855, Stanton and Blatch, eds., 2:59–60; Susan B. Anthony to William Lloyd Garrison, March 8, 1859, Papers of Susan B. Anthony, Special Collections, Vassar College Library, Poughkeepsie, N.Y., in *Papers*, ed. Holland and Gordon, reel 9, frame 227; Henry B. Stanton to Elizabeth Cady Stanton, October 1, 1860, Elizabeth Cady Stanton Papers, Theodore Stanton Collection, Mable Smith Douglass Library, Rutgers University, New Brunswick, N.J., in ibid., reel 9, frame 856; Elizabeth Cady Stanton and Anthony to Garrison, May 22 [1860], Garrison Papers, Boston Public Library, in ibid., reel 9, frames 676 and 677; see also Samuel J. May to Anthony, August 24 [1852], Ida Husted Harper Collection, Henry E. Huntington Library, San Marino, Calif., in ibid., reel 7, frame 316.

27. Susan B. Anthony to Lucy Stone [November 11, 1856], Blackwell Family Papers, Library of Congress, Washington, D.C. in ibid., reel 8, frame 791; see also Anthony to Stone, October 27, 1856, in ibid., reel 8, frame 614.

28. *New York Daily Times*, August 2, 1852, p. 2.

29. *Frederick Douglass's Paper*, October 30, 1851, p. 2.

30. *New York Daily Tribune*, October 28, 1850, p. 6; *Boston Weekly Telegraph*, n.d. [September 19–20, 1855], C. H. Dall Collection, Massachusetts Historical Society, Boston, Mass., in *Papers*, ed. Holland and Gordon, reel 8, frame 282.

31. *Chenango Union* [Norwich, New York], n.d. [February 6, 1855], Susan B. Anthony Scrapbook 1, Susan B. Anthony Papers, Rare Books Division, Library of Congress, in *Papers*, ed. Holland and Gordon, reel 8, frame 129.

32. Paulina Wright Davis to Stanton, [February] 9 [1852], Elizabeth Cady Stanton Papers, Library of Congress, in ibid., reel 7, frame 154.

33. Stanton, Anthony, and Gage, eds., 1:638.

34. *New York Daily Times*, November 26, 1856, p. 1; *New York Daily Herald*, November 27, 1856, p. 8; *New York Daily Tribune*, November 26, 1856, p. 5.

35. Lucy Stone in *Proceedings . . . New York . . . 1856*, 85.

36. *New York Daily Times*, May 14, 1858, p. 5. Reference to this statement, although not exactly the same quote, appeared in the *New York Daily Herald*, May 14, 1858, p. 3.

37. Wendell Phillips in *Proceedings . . . New York . . . 1856*, 18.

38. Martha C. Wright in *Proceedings of the Tenth National Woman's Rights Convention, Held at the Cooper Institute, New York City, May 10th and 11th, 1860* (Boston: Yerrinton and Garrison, 1860), 4.

39. Stanton in ibid., 70.

40. Ernestine Rose in ibid., 51.

41. *Proceedings of the Woman's Rights Convention, Held at the Broadway Tabernacle in the City of New York, Tuesday and Wednesday, September 6 and 7, 1853* (New York: Fowler and Wells, 1853), 21–33.

42. Quoted in Walter M. Merrill, *Against the Wind and Tide: A Biography of William Lloyd Garrison* (Cambridge: Harvard University Press, 1963), 132.

43. Ibid., 69–72, 193.

44. His responses to these two incidents are described in ibid., 103–108, 142.

45. *New York Daily Times*, September 7, 1853, p. 8; *New York Daily Tribune*, September 7, 1853, p. 5; *New York Daily Herald*, September 7, 1853, p. 2.

46. *Proceedings . . . New York . . . 1856*, 33, 39, 40–41.

47. See, for example, *New York Daily Herald*, November 27, 1856, p. 8, and *New York Daily Times*, November 27, 1856, p. 2.

48. Douglass changed the name of his paper to *Frederick Douglass's Paper* in 1853.

49. See *The Liberator*, XVIII (September 1, 1848), 137, and (September 15, 1848), 148.

50. John L. Thomas, *The Liberator, William Lloyd Garrison: A Biography* (Boston: Little, Brown, 1963), 128, 131–32, 181.

51. For a discussion of Douglass's interest in woman's rights, see Philip S. Foner, *Frederick Douglass on Women's Rights* (Westport, Conn.: Greenwood, 1976), 3–25.

52. *Frederick Douglass's Paper*, June 10, 1853, p. 2.

53. For general discussions of these periodicals, see Ann Russo and Cheris Kramarae, *The Radical Women's Press of the 1850s* (New York: Routledge, 1991); Bertha-Monica Stearns, "Reform Periodicals and Female Reformers, 1830–1860," *American Historical Review* 37 (July 1932), 678–99; Martha M. Solomon, "The Role of the Suffrage Press in the Woman's Rights Movement," in *A Voice of Their Own: The Woman's Suffrage Press, 1840–1910* (Tuscaloosa: University of Alabama Press, 1991), 1–16.

54. Russo and Kramarae, 11–13.

55. See, for example, Sun Flower, "Woman," *The Lily*, II (January 1850), 4.

56. Senex may have been Bloomer's husband, Dexter Bloomer. Norma Basch attributes the essays to New York Assemblyman Anson Bingham. See Norma Basch, *In the Eyes of the Law: Women, Marriage, and Property in Nineteenth-Century New York* (Ithaca: Cornell University Press, 1982), 193. My thanks to Patricia Holland of the Stanton-Anthony Papers, Amherst, Massachusetts, for this information. For examples of these essays, see "Equality of Rights to Woman," *The Lily*, III (August 1851), 60; (September 1851), 68; (October 1851), 76; (November 1851), 84; (December 1851), 92; IV (February 1852), 10; (March 1852), 20; "The Democratic Review on Woman's Rights," ibid., IV (April 1852), 28; (May 1852), 47–48; (June 1852), 52; (July 1852), 60; (August 1852), 68; (September 1852), 75; (October 1852), 82; (December 1852), 103; V (March 15, 1853), [4].

57. Davis to Stanton, [February] 9 [1852], Elizabeth Cady Stanton Papers, Library of Congress, in *Papers*, ed. Holland and Gordon, reel 7, frames 154 and 155.

58. "Prospectus," in ibid., reel 7, frame 156.

59. *New York Daily Herald*, September 10, 1852, p. 8.

60. *New York Daily Tribune*, September 14, 1852, p. 6; *Proceedings . . . Syracuse . . . 1852*, 18, 94–96.

61. *The Una*, I (February 1, 1853), 3–4.

62. Philadelphia *Evening Bulletin*, October 19, 1854, in *Papers*, ed. Holland and Gordon, reel 8, frame 69; see also Stanton, Anthony, and Gage, eds., 1:378.

63. Russo and Kramarae, 14–15.

64. *The Woman's Advocate*, December 15, 1855, p. 3; Stanton, Anthony, and Gage, eds., 1:388–89; see also Russo and Kramarae, 15.

65. For a discussion of Hasbrouck's editorial policy, see *The Sibyl*, I (July 1, 1856), p. 8; see also Russo and Kramarae, 15–16.

66. Alice Felt Tyler, "Jane Grey Cannon Swisshelm," in *Notable American Women: A Biographical Dictionary, 1607–1950*, ed. Edward T. James, 3 vols. (Cambridge: Harvard University Press, 1971), 3:416.

67. *Frederick Douglass's Paper*, December 16, 1853, p. 4.

68. Susan B. Anthony to Wendell Phillips, April 3, 1861, Wendell Phillips Papers, Houghton Library, Harvard University, Cambridge, Massachusetts, in *Papers*, ed. Holland and Gordon, reel 9, frames 1137–38.

69. Ibid.

70. For a more positive assessment of the influence of reform journals, see Solomon, 1–16.

71. Stanton and Blatch, eds., 2: 18–19.

72. *The Liberator*, XX (May 17, 1850), 80.

73. Paulina Wright Davis in *Proceedings of the Woman's Rights Convention, Held at Worcester, October 15th and 16th, 1851* (New York: Fowler and Wells, 1852), 7–8; see also Frances Gage in *Proceedings of the National Women's Rights Convention, Held at Cleveland, Ohio, on Wednesday, Thursday, and Friday, October 5th, 6th, 7th, 1853* (Cleveland: Gray, Beardsley, Spear, and Co., 1854), 5–6.

74. Paulina Wright Davis in *Proceedings . . . New York . . . 1853*, 24.

5. The Responses

1. *Proceedings of the National Women's Rights Convention, Held at Cleveland, Ohio, on Wednesday, Thursday, and Friday, October 5th, 6th, 7th, 1853* (Cleveland: Gray, Beardsley, Spear, and Co., 1854), 132–66.

2. Elizabeth Cady Stanton, Susan B. Anthony, and Matilda Joslyn Gage, eds., *History of Woman Suffrage*, 2 vols. (New York: Fowler and Wells, 1881), 1:144.

3. See *Proceedings of the Woman's Rights Convention, Held at the Broadway*

Tabernacle in the City of New York, Tuesday and Wednesday, September 6 & 7, 1853 (New York: Fowler and Wells, 1853) for a description of the disturbances.

4. New York *Evening Post* quoted in *The Liberator,* XXIII (September 30, 1853), 156.

5. "Mobs," *The Una,* I (October 1853), 154.

6. New York *Express* quoted in *The Liberator,* XXIII (September 16, 1853), 148; New York *Home Journal* quoted in ibid. (September 30, 1853), 156.

7. *Proceedings of the Ninth National Woman's Rights Convention Held in New York City, Thursday, May 12, 1859* (Rochester, N.Y.: A. Strong & Co., 1859).

8. See, for example, Eleanor Flexner, *Century of Struggle: The Woman's Rights Movement in the United States* (New York: Atheneum, 1972), 81–82; Keith E. Melder, *Beginnings of Sisterhood: The American Woman's Rights Movement, 1800–1850* (New York: Schocken, 1977), 148, 151; E. Claire Jerry, "The Role of Newspapers in the Nineteenth-Century Woman's Movement," in *A Voice of Their Own: The Woman's Suffrage Press, 1840–1910,* ed. Martha M. Solomon (Tuscaloosa: University of Alabama Press, 1991), 19.

9. *New York Daily Herald,* September 9, 1852, p. 1; September 14, 1852, p. 3.

10. *New York Daily Herald,* September 7, 1853, p. 1.

11. *New York Daily Herald,* September 8, 1853, p. 1.

12. *New York Daily Herald,* November 27, 1856, p. 7.

13. See, for example, *New York Daily Tribune,* October 25, 1850, p. 5; October 20, 1851, p. 8; September 7, 1853, p. 5; May 12, 1860, p. 10; *New York Daily Times,* September 9, 1852, p. 2; September 7, 1853, p. 7; *New York Times,* May 13, 1859, p. 1.

14. *New York Daily Herald,* September 9, 1852, p. 1; September 10, 1852, pp. 7–8; September 11, 1852, p. 8; September 12, 1852, p. 1; September 14, 1852, p. 3; *New York Daily Tribune,* September 9, 1852, p. 5; September 10, 1852, p. 5; September 11, 1852, p. 5; September 14, 1852, p. 6; *New York Daily Times,* September 9, 1852, p. 2; September 10, 1852, p. 2; September 11, 1852, p. 2.

15. *New York Daily Herald,* September 7, 1853, pp. 1–2; September 8, 1853, pp. 1–2; *New York Daily Tribune,* September 7, 1853, p. 5; September 8, 1853, pp. 5–6; *New York Daily Times,* September 7, 1853, pp. 7–8; September 8, 1853, p. 1.

16. *New York Daily Herald,* November 27, 1856, pp. 7–8; *New York Daily Tribune,* November 26, 1856, p. 5; November 27, 1856, pp. 6–7; *New York Daily Times,* November 26, 1856, pp. 1, 8; November 27, 1856, p. 2.

17. *New York Daily Herald,* May 14, 1858, p. 3; May 13, 1859, pp. 4–5; May 11, 1860, p. 3; *New York Daily Tribune,* May 14, 1858, p. 5; May 15, 1858, p. 5; May 13, 1859, p. 5; May 11, 1860, pp. 7–8; May 12, 1860, p. 10; *New York Daily Times,* May 14, 1858, p. 5; May 15, 1858, p. 4; *New York Times,* May 13, 1859, p. 1; May 11, 1860, p. 8; May 12, 1860, p. 3.

18. *New York Daily Tribune,* October 25, 1850, p. 4 and p. 5; October 26, 1850, p. 6; ibid., October 17, 1851, pp. 7–8; October 18, 1851, p. 6; October 20, 1851, pp. 7–8.

19. *New York Daily Tribune,* October 10, 1853, p. 1; October 19, 1854, p. 5; *New York Daily Times,* October 10, 1853, p. 1; October 19, 1854, p. 1.

20. *New York Daily Herald,* October 19, 1855, p. 4; October 20, 1855, p. 8; *New York Daily Tribune,* October 19, 1855, p. 5; October 20, 1855, p. 3; *New York Daily Times,* October 19, 1855, p. 4; October 20, 1855, p. 2.

21. *Daily Missouri Republican,* October 23, 1855; *Cleveland Daily Plain Dealer,* October 22, 1855.

22. See, for example, *New York Daily Times* notice of the woman's rights convention in Albany, February 15, 1854, p. 4; notice of the woman's rights

convention in Saratoga, August 19, 1854, p. 4; notice of the woman's rights convention in Saratoga, August 17, 1855, p. 1.

23. The New England Woman's Rights Convention held September 19, 1855, in Boston did receive a nine-line notice in the *New York Daily Times* on September 20, 1855, p. 3; the *New York Daily Tribune* devoted almost a whole column to a woman's rights convention held in Massilon, Ohio, in May of 1852; see *New York Daily Tribune*, June 4, 1852, p. 6; Greeley also covered the West Chester, Pa., woman's rights convention held in June of that year; see *New York Daily Tribune*, June 3, 1852, p. 5.

24. *New York Daily Tribune*, October 25, 1850, pp. 5–6; for other examples, see the four-and-a-half-column article on the Syracuse convention appearing in the *Herald*, September 12, 1852, p. 1, or the five-column article on the New York convention appearing in the *New York Daily Times*, November 27, 1856, p. 2.

25. Stanton, Anthony, Gage, eds., 1:805.

26. Quoted in Elinor Rice Hays, *Morning Star: A Biography of Lucy Stone, 1818–1893* (New York: Harcourt, Brace, and World, 1961), 87.

27. *New York Daily Herald*, September 14, 1852, p. 4.

28. Stanton, Anthony, and Gage, eds., 1:556; *New York Daily Herald*, September 6, 1853, p. 4.

29. *New York Daily Herald*, November 27, 1856, p. 4.

30. Stanton, Anthony, and Gage, eds., 1:805.

31. *New York Daily Herald*, September 14, 1852, p. 3; for another example, see ibid., September 6, 1853, p. 4 which describes the woman's rights convention as being preceded by "preliminary skirmishing" and anticipates the coming "battle of Amazons."

32. Ibid., September 14, 1852, p. 4.

33. *New York Daily Times*, August 2, 1852, p. 2.

34. *New York Times*, February 10, 1860, p. 4.

35. "Revilo," [West Chester] *Pennsylvania Farmer*, June 12, 1852.

36. "Woman's Rights" [West Chester, Pa.], *The Jeffersonian*, May 25, 1852.

37. *New York Daily Times*, May 14, 1858, p. 5; May 15, 1858, p. 4.

38. *New York Daily Herald*, November 27, 1856, p. 4.

39. Jean Fagan Yellin, *Women and Sisters: The Antislavery Feminists in American Culture* (New Haven, Yale University Press, 1989), 45, 46, 50–51; for a similar reference to Frances Wright, see Kathleen Edgerton Kendall and Jeanne Y. Fisher, "Frances Wright on Women's Rights: Eloquence Versus Ethos," *Quarterly Journal of Speech* 60 (February 1974), 65.

40. Nancy Sahli, "Smashing: Women's Relationships Before the Fall," *Chrysalis* 8 (Summer 1979), 17–27; Carroll Smith-Rosenberg, "The New Woman as Androgyne: Social Disorder and Gender Crisis, 1870–1936," in *Disorderly Conduct: Visions of Gender in Victorian America* (New York: Oxford University Press, 1985), 265–83.

41. *New York Daily Herald*, November 27, 1856, p. 4; September 14, 1852, p. 4; see also ibid., August 8, 1855, p. 2; September 6, 1853, p. 4.

42. Ibid., quoted in *The Jeffersonian* of West Chester, Pa., May 25, 1852.

43. *New York Daily Herald*, November 27, 1856, p. 4.

44. New York *Express* quoted in the *National Anti-Slavery Standard*, XIV (September 17, 1853), p. 66.

45. Ida Husted Harper, *The Life and Work of Susan B. Anthony*, 3 vols. (Indianapolis: Hollenbeck Press, 1898–1908), 1:78.

46. This connection was discussed by Joan Wallach Scott, "French Feminists Claim the Rights of 'Man': Olympe de Gouges in the French Revolution," lecture presented on April 2, 1991, Washington University, St. Louis, Missouri.

47. Abby Wettan Kleinbaum, *The War against the Amazons* (New York: New Press, 1983).

48. Ibid., 3.

49. Ibid., 1.

50. *New York Daily Tribune*, October 25, 1850, p. 4.

51. "Letter of Horace Greeley" in *Proceedings of the Seventh National Woman's Rights Convention Held in New York City, November 25 and 26, 1856* (New York: n.p., 1856), 55–57. This letter was also published in *New York Daily Times*, November 27, 1856, p. 2.

52. Harper, 1:122.

53. *New York Daily Tribune*, January 5, February 7, March 3, 1855.

54. Harper, 1:146–47.

55. *New York Daily Tribune*, May 15, 1858, p. 4.

56. *New York Daily Tribune*, May 14, 1860, p. 4; ibid., May 30, 1860, p. 4.

57. Parker Pillsbury to Elizabeth Cady Stanton [May 1860], quoted in Harper, 1:195; Lydia Mott to Stanton, June 16 [1860], Elizabeth Cady Stanton Papers, Theodore Stanton Collection, Mable Smith Douglass Library, Rutgers University, New Brunswick, N.J., in *The Papers of Elizabeth Cady Stanton and Susan B. Anthony*, ed. Patricia G. Holland and Ann D. Gordon (Wilmington, Del.: Scholarly Resources, 1991, microfilm, series 3), reel 9, frame 726.

58. *New York Daily Times*, October 18, 1851, p. 2.

59. *New York Daily Times*, September 8, 1853, p. 4; October 8, 1853, p. 4.

60. *New York Times*, March 18, 1859, p. 4; February 6, 1860, p. 4; February 10, 1860, p. 4.

61. Stanton, Anthony, and Gage, eds., 1:568–69.

62. Ibid., 1:555, 574.

63. *New York Daily Herald*, September 8, 1853, p. 1.

64. *Christian Inquirer* quoted in *The Liberator*, XXIII (September 30, 1853), 156.

65. *The Liberator*, XXIII (September 16, 1853), 148.

66. New York *Sun* quoted in *The Liberator*, ibid., 148.

67. New York *Home Journal* quoted in *The Liberator*, XXIII (September 30, 1853), 156.

68. *New York Times*, May 13, 1859, p. 1; May 14, 1859, p. 4. See also the *New York Daily Tribune*, May 13, 1859, p. 5, for another description of the interruptions.

69. *St. Louis Daily Missouri Republican*, September 10, 1853; October 23, 1855; May 17, 1860.

70. Ibid., October 26, 1850; September 16, 1852; October 14, 1853; October 20, 1854; May 14, 1858.

71. *Cleveland Daily Plain Dealer*, October 31, November 2, 1850; May 28, 29, June 1, 4, 1852; May 29, June, 1, 2, 3, 4, 1852; September 10, 1852; September 28, 1852; September 14, 1853; October 3, 1853; October 5, 6, 7, 8, 1853. The paper covered the 1858 national convention in New York. See ibid., May 17, 1858.

72. The *Daily Chicago Tribune* did not begin publication until 1849, and the microfilm collection of its issues is incomplete. For references to the 1853 New York convention, see *Daily Chicago Tribune*, September 12, September 19, 1853. For references to the 1853 Cleveland convention, see ibid., October 10, October 11, 1853. For the editorial discussing the 1858 New York convention, see ibid., May 18, 1858.

73. The paper's editor was William M. Swain who lived in New York while he served as editor of the Philadelphia paper. For information on Swain, see Frederic Hudson, *Journalism in the U.S., 1690–1872* (New York: Harper, 1873), 505–508. *Philadelphia Public Ledger and Daily Transcript*, August 1, August 10, 1848; October 25, 26, 28, 1850; October 20, 1851; September 9, 10, 17, 1852.

74. Ibid., September 9, 1853.

75. Ibid., October 15, 1853; October 19, 20, 21, 1854; October 18, 1855; November 27, 1856; May 14, 15, 1858; May 11, 12, 1860.

76. *Boston Daily Advertiser*, August 8, 1848; October 25, 1850; October 17, 18, 1851; September 8, 1853; October 21, 1854; November 26, 1856; May 14, 1858; May 14, 1859.

77. Theodore Stanton and Harriot Stanton Blatch, eds., *Elizabeth Cady Stanton as Revealed in Her Letters, Diary, and Reminiscences*, 2 vols. (New York: Harper, 1922), 2:18–19.

78. Ibid., 2:49–50.

79. *Albany Atlas*, n.d. [February 14–15, 1854], Susan B. Anthony Scrapbook 1, Rare Books Division, Library of Congress, in *Papers*, ed. Holland and Gordon, reel 7, frame 967; *Albany Evening Transcript*, February 16, 1854, ibid., reel 7, frame 970.

80. Martha C. Wright to Susan B. Anthony, July 9, 1856, Box 35, Folder 921, Garrison Family Papers, Sophia Smith Collection, Smith College, Northampton, Mass.

81. Martha C. Wright to Elizabeth Cady Stanton, May 26, 1860, Box 36, Folder 940, ibid.; for a similar comment, see Frances Gage in *Proceedings . . . Cleveland . . . 1853*, 7.

82. *New York Daily Times*, November 27, 1856, p. 2.

83. *Pittsburgh Saturday Visiter*, November 2, 1850, p. 166.

84. *National Anti-Slavery Standard*, XIV (October 22, 1853), 87.

85. "The Journal and Bloomer Dress," *Pittsburgh Saturday Visiter*, October 4, 1851, p. 146; see also "The Bloomer Dress," ibid., September 20, 1851, p. 138.

86. Jane Swisshelm, "Woman's Rights and the Color Question," *Pittsburgh Saturday Visiter*, reprinted in *The Anti-Slavery Standard*, XI (December 5, 1850), 112.

87. Elizabeth Cady Stanton, *Eighty Years and More (1815–1897): Reminiscences of Elizabeth Cady Stanton* (New York: European Publishing Co., 1898), 149.

88. *The Liberator*, XX (May 17, 1850), 80.

89. Paulina Wright Davis in *Proceedings of the Woman's Rights Convention Held at Worcester, October 15th and 16th, 1851* (New York: Fowler and Wells, 1852), 7.

90. Paulina Wright Davis in *Proceedings . . . New York . . . 1853*, 24; for a similar comment by Susan B. Anthony, see *Proceedings of the Tenth National Woman's Rights Convention, Held at the Cooper Institute, New York City, May 10th and 11th, 1860* (Boston: Yerrinton & Garrison, 1860), 4.

Conclusion

1. Ellen Carol DuBois, *Feminism and Suffrage: The Emergence of an Independent Women's Movement in America, 1848–1869* (Ithaca: Cornell University Press, 1978), 162–202; Eleanor Flexner, *Century of Struggle: The Woman's Rights Movement in the United States* (New York: Atheneum, 1972), 142–55.

2. William Leach, *True Love and Perfect Union: The Feminist Reform of Sex and Society* (Middletown, Conn.: Wesleyan University Press, 1989), xi-xiii, 7.

3. Cynthia Eagle Russett, *Sexual Science: The Victorian Construction of Womanhood* (Cambridge: Harvard University Press, 1989), 193–94, 205–206.

4. Aileen S. Kraditor, *The Ideas of the Woman Suffrage Movement, 1890–1920* (Garden City, N.Y.: Anchor Books, 1971), 38–39, 90–91.

5. Michael McGerr, "Political Style and Women's Power, 1830–1930," *Journal of American History* 77 (December 1990), 874–79.

6. Molly Ladd-Taylor, *Mother-Work: Women, Child Welfare, and the State, 1890–1930* (Urbana: University of Illinois Press, 1994), 43–44, 104–32.

7. Christine A. Lunardini, *From Equal Suffrage to Equal Rights: Alice Paul and the National Woman's Party, 1913–1928* (New York: New York University Press, 1986); Susan D. Becker, *The Origins of the Equal Rights Amendment: American Feminism between the Wars* (Westport, Conn.: Greenwood, 1981), Nancy F. Cott, *The Grounding of Modern Feminism* (New Haven: Yale University Press, 1987), 51–81.

8. See, for example, J. Stanley Lemons, *The Woman Citizen: Social Feminism in the 1920s* (Urbana: University of Illinois Press, 1973).

9. William Chafe, *The Paradox of Change: American Women in the Twentieth Century* (New York: Oxford University Press, 1981); Susan Ware, *Beyond Suffrage: Women in the New Deal* (Cambridge: Harvard University Press, 1981); Lois Scharf, *To Work and to Wed: Female Employment, Feminism, and the Great Depression* (Westport, Conn.: Greenwood, 1980); D'Ann Campbell, *Women at War with America: Private Lives in a Patriotic Era* (Cambridge: Harvard University Press, 1984); and Susan Hartmann, *The Home Front and Beyond: American Women in the 1940s* (Boston: Twayne, 1982).

10. Rosalind Rosenberg, *Beyond Separate Spheres: Intellectual Roots of Modern Feminism* (New Haven: Yale University Press, 1982).

INDEX

SYLVIA HOFFERT is Professor of Women's Studies and of History at the University of North Carolina at Chapel Hill. She is the author of *Private Matters: American Attitudes toward Childbearing and Infant Nurture in the Urban North, 1800–1860.*